THIS IS MODERN PHILOSOPHY

THIS IS PHILOSOPHY
Series editor: Steven D. Hales

Reading philosophy can be like trying to ride a bucking bronco – you hold on for dear life while "transcendental deduction" twists you to one side, "causa sui" throws you to the other, and a 300-word, 300-year-old sentence comes down on you like an iron-shod hoof the size of a dinner plate. *This Is Philosophy* is the riding academy that solves these problems. Each book in the series is written by an expert who knows how to gently guide students into the subject regardless of the reader's ability or previous level of knowledge. Their reader-friendly prose is designed to help students find their way into the fascinating, challenging ideas that compose philosophy without simply sticking the hapless novice on the back of the bronco, as so many texts do. All the books in the series provide ample pedagogical aids, including links to free online primary sources. When students are ready to take the next step in their philosophical education, *This Is Philosophy* is right there with them to help them along the way.

This Is Philosophy, Second Edition
Steven D. Hales

This Is Philosophy of Mind
Pete Mandik

This Is Ethics
Jussi Suikkanen

This Is Political Philosophy
Alex Tuckness and Clark Wolf

This Is Business Ethics
Tobey Scharding

This Is Metaphysics
Kris McDaniel

This Is Bioethics
Ruth F. Chadwick and Udo Schuklenk

This Is Philosophy of Religion
Neil Manson

This Is Epistemology
J. Adam Carter and Clayton Littlejohn

This Is Philosophy of Science
Franz-Peter Griesmaier and Jeffrey A. Lockwood

This Is Modern Philosophy
Kurt Smith

Forthcoming:

This Is Environmental Ethics
Wendy Lee

This Is Philosophy of Mind, Second Edition
Pete Mandik

THIS IS
MODERN
PHILOSOPHY

AN INTRODUCTION

KURT SMITH

WILEY Blackwell

Registered Offices
John Wiley & Sons, Inc., 111 River Street, Hoboken, NJ 07030, USA
John Wiley & Sons, Ltd, The Atrium, Southern Gate, Chichester, West Sussex, PO19 8SQ, UK

Editorial Office
9600 Garsington Road, Oxford, OX4 2DQ, UK

For details of our global editorial offices, customer services, and more information about Wiley products visit us at www.wiley.com.

Wiley also publishes its books in a variety of electronic formats and by print-on-demand. Some content that appears in standard print versions of this book may not be available in other formats.

For general information on our other products and services or for technical support, please contact our Customer Care Department within the United States at (800) 762-2974, outside the United States at (317) 572-3993 or fax (317) 572-4002.

Library of Congress Cataloging-in-Publication Data applied for
Paperback ISBN 9781118686904

Cover and Image Design: Wiley

Set in 10.5/13pt Minion by Straive, Pondicherry, India
SKY10036044_091522

CONTENTS

ACKNOWLEDGEMENTS

I would like to thank Professor Steven Hales, who first approached me about doing this project. He is the editor of the series in which this book is now a member, but equally importantly, he is a respected, amazing colleague. I thank Bloomsburg University of Pennsylvania for granting me Sabbatical to do this project. I would also like to thank Professor Daniel Garber, not only for graciously providing me the opportunity to spend my sabbatical at Princeton University as a visiting scholar, but for humoring me when I would propose yet some new plan for this book when I first set out to write it. I would also like to thank Professors Martha Bolton, Margaret Atherton, Deborah Boyle, David Cunning, and Kristopher Philips for pointing the way to Lady Mary Shepherd. I should thank my students for giving me the opportunity to learn how to teach this material. It was always with them in mind that I wrote this book. And, I thank the many editors at Blackwell Wiley for their help and patience.

INTRODUCTION

This book was written for the undergraduate student taking a course in Modern philosophy. Even so, readers interested in philosophy, the general reader to the graduate student wanting to better acquaint themselves with the period, should find this book to be more than friendly to their respective ends. Modern philosophy is typically taken by scholars to begin around the late sixteenth century and to end around the early nineteenth century. In a course focused on the Modern period, a student can expect to engage in a study of certain philosophical texts. The latter would in turn focus on a variety of philosophical "problems." Many of the problems of interest to philosophers of the period would today be categorized in metaphysics, epistemology, ethics, and politics.

Although there was tremendous intellectual activity in the Modern period – political, economic, literary, musical, mathematical, theatrical, culinary, and the like – a significant amount of time and energy was focused on what philosophers of the period called *natural* philosophy, which today is identified as the physical sciences. Natural philosophy focused on topics not directly related to questions about human nature. Modern natural philosophers worked in astronomy, physics, and in applied disciplines such as mechanics and engineering. Several now-famous natural philosophers emerged from the Modern period, though due to our now drawing a distinction between philosophy proper and other disciplines, they are not immediately associated with philosophy. For example, Francis Bacon (1561–1626), Galileo Galilei (1564–1642), and Isaac Newton (1643–1727) were natural philosophers of the period. In addition to natural philosophy was what philosophers of the period called *moral* philosophy. Moral

This Is Modern Philosophy: An Introduction, First Edition. Kurt Smith.
© 2023 John Wiley & Sons, Inc. Published 2023 by John Wiley & Sons, Inc.

philosophy focused on topics specifically related to questions about human nature. Not only ethics and politics, but accounts of the possibility of knowledge, the function of human emotions, and, in general, studies in human psychology were classified as moral philosophy. John Milton (1608–1674) and Voltaire (1694–1778), whose names readers will recognize, are examples of moral philosophers of the period who today are studied in disciplines outside of philosophy proper.

To be counted among the natural and moral philosophers, one need not have been a professor of philosophy or a professional academic. In fact, most of the now-famous philosophers of the period studied other things or did something other than work in academia. For example, René Descartes (1596–1650) was a trained lawyer (though he never practiced), Elisabeth of the Palatinate was the Princess of Bohemia (1618–1680), Baruch Spinoza (1632–1677) was a lens-grinder, Gottfried Leibniz (1646–1716) was a court-librarian, Antoine Arnauld (1612–1694) was a theologian, Christina of the House of Vasa was the Queen of Sweden (1626–1689), John Locke (1632–1704) was a trained physician, and George Berkeley (1685–1753) was a Bishop. Among the philosophers studied in this book, only Immanuel Kant (1724–1804) was a professor of philosophy.

I.1 Knowledge as *Scientia*

Scientia was the Latin word that many philosophers of the Modern period used when talking about *knowledge*. The English word "science" comes from this Latin word. Of course, today, the word "science" refers to certain disciplines taught in buildings very likely located together on campus – astronomy, physics, chemistry, biology, medicine, and so on – and very likely conjures up images of laboratories, equations scribbled on blackboards, bubbling test tubes, hissing Bunsen burners, dissected frogs soaking in smelly formaldehyde, and the like. But this is not how philosophers of the Modern period understood the term. For them, *scientia* referred to a *systematic body* of true propositions. "Proposition" is simply the philosophical term for a *declarative sentence*, or what is sometimes called a *statement*. It is the sort of sentence in a natural language that can be either true or false. So, "I like cake" is an example of a proposition, but so are "The mass of this body is four kilograms," "A triangle has three sides," "God is omniscient," and "A substance is more real than its properties." The first example (about liking cake) is taken from ordinary life, the others are taken from the sciences of physics, mathematics, theology, and metaphysics, respectively. Both natural and moral philosophy were taken to be sciences.

Knowledge was not taken to be simply some *list* of true beliefs. So, someone was not considered to have knowledge simply because one believed this or that to be true. In this context, "to believe something" simply meant that one took a proposition to be true. To believe that a proposition is true in no way guarantees that it is true. There is always the possibility that what someone believes to be true is false. For example, many children have believed that Santa Claus brings presents to their houses on Christmas Eve. To their dismay, they eventually discover that this proposition is false. We might say that they had held a false belief. *Believing* that Santa did such a thing did not *make* it true. In addition to having or not having a belief, then, we can say that "having a *true* belief" means that the proposition that one holds to be true *is* true. So, the belief about Santa is not a true belief. No doubt people believe that Barack Obama was the 44th U.S. President. That he was the 44th U.S. President is in fact true. So, if someone believes this, they hold a true belief. What makes this claim true, of course, is some fact of the matter; not simply someone's taking it to be true.

Specific to the Modern period's conception of *scientia*, someone has knowledge only if that someone can demonstrate a command over a system of true propositions, where by *system* it was meant that all of the propositions that constitute the science are interrelated, forming a *hierarchy*, some propositions supported by others more basic in the system. The paradigm example of a science in the period was Euclidean geometry. First, the building blocks of the system are *defined*, after which certain *axioms* can be laid down. Together, these (the definitions and axioms) constitute the system's *foundation*. The axioms are the system's principal or foundational propositions – they are the system's most basic propositions. The truth and meaning of the non-foundational propositions in the system are ultimately anchored in, and can be derived from, the foundational ones. All non-foundational claims *presuppose*, or, as it can also be said, *entail*, the foundational ones, in the sense that in every case in which a non-foundational claim is true, the foundational ones are true too.

Here is an example that should make the connection between the Modern period's notions of *knowledge* and *science* clearer. Suppose that someone keeps in his or her pocket a laundry list of geometrical propositions, and every proposition on this list is true. Let us say that this person has included in their list 17 propositions. Their confidence in the truth of the propositions listed stems in part from the fact that they have copied them directly from a geometry textbook. They take this textbook to be authoritative. While pointing to one of the propositions on this list, we ask this person, "Do you believe that this one is true?" They reply, "Yes, I believe that that one is true." We point to another, "And that one?" They reply, "Yes, that one too." Fine. And given that these propositions *are* true, this person can be said to hold true beliefs of geometry. We might say that this person holds at least 17 true beliefs.

But, does this person understand *why* these propositions are true? Do they understand *how* they are related, and, more importantly, how they are related to the axioms that constitute the foundation of the system in which they operate? Here is an example of the sort of thing this person would need to possess in order to be counted as someone who had geometrical knowledge. Let us say that one of the propositions on this list is a claim about a particular right triangle, the sides of which measuring 3, 4, and 5 in length, respectively (the particular unit of length here is irrelevant). And let us say that another on this list is the Pythagorean Theorem. The claim about the particular right triangle presupposes the Pythagorean Theorem. In other words, the Pythagorean Theorem is entailed by the claim about the particular right triangle. The Pythagorean Theorem must be true if the claim about the particular right triangle is true. By the "must," here it is meant that in no conceivable circumstance (defined in terms of our system) could it ever turn out that the claim about the particular right triangle was true but the Pythagorean Theorem was false. If the Pythagorean Theorem *were* false, then the claim about the particular (Euclidean) right triangle *could not* be true. Even so, the Pythagorean Theorem is not among the *most* fundamental propositions in Euclidean geometry, for the Pythagorean Theorem presupposes the axioms of Euclidean geometry; the axioms are entailed by the Pythagorean Theorem. It is not possible for the Pythagorean Theorem to be true but Euclid's axioms to be false. If the axioms *were* false, then the Pythagorean Theorem *could not* be true.

The logical relation of entailment goes the other way too. That is, geometers typically say that the axioms of Euclidean geometry entail the Pythagorean Theorem. So, why think that the axioms are more fundamental than the theorem, since each entails one another? Here is an answer: Suppose that we were to swap out the definitions and axioms of Euclid's geometry with those of Bernhard Riemann. It turns out that in Riemannian geometry, the Pythagorean Theorem (in its Euclidean form) is false! In Riemannian geometry, if we are considering a right triangle, the sum of the two shorter sides, each squared, does not equal the square of the hypotenuse (the longest side). What *grounds* the Pythagorean Theorem are the definitions and axioms of Euclidean geometry, where the very meaning of the terms used to express the theorem have their *origin* in the definitions and axioms. Use different definitions and axioms and the theorems change too. This was one reason why philosophers also used *presupposes* in discussions like the one here, since it suggests a bit more than the truth-preserving logical notion of entailment. To say that the Pythagorean Theorem presupposes the definitions and axioms of Euclid's geometry is to say that when we even *conceive* the theorem (within the context of Euclid's geometry) we are (trivially) employing the definitions and axioms of Euclid, for they provide the very material in terms of which we are able to conceive a (Euclidean) right triangle. One could not conceive the theorem without also conceiving what is expressed by the definitions and axioms. By contrast, the definitions and axioms can be conceived without our conceiving the theorem. This asymmetry is in part why it is that the definitions and axioms are taken to be more fundamental in this system.

In terms of *scientia*, then, the presupposition relation tells us that the axioms are more fundamental in the system than the Pythagorean Theorem, and that the Pythagorean Theorem is more fundamental in the system than the claim about the particular right triangle. Transitivity holds, and so the axioms are shown to be more fundamental than the claim about the particular right triangle. In fact, the axioms are the *most* fundamental in the system. Their truth depends on no other proposition in the system – they are self-evidently true. The hierarchy of the system of propositions is revealed to us in our recognizing how one proposition presupposes another.

So, the person who we said holds 17 propositions taken from geometry to be true may hold true beliefs, but if they do not understand how the propositions on this list are related, and specifically how they are related to the axioms (they do not know, for instance, which propositions *must* be true given the truth of the propositions on this list, or which propositions presuppose which), no one in the seventeenth, eighteenth, or nineteenth centuries would say that this person has geometrical *knowledge*. What is missing is an understanding of the "linking" relation that connects the propositions on this list. What is missing is an understanding of the hierarchical structure. When philosophers of the period are talking about our having knowledge, then, many of them are talking about our having access to and command over a specific hierarchical system of true propositions, where this system, structurally speaking, would look a lot like Euclidian geometry.

I.2 Ideas, Propositions, and Beliefs

Thus far we have been using the words "proposition" and "belief." It is important to know that philosophers in the period were keen on casting their theories of knowledge in terms of *ideas*. Propositions and beliefs were understood in terms of ideas. Descartes, for example, in a letter tells the Catholic priest Guillaume Gibieuf: "I am certain that I can have no knowledge of what is outside me except by means of the ideas I have within me . . ." (19 January 1642 letter to Gibieuf). Nicolas Malebranche (1638–1715) says something similar: "But as for things outside the soul, we can perceive them only by means of ideas . . ." (*The Search After Truth*, Book III, Part II, Chapter I, Article 1). About knowledge specifically, Locke says that ideas are the "objects of its [i.e., the mind's] contemplation . . . [and] are the original of all knowledge" (*An Essay Concerning Human Understanding*, Book I, Chapter 1, §. 24). Let us briefly look at the role that ideas played within the framework of Modern theories of knowledge. We will get a better sense of how these three philosophical items – *ideas*, *propositions*, and *beliefs* – are related. The aim here will be to find some common ground, even if only a little, among the philosophers we will be considering in this book.

The word "idea" comes to us from Attic Greek, the ancient Greek language of Plato and Aristotle. Plato uses it, for example, within the context of his theory of the Forms. The words "*idea*" and "*eidos*," used by Plato to refer to the Forms, are derivatives of the Greek verb "*eidein*," which meant *to see* or *to look at*. Although many of the philosophers of the Modern period could read Attic Greek, they very likely, when reading Plato and Aristotle, studied instead the Latin translations of the two. And even here, they very likely read commentaries and not the "original" texts all by themselves. The Latin word used to translate the Greek word "*idea*" was "*species*," the latter the derivative of the verb "*specere*," which meant *to see* or *to look at*. The English words "spectacle" and "spectator," for example, are derivatives of this Latin word. Like the Greek word "*idea*," the Latin word "*species*" denoted *that which appears* (an *appearance*). Students are probably familiar with both words as they are used today in English. The word "idea" is found in psychological discourse, for example, and usually refers to a *psychological* or *mental entity* (sometimes cast as a nonmaterial entity). When a mind is thinking about something, it is said to be thinking by way of its ideas. On the other hand, the word "species" is found in biological discourse, and refers to a *natural kind*. The notion of a kind was sometimes understood in terms of structure or form. That is, to be an instance of a kind meant that the thing expressed a certain structure or form. You and I are human beings, for example, insofar as we express a certain structure or form. This is a sense in which you and I are alike, we are members of a kind. But it is in our expressing that form or structure that we are also understood to be different from, say, an oak tree. The oak tree is an oak tree (and not a human being) insofar as it expresses a certain structure (a structure that is not identical to that of the human being). The idea *is* this form or structure. Both meanings, found in psychology and biology, were expressed (or included) in Plato's word "idea."

On Plato's view, the idea or Form of human being is more real than you and me, since it exists regardless of whether you and I exist. In fact, the Form can (and does) exist independently of all particular human beings. Even so, you and I cannot exist as the things we are (as the particular *human beings* we are) without the idea or Form of human being. So, the idea does not depend on us, but we depend on it. Instances or particulars presuppose kinds; just like claims about particular triangles presuppose the axioms of Euclidean geometry. And, for Plato, that meant that these kinds, or ideas, were more fundamental in the cosmos than particular things. In fact, Plato took the ideas to be the most real things in the cosmos – they were the substances on which everything else depended. The system of ideas is what made *knowledge* possible.

Aristotle also put a great deal of emphasis on ideas as forms or structures. Even so, he disagreed with his teacher, Plato, rejecting Plato's view that the ideas existed independently of and prior to all particular objects in the cosmos. On Aristotle's view, if there were no particular human beings, then the idea of human being would no longer exist in the cosmos. Philosophical analysis led Aristotle to hold that the form or structure of a thing is manifested in the cosmos only when this structure was "enmattered," where the result was a "unity" brought about in the form or structure *acting through* matter. This enmattered-structure was a *particular* object in the cosmos – it was an *individual*. Aristotle called it a *hylomorphic unity*; "*hyle*" = matter and "*morphos*" = structure or form. But for all that, he did not think that ideas (forms) and matter existed independently of one another. Although the two (conceptually) emerge from a philosophical analysis of particular things, and cannot be understood as existing apart from one another, the analysis shows that there is a sense in which they are *prior* to the individual or particular. That said, the particulars are where the rubber meets the road. In the *Categories*, Aristotle refers to them as *primary substances*, and refers to ideas or forms as *secondary substances*. So, unlike Plato who had held that ideas were *the* substances of the cosmos, and that particulars were simply occurring instances of the ideas, Aristotle held that particular things (e.g. you, me, an oak tree, an individual horse, and so on) were the primary substances, which presuppose ideas, despite the fact that ideas cannot be understood as existing "apart" from the particulars. For Aristotle, everything, including ideas, ultimately depended on the particulars.

Ideas also played a role in Aristotle's account of the possibility of knowledge. Roughly, his view went as follows. The mind, which emerges from a complex organization of matter (the principle of organization is the *psyche* or soul – so the mind and the soul were not identical for Aristotle), is affected by the environment that is interacting with one's body (the organized body from which one's mind emerges). The sensations that arise in the brain affect the mind. From such sensory experience, the mind can actively abstract the structure or form presented in sensory experience, specifically abstracting the form or structure of the "object" experienced. This form or structure counted as the nature or essence of the object. It is what makes the object *intelligible* to a mind. The mind, then, actively works to "manipulate" the abstracted forms, where the mind can understand how they are related to one another. Such a system of interrelated forms (ideas), a system rooted in first principles (foundational forms), is a *scientia* – a genuine *body* of knowledge. Understanding this system, seeing how everything in the system "hangs together," is what it is to have or to possess knowledge.

Philosophers of the Modern period were well aware of the disagreements between Plato and Aristotle. These disagreements would be echoed in the works of Medieval and Scholastic philosophers (who historically preceded the Modern philosophers). Such disagreements are found, for example, in comparing the works of Augustine (354—430 CE) and Aquinas (1225–1274 CE), the former adopting much from Plato, the latter much from Aristotle. Philosophers of the Modern period were well acquainted with these and other Medieval philosophers. That said, by the time of the Modern period, it is probably more accurate to say that there really were no "pure" Platonist or Aristotelian positions. As noted earlier, whatever Greek philosophy modern philosophers did read had been worked and reworked by way of a host of commentators, so that what philosophers of the Modern period inherited was more of an amalgam of Plato and Aristotle than anything. It would be better to say that there were Platonisms and Aristotelianisms (plural). In fact, Neoplatonisms of the period, which were mixtures of Platonisms and Aristotelianisms (versions of which go back to at least Plotinus [204–270 CE]), were found at every turn.

When philosophers of the Modern period refer to *ideas*, then, we will need to keep in mind that what they meant was very likely something that better aligned with some mixture of Plato and Aristotle. And, in fact, we will see just this. Descartes, for instance, will cast ideas as modes of the mind (mode = *way of being*; a mode of x can also be taken to be a property of x) and at the same time as expressing natures that are eternally true and immutable, such as the ideas of geometrical shapes. In casting them as *modes*, as modifications or ways of being a mind, ideas are taken as depending importantly for their existence on the existence of the finite mind (the mind they modify), on the particular mind that thinks them. No minds, no ideas. But, as in the case of the idea of the true and immutable nature of a geometrical figure (e.g. a triangle), the idea, understood as "object" represented or presented to the mind, does not depend in any way on the existence of any finite mind. In tying the idea to a particular mind (as a mode), the view sounds Aristotelian; but in tying the idea to something that exists independently of the mind (as an eternal – i.e. as a non-spatial, non-temporal – object), the view sounds Platonic.

In the Third Meditation, Descartes classifies his thoughts into various kinds. He wonders which kind of thought is the bearer of truth. The most basic kind of thought, he says, is an idea. "Some of my thoughts are as it were images of things, and that it is only in these cases that the term 'idea' is strictly appropriate – for example, when I think of a man, or a chimera, or the sky, or an angel, or God" (AT VII 37; CSM II 25). Descartes was among the first in the period to introduce the Greek word "idea" back into philosophical discourse. Notice that he says that ideas are "as it were" images of things, and not *literally* images. The sense in which ideas are images is in virtue of their *representing* or *presenting* or *exhibiting* (Descartes uses these terms interchangeably) objects directly and immediately to the mind. The idea of sweet, the idea of cold, and the idea of God are just as much ideas as is the idea of a triangle. Of course, we might think of the idea of a triangle as being visual in nature. But not all ideas are visual. In saying that ideas are "as it were" images (and not literally images), Descartes is able to sidestep the obvious question: what does sweet or cold or God *look* like? The idea of sweet, the idea of cold, and the idea of God are not visual images of anything, but are instead image-like – they are image-like insofar as they represent or present or exhibit things directly and immediately to the mind.

In the Second Set of Replies (appended to the *Meditations*), Descartes defines "idea" as follows: "I understand this term to mean the form of any given thought, immediate perception of which makes me aware of the thought. Hence, whenever I express something in words, and understand what I am saying, this very fact makes it certain that there is within me an idea of what is signified by the words in question" (AT VII 160; CSM II 113). An idea is the form of a thought. This form is what accounts for your being *aware of* something. It is part of the account of how something is made intelligible to the mind. In the Third Meditation, Descartes also says that ideas are the immediate objects of thought. This is repeated in his reply to Hobbes in the Third Set of Replies. There, Descartes says: "I am taking the word 'idea' to refer to whatever is immediately perceived by the mind" (AT VII 181; CSM II 127). Descartes took Hobbes' view to be that ideas, or *phantasms* as Hobbes calls them more often than not, are literal images located on extended (i.e. material) things. Descartes may be right about that. Even so, as Hobbes says in *De Corpore*, Part 2, Chapter VII, Article 1, when a man thinks, he or she thinks with his or her ideas (phantasms), which are not identical with the *things* that the ideas represent. So, even for Hobbes, and even supposing that they are always of or are always about extended (material) things, the "objects" that are immediately presented to the mind are ideas. So, in this very narrow sense, it would appear that his view agrees with Descartes's. Locke defines "idea" similarly: "It being that term which, I think, serves best to stand for whatsoever is the object of the understanding when a man thinks, I have used it to express whatever is meant by *phantasm, notion, species,* or *whatever it is which the mind can be employed about in thinking...*" (*An Essay Concerning Human Understanding,* Book I, Chapter 1, §. 8). We will see that this view about ideas being the "objects" of which a mind is immediately aware is an important element constituting a common ground among the philosophers we will be examining.

In the above passage taken from the Second Set of Replies, Descartes makes the connection between ideas and language: "whenever I express something in words, and understand what I am saying, this very fact makes it certain that there is within me an idea of what is signified by the words in question." This is a common theme that can also be found expressed throughout the period. The view is that our ideas (their contents – i.e. what they present or exhibit to the mind) serve as the *meanings* of our words. Our ideas (their contents) are what our words signify. And so, if one asserts a proposition, the meaning of what is asserted is the content of an idea. Although Hobbes disagreed with Descartes about many things, he agreed with Descartes about the connection between words and ideas—our words are signs that signify our thoughts (*De Corpore*, Part I, Chapter II, Articles 2 and 3). Locke also says something similar, namely that our words, if meaningful, signify ideas (*An Essay Concerning Human Understanding,* Book III, Chapters 1 and 2). As we will see down the road, like Hobbes and Locke, Hume will suggest that this ideational theory of meaning ought to play a central role in the doing of philosophy (*A Treatise of Human Nature,* "Abstract," and *An Enquiry Concerning Human Understanding,* close of Section II). For, if it turns out that the words that someone uses in making a claim have no corresponding ideas (either the word is not "annexed" to an idea or the word is "annexed" to an idea, but the idea is empty), it will follow that the words that this someone uses are meaningless. And, if the words that this someone uses are meaningless, it will follow that this someone is not *claiming* anything after all. This will serve to show (at least according to

Hobbes, Locke, and Hume) that much of what philosophers took themselves to be "claiming," specifically within the context of doing metaphysics, was in the end meaningless, and should be abandoned.

The relationship between *idea*, *proposition*, and *belief* can now be made clearer. In line with everything just said, especially when we are being technical, we will take a proposition to be a statement whose meaning is the content of an idea, where if one holds that the proposition being asserted is true, one is said to have a belief. So, just to be clear before moving forward: *to believe something is to hold that some proposition is true, where the meaning of the proposition being asserted is an idea (its content).* Of course, we will see important variations of this. So, Hume, for example, will say that a belief is an idea whose force and vivacity is strong, which accounts for why the one whose idea it is holds that the idea represents something that is true. That said, even though today we attribute truth to propositions, in what follows we will take "true proposition," "true belief," and even "true idea," as coextensive phrases, unless stated otherwise. For, as we will see, many of the philosophers who we will be examining, when addressing their readers in nontechnical language, used these sorts of phrases when working out their respective theories of knowledge.

I.3 The idea of a Modern Philosophy Course

The idea of a Modern philosophy college course is relatively new – maybe a little over a century old. Whose work gets included in such a course continues to evolve, but there are some basic figures and important works and "problems" that have remained central. A typical course, whether semester or quarter, will very likely include the following philosophers:

René Descartes (1596–1650)
John Locke (1632–1704)
Immanuel Kant (1724–1804)

Although Bacon and Galileo preceded Descartes, and are considered Modern philosophers, neither Bacon nor Galileo are typically included in the basic Modern philosophy course – although some professors who specialize in the history of philosophy of science may include them. And although Newton is certainly as important a figure as are Hobbes and Locke, the basic course typically does not include Newton either. The "book-ends" of the basic Modern philosophy course are usually Descartes and Kant. So, the typical course as it has evolved over the past century or so, if it is geared to deal with the entire period, begins with Descartes and ends with Kant.

Between Descartes and Locke we might find included Malebranche, Spinoza, or Leibniz; and between Locke and Kant: Berkeley, Hume, or Reid. The first group, the group between Descartes and Locke, though not counting Locke, constitutes what has become known as the Continental Rationalists, where Descartes is considered the first among the Modern rationalists. The second group, the group between Locke and Kant, though not counting Kant, constitutes what has become known as the British Empiricists, where Locke is considered the first among the Modern empiricists (though Hobbes runs a close second). There are courses that focus specifically on the rationalists, others that focus specifically on the empiricists, and yet others still that focus on just a single figure or a single work. Kant, the only professional philosopher of the group (Newton was a professor at Cambridge, so, he would certainly count, but since we would not be studying Newton, he is not in our group – the group we will be studying), and so Kant will be the outlier. As we will see, he in effect argued that there is a sense in which both groups, rationalists and empiricists, were essentially right, and that their views need not be taken as mutually exclusive. He makes his case for this in his *Critique of Pure Reason*.

Some scholars have argued that the distinction between rationalism and empiricism is not something that was clearly recognized by the philosophers of the Modern period. It has been argued that it is a distinction fabricated by twentieth-century historians of philosophy, and then imposed on the philosophers of the Modern period. Although there is some merit to this argument, philosophers of the period can nevertheless be seen as recognizing at least some of the philosophical differences that hold between the two categories. Let us pause and look more closely at this distinction, along with a few other "isms" associated with the period, before bringing this Introduction to a close.

I.4 Rationalism and Empiricism

The basic difference between rationalism and empiricism is this: rationalism holds that the very *possibility* of knowledge is rooted in certain things inherent in the human mind. Descartes, for instance, held that the mind came furnished, so to speak, with certain ideas. He referred to these ideas as "innate." These ideas serve to "structure" sensory experience. It was by way of these ideas, then, that the human mind makes the sensible world intelligible to itself. By contrast, empiricism holds that the very *possibility* of knowledge is rooted in sensation. The mind has no inherent structure. Nothing is essentially innate. It is, as Locke famously claimed, a *tabla rasa* (a blank slate). Without the particulars of sensory experience, such as seeing colors and hearing sounds, the human mind would be empty, so to speak. It is from the particulars of sensory experience that the human mind derives its abstract concepts or ideas.

Here is another way to think of the difference: the rationalist thinks that your mind imposes its structure, the structure inherent in it, on sensory experience, making the world around you intelligible. An important assumption for this view is that this structure corresponds in all the right ways to the structure of the world (otherwise, how could you be said to have knowledge of the world?). By contrast, the empiricist thinks that the world around you imposes its structure on your mind by way of sensory experience. An important assumption here is that the structure that your mind ultimately receives corresponds in all the right ways to the structure of the world (otherwise, how could you be said to have knowledge of the world?). Both views hold that the correspondence of the structure of your mind and the world account for the possibility of knowledge of the world. Where they differ, then, is with respect to the origin of the structure that now resides in your mind. Rationalists say that it was "in" the mind even *before* having your first sensory experience, whereas empiricists reject that and say that it emerged only *after* having your first sensory experience.

In the "Preface" of his *New Essays on Human Understanding* (finished in 1704 and published in 1765), Leibniz makes clear some differences that he finds to hold between his view and that of Locke's. One difference looks similar to the one drawn above, between the rationalist and the empiricist. Leibniz writes:

Our disagreements concern points of some importance. There is the question whether the soul itself is completely blank like a writing tablet on which nothing has yet been written – a *tabla rasa* – as Aristotle and the author of the *Essay* (i.e. Locke) maintain, and whether everything which is inscribed there comes solely from the senses and experience; or whether the soul inherently contains the sources of various notions and doctrines, which external objects merely rouse up on suitable occasions, as I believe and as do Plato and even the Schoolmen and all those who understand in the sense the passage in St. Paul where he says that God's law is written in our hearts . . ..

(*New Essays*, Preface, marginal number 48)

This is but one distinction to keep in mind, then, as you work through this book. In this book, you will find an examination of at least one important rationalist, Descartes, and an examination of several important empiricists, Hobbes, Locke, Berkeley, Hume, and Shepherd. There is also an examination of Kant's view.

I.5 Some Other "isms" of the Period

The distinction between rationalism and empiricism appears to be primarily epistemological – for each accounts differently for the possibility of knowledge. "Epistemology" refers to an area of philosophy that deals with theories of *knowledge*. But the distinction is not solely epistemological. Philosophers also differed with respect to their ontologies. "Ontology" refers to the study of theories of *being*. As philosophers today would put it, they differed with respect to their metaphysical commitments. "Metaphysics" refers to an area of philosophy that deals with theories of *reality*. Ontology is included in the area of metaphysics. Metaphysical commitments in many cases served to underwrite the epistemology. Although philosophers today (and philosophy courses today) typically keep epistemological and metaphysical questions separate, this was not always the case for philosophers of the Modern period.

The following are some other "isms" associated with the period that are related to various metaphysical commitments.

I.5.1 Monism and Dualism

Monism, as the name suggests ("mono" = one), was the view that at bottom (or ultimately) there exists one and only one kind of substance in the cosmos. There were two widely held types of monism:

1. Materialism
2. Idealism

Materialism is the view that the only kind of substance that exists in the cosmos is corporeal (bodily or material). Such a substance is essentially a thing that is extended (in three dimensions – in length, breadth, and depth). By contrast, *idealism* is the view that the only kind of substance that exists in the cosmos is mental or nonmaterial (sometimes said to be "spiritual").

Such a substance is essentially a thing that perceives or thinks. Now, a materialist *can* allow for minds, or immaterial things, but those things arise or emerge out of the interaction of bodies. Minds are not substantial (they cannot exist on their own). Minds depend for their being on the being of matter. No bodies, no minds. Likewise, an idealist *can* allow for bodies, or material things, but those things arise or emerge out of the perceptions of minds. Bodies are not substantial (they cannot exist on their own). Bodies depend for their being on the being of minds. If no minds, no bodies. The important thing to stress is that for the materialist all things ultimately can be explained by an appeal to matter, whereas for the idealist all things ultimately can be explained by an appeal to mind. Hobbes and Pierre Gassendi are good examples of materialists; Leibniz, Berkeley, and Hume are good examples of idealists.

By contrast, *dualism* ("dua" = two) is the view that at bottom (or ultimately) there exists exactly two kinds of substance in the cosmos. Interestingly enough, the two kinds of thing are minds and bodies. That is, a dualist holds that minds can exist independent of bodies, and vice versa. One does not essentially depend on the other. This is different, then, from a monist – a materialist, say – who may allow for the existence of mind, but rejects the claim that a mind can exist independent of matter. Likewise for the idealist, where they may allow for the existence of body, but will reject that body can exist independent of mind. So, neither the materialist who allows for mind nor the idealist who allows for body are dualists. Full-blown dualism requires that the two kinds of substance be able to exist independent of one another. So, if no minds, there could in principle be body; or if no bodies, there could in principle be mind. But since both are substantial, such hypotheticals (for the dualist) are pointless. For, given that mind and matter are each substantial, they cannot come to be nor cease to be. This means that if dualism is true, the case would not arise where there is no longer mind or no longer body. Unless ordained by God, the view is that there could never be a time when minds simply vanished, leaving only bodies remaining; or there could never be a time when bodies simply vanished, leaving only minds remaining. Instead, being finite substances, they are brought into existence by the divine being – so, they are brought into existence by way of divine *creation* – and they can only cease to be by way of divine *annihilation*. So, for the dualist, no *natural* process could produce or destroy mind or body. At least this was the typical sort of view found in the period. Descartes is a good example of a dualist.

I.6 The Problem of the External World

It was noted above that in a philosophy course focused on the Modern period that the course would very likely be geared around certain philosophical "problems." With this in mind, it is worth mentioning that there are some interesting differences with respect to the character of ordinary, everyday problems, and the character of *philosophical* problems. For instance, suppose someone asks you: "How high is Mount Whitney?" This is an example of a simple, ordinary, everyday question. Even so, very likely the answer is not something that you would know off-hand. But you know exactly what this person is asking, and you know what an answer should look like. What is more, you very likely know how to go about getting the answer – *Google* it, or find a website online dedicated to reporting the heights of mountains, or consult a book, or ask your friend who recently hiked Whitney, and so on. Philosophical problems are different.

Ludwig Wittgenstein (1889–1951) once wrote: "A philosophical problem has the form: 'I don't know my way about'" (*Philosophical Investigations*, 123). We might say that when properly worked up, a philosophical problem is *perplexing*. This has nothing to do with its being difficult to answer. So, do not confuse difficulty with perplexity. As Wittgenstein says in the passage just quoted, one of the features that makes a philosophical question perplexing is that if you understand the problem at hand, you have absolutely no bearing on *how* to answer it, or what an answer would even look like. He says something related to this in *The Blue Book* about what he refers to as *philosophical bewilderment*, where such problems, he says, "produce in us a mental cramp. We feel that we can't point to anything in reply to them and yet ought to point to something" (*Blue Book*, p. 1). So, for example, you believe that there is a world that exists independently of your perceiving it, even independently of your *conceiving* it. The world exists utterly independently of you. What belief could be more simple and fundamental than that? Here is the philosophical question: other than your having been told this, how do you *know* that there is a world that exists independently of your mind? How exactly will you go about demonstrating to yourself that there in fact exists a world independently of your mind – that is, independently of your conceiving it? Do you *imagine* the world without you in it? But in imagining it are you not still conceiving the world? So, what next? Clearly, in being such a fundamental belief, you would think that it would be easy to demonstrate its truth. But, as Wittgenstein says, you feel that you cannot point to anything, and yet feel that you ought to be able to point to *something*. What could be more obvious than that there exists a world independent of you? The "perplexity" here is borne out by your feeling that you ought to have an answer to something so obvious but realize that you do not even know what an answer would look like. Notice how different this is from that question about the height of Mount Whitney.

Philosophers of the Modern period raised several very exciting and challenging philosophical questions. Too many to work through in a single book. But many of them turn out to be related. Specifically, they are related to the question just raised in the previous paragraph, a philosophical problem that we will call for lack of a better name *The Problem of the External World*. Although this can be treated as a single problem, it can also be cast as a kind of "umbrella" problem, under which several other problems lurk. Or it can be cast as a general category of more specific problems that form a kind of "family" of related philosophical problems. For example, related problems are: If there is a world that exists independently of my mind, what is its nature? Is it material? Immaterial? How can that be determined? Is my experience a *representation* of anything? What is conceptually involved in thinking that it is? Does my experience of the world, assuming it to be a representation of the world, correspond to the way the world actually is? If there are bodies, for instance, do they possess the sizes, shapes, colors, smells, and so on, as my mind represents them as having? Again, how could that be determined? Do such questions presuppose a distinction between appearance and reality? Where does *that* distinction come from? Does this distinction not in turn presuppose that we already understand the difference between what we are calling *appearance* and *reality*? The questions multiply. Are there other minds like mine? Or, is it like when dreaming? – although in dreams I have the experience of talking with others, for example, I typically (when awake) do not take them to be "real" people. Even so, they *seem* to be real. But, again, this assumes I know what is *real* and what it *seems like* to be real (and being awake and dreaming). Why *must* the people I experience when awake be "real" people? What is the difference between being awake and dreaming anyway? And the questions multiply.

The central philosophical problem that will serve as the thread that ties everything together in this book will be The Problem of the External World. It is a problem that each of the philosophers examined here – Descartes, Hobbes, Berkeley, Hume, Kant, and Shepherd – took very seriously. In allowing this problem to guide our examination, we will take up some of those other related questions mentioned in the previous paragraph. By book's end, a reader should have a basic but solid understanding of philosophy as it was done in the Modern period.

I.6.1 A Quick Note About This Book

As noted earlier, a typical Modern philosophy course will likely include a study of the views of Descartes and Kant, since they are good examples of the work being done in the beginning and ending of the period. The rub is who to include in between. As also noted, between Descartes and Kant, professors typically include Locke. This way, students get a good example of a "rationalist" (Descartes), and a good example of an "empiricist" (Locke), and then a good example of a philosopher who considered both (Kant). But some think that this is biased toward epistemology. To avoid this, professors sometimes include Hobbes, Leibniz, or Berkeley, where the aim is to widen the focus to include ontology – in which case, Descartes is the example of the dualist, and one of these others an example of a monist. Of course, some think that this is biased toward metaphysics. Yet, other professors will avoid epistemology and metaphysics altogether, and instead focus on moral systems or on political treatises. In these cases, Descartes is almost certainly abandoned for someone like Hobbes (since Descartes wrote almost nothing concerning moral or political matters), though Kant would likely remain on the list. The challenge of putting together any book for undergraduates to use in an upper-division course in Modern philosophy is that no book would be able to cover the breadth of interests. Even so, a decision about what to study, who to include, and so on, had to be made. Focusing on The Problem of the External World, the decision is made a bit simpler, for we can turn to studying philosophers who had dealt specifically with *that* problem.

The working idea of this series was in part to address the costs of books for a class, by locating the primary texts online, which would be free to students, so that if a professor wished, they could order just one book – a book from this series. The host of primary texts would now be free to the student. I have located for the student all of the online primary texts that we will be using, and links to the relevant texts are included at the ends of each chapter. So, no need to require students to purchase the *Meditations* (Descartes), the *Essay* (Locke), the *Treatise* (Hume), the *First Critique* (Kant), and so on. This can be quite an investment. The typical alternative to this is to require students to purchase a "reader" that includes the primary texts. The challenge here is that such readers fail to include the specific material that a professor wishes to cover, and so there is always the problem of how to supply students with the missing texts. Besides, most of the readers include translations of texts whose copyrights have long expired. These will typically be the very texts found for free online! So, ideally, a professor could order just this book.

Of course, it is more than likely that a professor, if they are like me, would not want to order just this book, and would instead prefer to be the one who leads students through the primary texts. A book like this, then, would either be redundant or an obstacle. If the former, the professor can think of the book as serving as detailed notes for the students, and can serve to prepare them for upcoming discussions; if the latter, the professor can use what is said in this book as a foil to establish his or her own view of the material. Either way, this book can be useful to both the professor and student.

In earlier drafts of this manuscript, a reviewer noted that the book included only men. The reviewer had a point! As with many in my generation (and before), familiarity with the work of women philosophers of the Modern period is (and has been) seriously lacking. It has only been relatively recently that scholars – for instance, Margaret Atherton, Martha Bolton, Deborah Boyle, David Cunning, Karen Detlefsen, Jane Duran, Jessica Gordon-Roth, Alan Gabbey, John Grey, Sarah Hutton, Christia Mercer, Carolyn Merchant, Eileen O'Neill, Lisa Shapiro, Emily Thomas, to name several – have begun to bring to light their contributions. It is exciting! The remarks of the reviewer prompted me to search for a woman philosopher of the period whose work fit in with our study of The Problem of the External World. It was by way of my correspondence with Professor David Cunning that the work of Lady Mary Shepherd was brought to my attention. I am indebted to him, and to several others – Professors Margaret Atherton, Martha Bolton, Deborah Boyle, and Kristopher Philips – for additional guidance on how to present some of the details.

Although the following six chapters focus primarily on the views of Descartes, Hobbes, Berkeley, Hume, Kant, and Shepherd, the reader will find a host of discussions throughout the book that include others. So, those interested in Locke, for instance, will find his view discussed here. Readers will also find that the larger chapters are Chapters 1, 3, and 5, the chapters on Descartes, Berkeley, and Kant. Chapters 2, 4, and 6, the chapters on Hobbes, Hume, and Shepherd, are relatively shorter. Perhaps in future additions, the book can include studies of Anne Conway (1631–1679), Lady Margaret Lucas Cavendish (1623–1673), Malebranche, Leibniz, Spinoza, Anton Wilhelm Amo (c. 1703–1759), Thomas Reid (1710–1796), and the like. Chapter 1, the chapter on Descartes, is by far the longest. This was on purpose, for it is the chapter in which the philosophical stage is set for the chapters that follow. The book, as it moves forward, builds on things established in previous chapters. So, the chapters, although independent, together form a coherent narrative.

In the Epilogue, the philosophical views from each of the six chapters are explicitly, though only briefly, juxtaposed, for one last look at how they are similar and how different. The comparison is done by way of an important analogy introduced by Socrates at the close of Book VI of Plato's *Republic* – the analogy of the Divided Line. It is hoped that the use of this analogy will help readers further "locate" other important philosophers, independent of the historical periods in which they lived and worked.

1

RENÉ DESCARTES

Descartes (pronounced *Day Kart*) was born 31 March 1596, in the small 1.1
town of La Haye, France. At the age of 10, he entered the Jesuit College of La
Flèche. He completed his studies there in 1614 and entered law school at the
Université de Poitiers, earning his Baccalaureate and License in Canon and
Civil Law in 1616. Instead of practicing law, however, he joined the army of
the Dutch Prince, Maurice of Nassau (1567–1625). After military service, he
lived in Paris, moving to the Netherlands around 1628. He lived most of his
adult life in the Netherlands, writing several important philosophical works.
He is famous for having made important connections between geometry
and algebra, for introducing into physics a new conception of matter, for
suggesting that living things were basically fancy machines, and for showing
how it was possible to acquire knowledge. He died 11 February 1650, while
employed by the Court of Queen Christina of Sweden (1626–1689).

1.1 Descartes's First Principle

In Part One, Article 7 of the *Principles of Philosophy* (1644),[1] Descartes claimed: 1.2

> . . . [I]t is a contradiction to suppose that what thinks does not, at the very
> time when it is thinking, exist. Accordingly, this piece of knowledge – *I am*

---

[1] In this chapter, although I provide links to free online readings, I will be using *The
Philosophical Writings of Descartes*, 3 vols., translated by John Cottingham, Robert
Stoothoff, and Dugald Murdoch, referred to as CSM (vol 3 includes Anthony
Kenny, so CSMK), Cambridge: Cambridge University Press, 1988. I will also use
Oeuvres de Descartes, 11 vols., edited by Charles Adam and Paul Tannery, referred
to as AT, Paris: Librairie Philosophique J. Vrin, 1983. Citations, then, will refer to
the AT and CSM volume and page numbers.

This Is Modern Philosophy: An Introduction, First Edition. Kurt Smith.
© 2023 John Wiley & Sons, Inc. Published 2023 by John Wiley & Sons, Inc.

thinking, therefore, I exist – is the first and most certain of all to occur to anyone who philosophizes in an orderly way. (AT VIIIA 7; CSM I 194–195)

1.3   The heading of Article 7 would foreshadow this claim, though it specifically
cast the claim in terms of *doubt*: "It is not possible for us to doubt that we
exist while we are doubting" (Ibid.). Of course, given that doubting is a species of thinking, the point of both formulations seems to be fundamentally
the same. In Part One, Article 49 of the *Principles*, Descartes would go on to
classify as an *eternal truth* the proposition "He who thinks cannot but exist
while he thinks," which, again, looks to be an alternative formulation of this
first and most certain piece of knowledge. The name of the class of propositions speaks for itself – eternally true propositions are *always* true, which is
another way of saying that they *cannot ever* be false. If it was not possible for
a statement to be false, then it was considered to be *necessarily* true. It is in
this category that he would also classify all mathematical propositions.

1.4   Descartes first proposed the above eternal truth several years earlier, though
he did not refer to it as such, in Part Four of the *Discourse on Method* (1637),
claiming that it was the "first principle" of his philosophy. This no doubt anticipated his later calling it a first and most certain piece of knowledge. In the
Discourse, he reported that he became aware of the importance of this first
principle when engaged in a philosophical exercise, a kind of thought experiment in which he had attempted to think everything false. He recounted:

> But immediately I noticed that while I was trying thus to think everything
> false, it was necessary that I, who was thinking this, was something. And
> observing that this truth "*I am thinking, therefore I exist*" was so firm and sure
> that all the most extravagant suppositions of the skeptics were incapable of
> shaking it, I decided that I could accept it without scruple as the first principle
> of the philosophy I was seeking. (*Discourse*, Part Four: AT VI 32; CSM I 127)

It is important from the outset to note that this insight – the insight that if "I
am thinking" is true, "I exist" cannot be false – is not solely the insight into
each of the individual, simpler claims – "I am thinking," or "I exist" – though
clearly they are elements of the insight. No, the insight is ultimately an insight
into the *connection* between one's thinking and one's existence; or, in terms
of the truth of propositions, between "I am thinking" and "I exist" – where "I
am thinking" is understood as guaranteeing the truth of "I exist."

1.5   Even so, some critics expressed concerns over the simpler claims "I am
thinking" and "I exist" – namely, that before any connection between them
could be understood, one would first have to understand what one meant by
"thinking" and "existence." Descartes, they complained, had failed to define
these terms. So, how could any connection between *them* be understood? To

these critics, who had authored "objections" to his *Meditations on First Philosophy* (1641), a work that would be published in the interim between the *Discourse* and *Principles*, and a work at which we will look more carefully shortly, Descartes had replied that when one *thinks*, one could not fail to understand that *that* was what one was doing. Likewise, one's own existence was so obvious to oneself that nothing could be clearer. Descartes wrote:

> Thus when anyone notices that he is thinking and that it follows from this that he exists, even though he may never before have asked what thought is or what existence is, he still cannot fail to have sufficient knowledge of them both to satisfy himself in this regard. (Sixth Replies: AT VII 422; CSM II 285)

So, on Descartes's view, one does not require definitions of "thinking" or "existence" in order to understand that one thinks or exists. Such things are self-evident. In his study of Descartes's *Meditations*, Edmund Husserl (1859–1938) had identified the certainty associated with such experience as *apodictic* certainty (Husserl 1960). On Husserl's reading, there was an *unimaginableness* associated with the "object" given to one in one's experience, such that when given, one could not imagine that what was given was not what was given. If one thinks of the number 1, he or she would find it impossible to imagine that perhaps it is not the number 1 but the number 3 or a triangle that was being thought. For, supposing one raised the concern and asked, "perhaps this isn't the number 1 that I'm thinking about," in being able to form that very thought, he or she would have to know what it was that he or she might be mistaken about. One could be mistaken or wrong about a lot of things, but not about something like this (we might cast this particular case in terms of a principle of identity: A = A). In the *Principles*, Descartes again would emphasize that knowing what *thinking* is, or what *existence* is, did not require that one first be given philosophical definitions. He wrote:

> Matters which are very simple and self-evident are only rendered more obscure by logical definitions, and should not be counted as items of knowledge which it takes effort to acquire. (*Principles*, Part One, Article 10: AT VIIIA 8; CSM I 195–196)

He then offered what *thinking* and *existence* are as examples of the very simple and self-evident items he was talking about in this passage. Definitions of such items would only serve to muddy the waters, making obscure that which was already clear.

In two works, unpublished during his lifetime, *Rules for the Direction of the Mind* (c. 1628, though there is evidence that suggests he returned to this work later, sometime after 1634), and a dialogue, *The Search for Truth* (the   1.6

date it was written is unknown), he would make similar claims. For example, in the *Rules*, he wrote:

> By "intuition" I do not mean the fluctuating testimony of the senses or the deceptive judgment of the imagination as it botches things together, but the conception of a clear and attentive mind, which is so easy and distinct that there can be no room for doubt about what we are understanding . . .. Thus everyone can mentally intuit that he exists, that he is thinking, that a triangle is bounded by three lines, and a sphere by a single surface, and the like. (*Rules*, Rule Three: AT X 368; CSM I 14)

And, in the *Search*, the character Eudoxus says:

> . . . [T]here are, in my view, some things which are made more obscure by our attempts to define them: since they are very simple and clear, they are perceived and known just on their own, and there is no better way of knowing and perceiving them . . . doubt, thought and existence can be regarded as belonging to the class of things which have this sort of clarity and which are known just on their own.
>
> I would never have believed that there has ever existed anyone so dull that he had to be told what existence is before being able to conclude and assert that he exists. The same applies to doubt and thought. (*Search*: AT X 523-24; CSM II 417)

To be clear, then, the insight, his first principle, is neither the insight that "I am thinking" nor that "I exist" are true, separately, but instead is the insight into the *connection* that holds between these two simpler claims. This cannot be stressed enough. What is more, as has also been suggested, which will be made clearer in what follows, this connection was also something that one "intuited," to use a term from the *Rules*. That is, one might be said to intuit that one thinks and that one exists, but, according to Descartes, if one philosophizes in the right way, one will *also* intuit the connection between them, such that one would clearly understand that if "I am thinking" is true, "I exist" is also true (cannot be false) – the former guaranteeing the truth of the latter. That's the insight: that's his first principle!

1.7   To several anonymous critics of the *Meditations*, whose objections were compiled by Marin Mersenne (1588–1648), forming the Second Set of Objections, Descartes wrote:

> Now awareness of first principles is not normally called "knowledge" by dialecticians. And when we become aware that we are thinking things, this

is a primary notion which is not derived by means of a syllogism. When someone says "I am thinking, therefore I am, or I exist", he does not deduce existence from thought by means of a syllogism, but recognizes it as something self-evident by a simple intuition of the mind. This is clear from the fact that if he were deducing it by means of a syllogism, he would have to have had previous knowledge of the major premise "Everything which thinks is, or exists"; yet in fact he learns it from experiencing it in his own case that it is impossible that he should think without existing. (AT VII 140; CSM II 100)

In this passage, Descartes denied that the insight was an *argument*. But, is this a problem? For, his denial would appear to conflict with how the principle was proposed – *I am thinking, therefore, I exist*. That certainly looks like an argument. Let us look closer at this.

In the *Discourse*, as we already know, Descartes had initially proposed   1.8
the principle in its now famous and more familiar form:

> *I am thinking, therefore I exist*
> *Je pense, donc je suis* (the original French formulation)
> *ego cogito ergo sum* (the translated Latin formulation)

His use of the conclusion indicator "therefore" (French: *donc*; Latin: *ergo*) did more than to suggest to early readers, who were reading the *Meditations* in light of having read the *Discourse*, that Descartes's first principle was an argument, and presumably a valid one at that, since the claim seemed to be that if the premise "I am thinking" was true, the conclusion "I exist" could not be false.

If his first principle was an argument, however, a potential problem   1.9
lurked, the trouble being that arguments themselves were not usually understood as being first principles. Descartes himself seemed to agree with this, as seen in the passage just quoted, where he had denied that his first principle was an argument. Typical for the period, arguments were understood as logical instruments employed by philosophers to derive other statements, which, of course, included deriving statements *from* first principles. But a first principle (or generally, a *principle*), like an axiom in geometry, was taken to be self-evidently true; and so, arguments were not employed in securing their truth – the greater point being, they themselves were not understood to be arguments. Although not perfectly clear, perhaps some early readers of the *Meditations* might have been willing to grant Descartes that "I am thinking" and "I exist," taken separately, met the first principle criterion, but, as has been noted, several critics were in fact

unwilling to grant even this, and claimed that definitions were needed. But what is crystal clear is that none of his critics were willing to let the inference that "therefore" suggested count as a first principle – the epistemic status of inferences, as opposed to self-evident statements, were another epistemological kettle of fish.

1.10   Pierre Gassendi (1592–1655), for example, author of the Fifth Set of Objections appended to the *Meditations*, complained that the way Descartes had established the first principle in the Second Meditation was unnecessarily cumbersome for the reader, and suggested that it would have been clearer had it took the more familiar form as offered in the *Discourse*. He suggested that the argument in the Second Meditation should have gone something like this:

1.   Whatever thinks acts.
2.   Whatever acts exists.
3.   Therefore, whatever thinks exists.

The trouble with this, assuming that it was the argument Gassendi was suggesting, is that the argument does not conclude "I exist," but only that "Whatever thinks exists." It also lacks the crucial premise "I am thinking." If we are charitable, however, we might read Gassendi as having instead suggested the following argument, which, it should be kept in mind, would not have taken the then standard form of a Categorical Syllogism, though it would have run close to taking the common form of *Modus Ponens*. Charitably, then, the argument Gassendi may have been suggesting in his criticism was this:

1.   Whatever thinks, exists.
2.   I am thinking.
3.   Therefore, I exist.

This argument at least includes as a premise "I am thinking" and includes the conclusion "I exist." But, as we can see, it requires a premise that is not explicitly introduced by Descartes, namely Premise (1), which in the prior formulation was the argument's *conclusion*, statement (3); but what is more, it is a premise that Descartes had said, in the earlier quoted reply to critics, was not something the reader would have had to rely on in order to have had the insight into his first principle.

1.11   We might rework this second rendering of Gassendi's suggested argument to avoid the problematic Premise (1).

1. If I am thinking, I exist.
2. I am thinking.
3. Therefore, I exist.

Here, Premise (1) makes the argument perfectly conform to *Modus Ponens*. And, it is not the potentially problematic general claim "Whatever thinks, exists." But, notice that Premise (1) seems to express the insight itself – it is Descartes's first principle, minus the "therefore," and formulated as a conditional statement. It expresses the connection between "I am thinking" and "I exist," a connection that he said one could intuit. So, perhaps Descartes was claiming that his philosophical thought experiment had revealed to him that this *conditional statement* was true. Let us consider this interpretation further.

The logic of conditional statements was well known among those who attended school in the seventeenth century. A conditional statement has two parts: the "if" part, which is called the *antecedent*, and the "then" part, which is called the *consequent*. Let p be the antecedent and q the consequent, where the conditional is "*if p, then q.*" We can assign truth (T) and falsity (F) to p and q, which will allow us to make the following table (Table 1.1), which defines the logical connection between p and q:

1.12

Table 1.1 Truth-table for conditionals.

p	q	If p, then q
T	T	T
T	F	F
F	T	T
F	F	T

Here is how to read this table. Start with the first row: The antecedent p has been assigned true (T) and the consequent q has been assigned true (T). If both are true (T), then the conditional statement "*If p, then q*" is true (T). Now, the second row: Here, the antecedent has been assigned true (T) and the consequent has been assigned false (F). If the antecedent is true (T) and the consequent is false (F), the conditional statement "*If p, then q*" is false (F). The third row: The antecedent has been assigned false (F) and the consequent true (T). If the antecedent is false (F) and consequent true (T), the conditional statement "*If p, then q*" is true (T). Lastly, the fourth row: If both the antecedent and consequent are false (F), the conditional statement

"*If p, then q*" is true (T). Notice that there is only one scenario in which a conditional statement is false (F) – when its antecedent is true (T) and its consequent is false (F).

1.13   If we allow Descartes's first principle to take the form of Premise (1) of our third formulation of Gassendi's suggestion, as the conditional statement "If I am thinking, I exist," what Descartes would seem to have been claiming is that his philosophical thought experiment had revealed to him that this statement is true, and necessarily so, which would mean that in every conceivable case in which its antecedent "I am thinking" is true, its consequent "I exist" was not false. For, if "I exist" *could* be false while "I am thinking" is true, the first principle, cast in the form of a conditional statement, would be false! But, since it is a first principle, and so *necessarily* true, it could never turn out that when "I am thinking" is true, "I exist" was false. So, how does Descartes's philosophical thought experiment reveal that this claim, "If I am thinking, I exist," is necessarily true (i.e. always true)? We will turn to answering this question in a moment, but before we do, let us weigh our reading Descartes's principle as an argument against our reading it as a conditional statement. In the end, it may not matter which reading we adopt. But as scholars-in-training, it is important that we make sure that our reading is both faithful to the texts and charitable to their author.

1.14   Is there any textual evidence that might further support our reading Descartes's first principle as the statement, *If I am thinking, I exist*, instead of reading it as one of the arguments considered above?

1.15   Recall an earlier quoted passage from the *Rules*. There, in the passage taken from Rule Three, Descartes had introduced the notion of *intuition*, where he had said that it was the conception of a clear and attentive mind. The thing conceived is so obvious and clear that one cannot doubt what was being conceived. When thinking, Descartes said, everyone can intuit that he or she thinks, and what is more, that he or she exists. Also in Rule Three, Descartes would go on to contrast intuition to what he called *deduction*. In fact, on his view, intuition and deduction are the only two ways by which we can come to have knowledge. Well, we know that intuition is at the very least the immediate and clear cognizing of the truth of a simple proposition. And, as we will see in the passage that follows, deduction is at the very least the making of inferences. But, are they mutually exclusive? If something is an intuition, will that rule out its being an inference, and vice versa? And, if intuition is limited to the cognizing of single, simple propositions, and deduction is limited to inferring one proposition from another, will this put pressure on Descartes's rejecting that his first principle was an argument, something that looked to be best classified as an instance of deduction? Let us see. In Rule Three, Descartes wrote:

. . . [The] distinction [between intuition and deduction] had to be made, since very many facts which are not self-evident are known with certainty, provided they are inferred from true and known principles through a continuous and uninterrupted movement of thought in which each individual proposition is clearly intuited. This is similar to the way in which we know that the last link in a long chain is connected to the first: even if we cannot take in at one glance all the intermediate links on which the connection depends, we can have knowledge of the connection provided we survey the links one after the other, and keep in mind that each link from first to last is attached to its neighbor. Hence we are distinguishing mental intuition from certain deduction on the grounds that we are aware of a movement of a sort of sequence in the latter but not in the former, and also because immediate self-evidence is not required for deduction, as it is for intuition; deduction in a sense gets its certainty from memory . . . (*Rules*, Rule Three, AT X 369–370; CSM I 15)

So, why is the first principle not an instance of deduction? Recall that Descartes had said that as a result of his philosophical exercise, we *intuit* the connection between "I am thinking" and "I exist." About that, still in Rule Three, Descartes further wrote:

The self-evidence and certainty of intuition is required not only for apprehending single propositions, but also for any train of reasoning whatever. (*Rules*, Rule Three, AT X 369; CSM I 14)

He appeared to extend intuition to include the clear cognizing of a connection between two claims, which, we will see, was cast as the cognizing of an *inference*. So, *both* intuition and deduction look to be part of Descartes's account of the reliability of inference making. From what he says in the above passage, it would appear that he thought that some instances of intuition could include the relating of simple propositions – such as what occurs when intuiting the connection between "I am thinking" and "I exist" – where this, strictly speaking, would not be an instance of deduction proper. How so? For starters, with respect to deduction, one is aware of a *movement* of the mind, from one proposition to another; whereas, by contrast, with respect to intuition, one is not aware of any movement, but instead the connection and the items connected are immediately perceived or cognized all at a single go. The certainty of intuition arises from immediately given self-evidence, whereas the certainty of deduction in part arises from memory. Apparently, deduction does not require any self-evident elements. What are we to make of this?

1.16   In the Fifth Meditation, Descartes had considered a limitation of deduction, or of argumentation generally, that may help clarify how deduction proper differs from intuition. He wrote:

> ... [I]t is not necessary for me to think that all quadrilaterals can be inscribed in a circle; but given this supposition, it will be necessary for me to admit that a rhombus can be inscribed in a circle – which is patently false. (AT VII 67; CSM II 46)

A rhombus is a quadrilateral (a four-sided shape), though it is not inscribable in a circle. Even so, *if* one were to assume that "All quadrilaterals can be inscribed in a circle" was true, then from that and the claim "A rhombus is a quadrilateral," it would *necessarily* follow that "A rhombus can be inscribed in a circle." The argument would go like this:

All quadrilaterals can be inscribed in a circle.
A rhombus is a quadrilateral.
Therefore, a rhombus can be inscribed in a circle.

Deduction is strange indeed. The above argument about the rhombus is valid, in that it is not possible for its premises to be true and its conclusion false at the same time. That would seem to be behind Descartes's noting that any argument of this form would *necessarily* yield the conclusion. In this particular case, given this is a valid argument, and its conclusion is false, it would follow that at least one premise is false. Why? A valid argument cannot allow all true premises and a false conclusion. So, if the conclusion is false, given this is a valid argument, it cannot be the case that all of its premises are true – at least one would have to be false. This result was usually the point of making what philosophers of the period referred to as a *reductio ad absurdum*: a valid argument with a false conclusion (usually a contradiction), which required that at least one of the premises be given up as false. We find this form of argument used as far back as Plato, and it was widely taught in seventeenth-century schools. The logical properties of a valid argument with a false conclusion were widely known to Descartes and his contemporaries. So, he would not have been saying anything new in his assessment of the argument about the rhombus. Why might he have introduced it in his discussion?

1.17   As with any valid form of argument, there is no guarantee that any of the premises are true; the only guarantee is that *if* all the premises are true, the conclusion will be true, too. In other words, for a valid form of argument, there is no *conceivable* scenario in which its premises are true and the conclusion is false. That said, if someone did not know that "All quadrilaterals can be inscribed in a circle" was false, but instead took it to be true, which was Descartes's point, the argument would require that this same someone hold (or tentatively entertain), at least as long as he or she held the premises to be true, that "A rhombus can be inscribed in a circle" is true – despite its being patently false! What this analysis reveals is that deduction, a movement from a premise or premises to a conclusion, guarantees only that *if* the premise or premises were true, the conclusion would be true, too. The thing that deduction proper does not require is that we know that the premise is, or premises are, true. By contrast, intuition, assuming that we apply this notion to inferences, seems to require that we know that all of the premises *are* true. They are self-evidently true. We would be looking at a valid argument with actually (not simply possibly) true premises, which is how logicians define a *sound* argument. But, in denying that his first principle was an argument, it seems that Descartes would also reject its being cast as a sound argument.

With the above in mind, let us return to our trying our hand at interpreting Descartes's first principle as a conditional statement instead of interpreting it as an argument. In this case, intuition would require that the antecedent statement (analogous to the premise of an argument) would be known to be true (it would be *self-evidently* true), the consequent statement (analogous to the conclusion of an argument) would be known to be true, too, and that the way in which the two are connected is such that in every conceivable case in which the antecedent was true, the consequent was true, too. Every element of the intuition – "I am thinking," "I exist," and the connection between them – is intuited at a single go. There is no "movement" of the mind from "I am thinking" to "I exist," as would happen in the case of deduction proper. 1.18

Let us now turn to the philosophical exercise that Descartes claimed had revealed to him the first principle. As suggested earlier, we find the best account of it in the *Meditations*. 1.19

In the First Meditation, Descartes walked his readers through the intellectual exercise that he had only mentioned in the *Discourse*. Recall, the exercise involved the attempt to think everything false. What Descartes said the reader would discover is that try as he or she might, one thing that could not be thought false was his first principle. As we get into this, it is worth noting that the now famous phrase (*I am thinking, therefore I exist*) did not appear in the *Meditations*. So, what gives? Some scholars have thought that this was not an oversight or a mistake on Descartes's part. Finnish philosopher Jaakko Hintikka (1929–2015), for instance, cast the *Meditations'* 1.20

version in terms of its being a kind of *performance*. So, in line with Descartes, he does not take the insight to be an argument, but instead views it as a kind of "aha!" moment had by the reader. The exercise sets the stage, so to speak, and the insight into the first principle is revealed to the reader by way of the performance that he or she undertakes after having immersed him or herself into the First Meditation. Now, the philosophical exercise was a rather radical sort of thought experiment – the challenge of overcoming the possibility of a supremely powerful being who had created Descartes with the aim of deceiving him, getting him to believe something to be true that was in fact false. Let us look at this carefully.

1.21   As Descartes would demonstrate at the opening of the Second Meditation, assuming even this most radical scenario as introduced in the First Meditation, there was one thing that this hypothesized supremely powerful deceiver could not deceive him about. Descartes reasoned:

> But there is a deceiver of supreme power and cunning who is deliberately and constantly deceiving me. In that case I too undoubtedly exist, if he is deceiving me; and let him deceive me as much as he can, he will never bring it about that I am nothing so long as I think that I am something. So, after considering everything very thoroughly, I must finally conclude that this proposition, *I am, I exist*, is necessarily true whenever it is put forward by me or conceived in my mind. (AT VII 25; CSM II 17)

As noted above, we do not get the principle as it had been famously proposed in the *Discourse*. In this Second Meditation passage just quoted, we are told that, if one reflected on the matter, one would be struck by the fact that *necessarily* the statement "I exist" is true *on the condition that* one's own existence was being thought about. So, how does the bit about the supremely powerful being who is aiming to deceive us yield the first principle exactly?

1.22   Start by our supposing that since no perfectly benevolent being would ever aim at deceiving anyone, the supremely powerful being in our thought experiment, in being *essentially* a deceiver, must be considered evil. So, we are hypothesizing a supremely powerful *evil* being. Suppose that you were created by this supremely powerful evil being. Its aim is to deceive you at every possible opportunity.

1.23   Next, we should consider how to take "truth" and "falsity" here. Although Descartes did not make explicit what he meant by these in the *Meditations*, his examples offer some hint as to how he thought the reader would have understood such terms. As suggested in his Third Meditation discussion of the difference between his ideas of a goat and a chimera, for example, we can glean that the issue under discussion, namely truth and falsity, and to what kind of thought they are associated, that he had in mind something like a correspondence view of truth – where one difference between the ideas is that while the idea of a goat is typically taken to correspond to a real thing, a goat, the idea of the chimera is typically taken to not correspond to anything at all, at least not to anything that exists "outside" the mind (AT VII 37; CSM II 26). And, we can glean a similar point from his Third Meditation discussion of the difference between the two ideas of the sun that he possesses, where he judges that one better corresponds to the object it represents, insofar as it better *resembles* it (AT VII 39; CSM II 27).

Now, a well-known account of truth was an Aristotelian correspondence   1.24 account. This view tells us that a statement's truth is determined by some corresponding fact. A *fact* is a piece of reality; a *statement* is a piece of language. Truth in this context is understood as a *relation* holding between a statement and a fact (Figure 1.1):

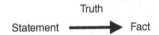

Figure 1.1 Correspondence Theory of Truth.

This view of truth – a correspondence account – was very likely an account Descartes ran across while a student at La Flèche. That he had adopted some view like this is suggested, in addition to the sorts of Third Meditation examples just mentioned, in a letter to his friend Claude Clerselier (1614–1684), dated 1649, where Descartes explained to Clerselier what he meant when discussing truth and falsity: "Truth consists in *being*, and falsehood only in *non-being*..." (AT V 356; CSMK III 377). In the Fifth Meditation, he wrote: "for it is obvious that whatever is true is something" (AT VII 65; CSM II 45). Such remarks support our thinking that Descartes took a statement to be true if it corresponds to reality (being), and is false if it fails to correspond to reality, which amounts to saying that it corresponds to nothing (nonbeing).

With the deceiver and a tentative account of truth and falsity on the table,   1.25 we are ready to better understand the import of Descartes's philosophical exercise. So, start by considering the statement:

Michelle is at her yoga studio.

Given the correspondence notion of truth, this statement is true if, and only if, it is a fact that Michelle is at her yoga studio. Otherwise, this statement (*Michelle is at her yoga studio*) is false. Now, we are assuming that there is a supremely powerful being, which in part means that this being can do anything that is *logically possible* (anything that is *conceivable*). This is a view that Descartes and his contemporaries would have run across in their having read Aquinas' *Summa Theologica*. So, again, Descartes would not have been introducing anything new to his readers here. Now, imagine that you are wondering whether the statement about Michelle is true. Let us say that you have under the *contacts* menu in your iphone the phone number (a landline) to her studio. You call that number and Michelle answers. "Good," you say to yourself, "she is at her yoga studio; so the statement is true." But, we can imagine that the supremely powerful being, prior to your making the call, say, reprogrammed your iphone so that although you thought that you were calling her yoga studio, you were actually calling her personal cellphone. She was actually standing in the organic food isle at the grocery store when you called. She was not at her studio. So, the statement *Michelle is at her yoga studio* was false. But, since you were (and remain) unaware of the supremely powerful being's activities, you continue to believe that the statement *Michelle is at her yoga studio* is true! The supremely powerful evil being has succeeded at deceiving you.

1.26   Let us say that the supremely powerful evil being will attempt to deceive you whenever possible. That is, if a scenario of deception is conceivable, assume that the supremely powerful evil being will take advantage of this and will succeed at deceiving you, at making this possible scenario an actual one. By the close of the First Meditation, in light of this thought experiment, Descartes admitted that things looked quite grim for anyone who claimed that knowledge was possible. For, according to Descartes, knowledge was possible only if there was at least one thing, no matter how trivial or slight, that one could not be wrong about – that is, it could not be false when held to be true. If nothing met this criterion, then all bets were off with respect to the possibility of our ever having knowledge.

1.27   As seen in the above quote taken from the opening of the Second Meditation, Descartes's own analysis revealed to him that there was at least one thing that this supremely powerful evil being could not deceive him about. At least, Descartes was not able to conceive the conditions necessary for deception in this case.

1.28   Here is how his philosophical exercise revealed this. We understand that "I exist" would be true if I in fact exist. On the flipside, we also understand that "I exist" would be false if I do not exist. Of course, if the latter is the case, I would not be in a position to entertain the statement "I exist." That, in part, is Descartes's point. Let us say that the supremely powerful evil being wished to deceive you about this statement, about "I exist" – it wants to get you to think that it is true when in fact it is false. Well, if the supremely powerful evil being is going to deceive you, clearly you will have to exist; otherwise, *who* is this supremely powerful being deceiving? We have already determined that "I exist" is false if, and only if, I (well, you in this case) do not in fact exist. So, this statement would be false (where the "I" in the statement refers now to you), if you do not exist. Therefore, in order to make the statement "I exist" (in reference to you) false, the supremely powerful evil being will have to make it such that you do not exist. But, if this is the statement the supremely powerful evil being wishes to deceive *you* about, it will have to be the case that you *do* exist. Otherwise, there is no one there to be deceived. So, in order to pull off the deception, the supremely powerful evil being will have to make it such that you do and do not exist at the same time. Well, that is a contradiction; it is logically *im*possible! Or, in other words, the case (that you do and do not exist at the same time) is *in*conceivable! The stipulation, recall, was that the supremely powerful evil being can *do* anything logically possible (conceivable). Since the case at hand is inconceivable, it is not the sort of thing that *can* be done. It is not among the things that any being, including a supremely powerful one, can *do*. (In fact, the "it" in the previous two statements does not refer to anything!)

To say that the supremely powerful being *cannot do* it makes it sound like   1.29
this being is not supremely powerful after all. But, as Aquinas would make clear, saying it that way would be a mistake. For, we are not actually pointing out something that this being cannot *do* – for the simple reason that there is no *something* there. "I exist and I do not exist at the same time" does not refer to or pick out some possible state of affairs. There is no way for anyone to even think the scenario required for deception here. Since the possibility of your being deceived about "I exist" requires the impossible state of affairs, and the latter cannot ever come about (it cannot even be thought!), your existence (while thinking about your existence) is one thing that the supremely powerful evil being cannot deceive you about. At least, you would have absolutely no grounds for thinking that such a being could deceive you on this matter. And, if you cannot even conceive the possibility of "I exist" being false, so long as you take it to be true, the only alternative is that is must be true and that you cannot ever be wrong about it! Now, this does not guarantee the past or future, so the philosophical exercise does not show that you cannot be deceived about whether you existed in the past or will exist in the future. It is limited to showing that your existence is guaranteed only at the moment you reflect on your existence.

Recall that Descartes had claimed that this insight – *If I am thinking, I*   1.30
exist – is among those found in the category of eternally true propositions, a category that includes the propositions of mathematics. So, in this category we would find claims such as "Two added to three equals five," "A square has four sides," "The interior angles of a Euclidian right triangle equal the sum of two right angles," and so on. What he noticed about such

claims was that when he considered them directly, he was compelled to affirm their truth. That is, when directly before the mind, they were so clear and distinct that they compelled his will to declare that they are true.

1.31   At the opening of the Third Meditation, thinking specifically of his first principle established in the Second Meditation, he wrote:

> In this first item of knowledge there is simply a clear and distinct perception of what I am asserting; this would not be enough to make me certain of the truth of the matter if it could ever turn out that something which I perceived with such clarity and distinctness was false. So, I now seem to be able to lay it down as a general rule that whatever I perceive very clearly and distinctly is true. (AT VII 35; CSM II 24)

And all of this would be great, if it were not for the fact that we have yet to overcome the threat of the supremely powerful evil deceiver. For, even though we may agree that there are certain items that when considered by us *directly* are such that we cannot even conceive their being false, which gives us every confidence in our holding that they are true – items such as *If I am thinking, I exist*; *I am at the very least a thing that thinks*; *Two added to three makes five*; *A square has four sides*; *The nature of mind is to think*; *The nature of body is to be extended* (in length, breadth, and depth), and so on – the story about that supremely powerful evil being is still on the table. We have yet to show that in such matters as those just mentioned that this evil being has not created us so that when we add two and three, for instance, and get five, that their sum is not five but is some other number unknown to us. Perhaps we have been created in such a way that when we add two and three and get five, the evil being gets a big kick out of it, knowing that we cannot even imagine being wrong about the sum, and yet we *are* wrong about it. Perhaps this supremely powerful evil being has made us such that we cannot conceive a case in which we exist and do not exist at the same time, but such a case is nevertheless conceivable (to beings other than ourselves). Descartes was clearly aware of this lingering issue. He wrote:

> But what about when I was considering something very simple and straightforward in arithmetic or geometry, for example that two and three added together make five, and so on? Did I not see at least these things clearly enough to affirm their truth? Indeed, the only reason for my later judgment that they were open to doubt was that it occurred to me that perhaps some God could have given me a nature such that I was deceived even in matters which seemed most evident. And whenever my preconceived belief in the supreme power of God comes to mind, I cannot but admit that it would be easy for him, if he so desired, to bring it about that I go wrong even in those matters which I think

I see utterly clearly with my mind's eye. Yet when I turn to the things themselves which I think I perceive very clearly, I am so convinced by them that I
spontaneously declare: let whoever can do so deceive me, he will never bring
it about that I am nothing, so long as I continue to think I am something; or
make it true at some future time that I have never existed, since it is now true
that I exist; or bring it about that two and three added together are more or less
than five, or anything of this kind in which I see a manifest contradiction.
(*Meditations*, Third Meditation: AT VII 36; CSM II 25)

So, we still have some important philosophical work to do. Now, we will
have to admit that when *directly* considered, the abovementioned items are
such that we cannot conceive the conditions that would render them false.
Consequently, our grounds for doubting their truth are not found in anything that we think directly in those items. In fact, as just admitted, we cannot conceive the conditions that would render them false. For instance, we
cannot conceive the case in which we exist and do not exist at the same
time, or that two added to three is not five, or that a triangle does not have
three sides. Rather, our grounds for doubting their truth are tied to a story
about the possibility of a supremely powerful evil being who created us with
the aim of deceiving us and not about what we directly or immediately conceive. We are satisfied that when we add two and three their sum is five. The
trouble is that perhaps that satisfaction is a result of the supremely powerful
evil being's design. As stories go, that is admittedly a pretty thin thread on
which to hang anything. But, it is still something that we must address. Why
think that we can trust our being satisfied in such cases, that we can trust
our being certain, when it is possible that our rational faculty has been
designed to go wrong? About this, Descartes wrote:

And since I have no cause to think that there is a deceiving God, and I do not
yet even know for sure whether there is a God at all, any reason for doubt
which depends simply on this supposition is a very slight, and, so to speak,
metaphysical one. But in order to remove even this slight reason for doubt, as
soon as the opportunity arises I must examine whether there is a God, and, if
there is, whether he can be a deceiver. For if I do not know this, it seems that
I can never be quite certain about anything else. (Ibid.)

All of this talk about a creator, whether it be a trustworthy creator or not,
and so on, can be philosophically distilled into the following concern: If we
can settle the issue about the origin of our mind and its capacities to intuit
and deduce, we can then settle the issue about whether we can trust those
capacities. If we cannot determine this, we will always be able to doubt,
though admittedly indirectly, the items that, when directly intuited, compel

us to declare their truth. What is worse, of course, is that if a supremely powerful evil being were our origin, we would be in trouble, epistemologically speaking. We might as well pack it up and go home. So, we want to at the very least debunk that possibility as soon as possible.

1.32   But, why think that anything other than himself was his origin? Perhaps Descartes and not some evil being is the origin of his own mind. In the Third Meditation, Descartes wondered whether he might be the origin of his own mind and its capacities (AT VII 46–47; CSM II 32). He was quick to note, however, that if he were its origin, he would have certainly made it so that he would know that he was his origin. And, he certainly would not have created himself to want or to lack anything. It went without saying, of course, that this very investigation, his searching for answers, demonstrated that he lacked all sorts of things. And, although he does not spell it out, clearly the other issue would be the looming contradiction that in order to be his own origin, he would have to exist before he existed. That is, if he created himself, then he would have had to have existed before he created himself. But, perhaps he is an infinite being and just does not know it. For, since an infinite being never does not exist, the very concept of origin is rendered meaningless. So, if he were an infinite being, the worry over origins could be dispelled, and so the bit about existing before he existed could be set aside. So, is he an infinite being? Well, if he were, which in terms of being an infinite *mind* would at least manifest as his being *omniscient* (all knowing), it would be odd indeed if he knew everything *but* the fact that he was an infinite mind. For, as he honestly (and modestly) admits in the *Meditations*, he certainly does not know everything. But, let us say that his being infinite was manifested in terms of power instead of knowledge. Well, if he was *omnipotent* (all powerful), he certainly would have the power to make himself smart enough to know that he was an infinite being. And, he certainly would not have had any need to work through six meditations to get any answers. So, what is the origin of his mind and its capacities to think? Ruling out that its origin is a supremely powerful evil being would make things less worrisome, perhaps, but the issue about origins would still remain. For, until we can settle that, worries, no matter how slight, are still in play.

1.33   Now, several paragraphs later, still in the Third Meditation, Descartes saw another and equally important philosophical reason for considering whether there exists a God who is not a deceiver, and who is the origin of his mind and its capacities. This reason, as we will see, is also importantly related to what in our Introduction was referred to as the *Problem of the External World*. For, whatever is responsible for creating Descartes's mind and its capacities, if not himself, would, by this very fact, be something that existed prior to, and hence independently of, his mind. That is, the origin of his mind must be something other than his mind. Such a proof, if one could be made, would demonstrate that there exists at least one thing other than his mind. This would be the first of several proofs Descartes offered in support of the claim that there exists a world "outside" his mind, where by "outside," as noted in this book's Introduction, it was taken to mean at the very least "independent" – so, an external world, a world that existed outside one's mind, would be a world whose existence in no way depended on one's mind.

But how might Descartes go about such an investigation? In a letter to   1.34
Guillaume Gibieuf (1583–1650), dated January 1643, Descartes wrote: "I am certain that I can have no knowledge of what is outside me except by means of the ideas I have within me" (AT III 474; CSMK III 201). This may explain what went into his reasoning that if in examining his ideas he found one that he could not account for

> ... and hence that I myself cannot be its cause, it will necessarily follow that I am not alone in the world, but that some other thing which is the cause of this idea also exists. But if no such idea is to be found in me, I shall have no argument to convince me of the existence of anything apart from myself. For despite a most careful and comprehensive survey, this is the only argument I have so far been able to find. (AT VII 42; CSM II 29)

So, let us now turn to Descartes's analysis of his ideas, and see how that analysis will result in producing a proof for the existence of an infinite being. This being, as will become clear, is not Descartes, of course, but is what theologians refer to as *God*. This proof, as we will see, is importantly related to Descartes's establishing the origin of his mind (specifically his faculty of reason), which in turn allowed him to secure the trustworthiness of his faculty of reason. To do this, we will want to look first at Descartes's view of ideas, and the role they played in his philosophical system. As part of our examination, we will also want to make clearer Descartes's ontology, which will include two distinct kinds of "reality," *formal* and *objective reality*, and the three "levels" of each: *mode*, *finite substance*, and *infinite substance*.

1.2 Preliminaries on Ideas and the Ontology

As just mentioned in the last section, in a letter to Gibieuf, Descartes had   1.35
told his friend about the importance of *ideas* in his philosophical system: "I am certain that I can have no knowledge of what is outside me except by means of the ideas I have within me" (AT III 474; CSMK III 201). So, if he is going to address the Problem of the External World, he will appeal no doubt to ideas. Let us keep that in mind as we proceed.

1.36   Descartes was in fact among the first philosophers of the period to reintroduce the word "idea" back into philosophical discourse. The word has its origins in the ancient Greek language of Plato and Aristotle. Philosophers prior to Descartes, those working in the earlier Medieval and Scholastic periods, preferred to use the Latin word *species*, which they had settled on as their translation of the Greek word *idea*. This Latin word is probably familiar to you, if you have taken a course in biology. *Species* refers to a *kind* of thing. And, that is in part what the medievals and scholastics meant by it. A species of animal is a kind of thing. If we replaced the Latin with the Greek, we might instead say: the *idea* of animal is a kind of thing. In fact, said this way, we would be expressing one sense in which Plato and Aristotle intended the term.

1.37   According to ancient and medieval views, the idea of animal is the *form* of animal. If something is an animal, it is an instance of this form or idea. If we think of this form as being a pattern of organization, where matter is what is organized, we now come close to how Aristotle used the term. On his view, when matter is organized in a certain way, in the pattern of animal, say, the result would be an *individual* animal, which would be an instance of the form animal. The existent individual *things* in the universe, according to Aristotle, were each a *unity* of matter and form. So, take matter and organize it in the pattern we refer to as "dog," and there will now exist an individual dog. Take the same matter and now organize it in the pattern we refer to as "oak tree," and there will now exist an individual oak tree. Every existent individual thing in the universe is an instance of some kind.

1.38   Now, Plato and Aristotle disagreed about the ontological status of ideas. On Plato's view, ideas (the *Forms*) were the most real things in the universe. Without them, nothing existed. They were the *substances* of the cosmos. That is, if no ideas, then there could never be instances of dogs, oak trees, rivers, and so on. Every existent thing in the cosmos depended on the ideas. The ideas stood prior to any material instances (individuals). So, the idea of dog stood prior to there being any particular dogs.

1.39   When you and I think of a dog, according to both Plato and Aristotle, we are in some way accessing the idea of dog. But, the idea is not yours or mine. It is neither spatial nor temporal. It is eternal. According to Plato, it does not exist here or there, or in your head or in mine. But, through our faculty of the intellect, we can access ideas. Even if there were no existent instances of dog (i.e. no particular dogs), the idea of dog would remain. We could in principle still *think* of a dog. This in part shows how it is that ideas are the most real entities in the universe, according to Plato, since all individual (material) things in the universe depend on ideas for their being what they are, whereas ideas do not depend on individual (material) things for their being. Ideas would exist regardless of whether there were ever any (material) instances of them.

Aristotle, however, would not grant ideas that sort of ontological status.   1.40
To be sure, the idea or form of dog accounted in part for a particular instance,
an individual dog, and it is what made the thing intelligible to us (as a dog),
but we (as human beings) never encounter an idea independently of individual things, or apart from a pattern's being "enmattered." What we encounter are particulars, individual dogs and oak trees. We never encounter
"doghood," say. As my professor Chuck Young used to say, you cannot
scratch doghood behind the ears. According to Aristotle, ideas always are
accompanied with matter. An individual thing is a unity of idea (form) and
matter. For Aristotle, such individuals are the most real things in the universe. They are matter (*hyle*) informed or structured (*morphos*), or, as he
would put it, an individual is a *hylomorphic unity*. Without matter and idea
(form), there are no individuals. But here, matter and idea look to be philosophical abstractions, the results of analysis, taken from our encounters with
individuals. So, where Plato had said that the *kinds* were the most real things
in the universe, Aristotle said that the *particulars* (instances of kinds) were
the most real things. For Aristotle, the particulars of the cosmos were the
primary substances, everything else depending on them.

So, did Descartes adopt one of these views? Well, he seems to have devel-   1.41
oped a view that included a little of both. This would not have been a new
view, however, we find it going back to at least the third-century CE, when
the ancient Roman philosopher Plotinus (205–270 CE) held something like
it, a view that philosophers now refer to as *Neoplatonism*. And, several
prominent philosophers of the modern period appear to have adhered to
some version of Neoplatonism. Descartes might certainly be counted
among them. Let us now turn to looking carefully at Descartes's view on
ideas, with the aim of examining his assessment of his idea of the infinite
being. This will fit in with the theme of our book, with our exploration into
the Problem of the External World.

Before setting out in the Third Meditation to examine whether God   1.42
exists, and is no deceiver, and is the origin of his mind, Descartes said that
a point of order needed to be addressed:

> First, however, considerations of order appear to dictate that I now classify
> my thoughts into definite kinds, and ask which of them can properly be
> said to be the bearers of truth and falsity. Some of my thoughts are as it
> were images of things, and it is only in these cases that the term "idea" is
> strictly appropriate – for example, when I think of a man, or a chimera, or
> the sky, or an angel, or God. Other thoughts have various additional forms:
> thus when I will, or am afraid, or affirm, or deny, there is always a particu-
> lar thing which I take as the object of my thought, but my thought includes

something more than the likeness of that thing. Some thoughts in this category are called volitions or emotions, while others are called judgments. (AT VII 37; CSM II 26)

He characterized ideas as "as it were images." The Latin is *tanquam rerum imagines*. Strictly speaking, the idea of sweet or the idea of cold, for instance, are not images – well, they are not *visual* images. Even so, such ideas nevertheless *represent* or *exhibit* to the mind *something* (sweetness and coldness in the cases just mentioned). It is just that the representing or exhibiting here is not a visual representing. But insofar as ideas represent or exhibit things to the mind, they are "like" images. That seemed to be his point.

1.43   So, an idea, ontologically speaking, is what accounted for an *object's* being represented (or directly presented) to the mind in a moment of consciousness (Descartes uses *represented*, *presented*, and *exhibited* interchangeably). Such an "object" is that of which the mind is directly aware. The objects represented can vary: his list above includes just a few – a man, a chimera, the sky, an angel, and God. We also can have ideas of simpler objects: the idea of hot or cold, the idea of a color, the idea of sweet, and so on. The "what" of thought is given by way of an idea. So, if one asks, "What are you thinking about?," the answer would involve your referring to an idea that is before your mind. Descartes will later claim that the mental capacity or faculty responsible for directly "producing" ideas in a mind is the *intellect* or the *understanding*.

1.44   Now, according to the passage just quoted, ideas are a special kind of thought, but there are more complex thoughts, the latter nevertheless including in them an ideational component. They will include an *object* of thought. These more complex thoughts involve both essential faculties of the mind: the understanding, just mentioned, and the will. The will is associated with a second faculty of mind, the volitional faculty, which is a faculty of activity (suggesting that the understanding, as a faculty, is passive in some sense). A complex thought, then, will include an ideational element, which will be associated with the faculty of the understanding, and a willing element, associated with the volitional faculty. The latter's activity is "directed at" the object of thought, at an idea. Consider the following complex thoughts, expressed by the following statements:

I affirm the Pythagorean Theorem.
I fear the tiger.
I desire pizza.

Let us look at each. In the first, the Pythagorean Theorem is the object of the thought, which is given by way of some idea. That is the ideational element. Now, when I *affirm* what is presented to me in thought (via the idea), I exercise the volitional faculty. In the second, the tiger is the object of the thought, which is given by way of some idea. That is the ideational element. When I fear what is presented to me in thought (via the idea), I exercise the volitional faculty. And, in the third case, the pizza is the object of the thought, which is given by way of some idea. As in the other cases, that is the ideational element. When I desire what is presented to me in thought (via the idea), I exercise the volitional faculty. Descartes is not clear about what accounts for the differences between affirming, fearing, and desiring, given they are exercisings of the same faculty, but he is clear to suggest that fearing *x*, for instance, is typically called an *emotion*, and affirming *x* is typically called a *judgment*, where "*x*" here is our stand-in for an idea. Perhaps the differences in volitional exercisings are best understood in terms of the ideational elements given in a thought. Scholars are still debating about how to read Descartes on this issue. Even so, many scholars would agree that if we look carefully at Descartes's discussions of such things, we will discover that the thoughts of human beings are, on his view, to be classified in the *complex* category. Every complete thought will include an ideational (intellectual) *and* a volitional element.

But let us return to Descartes's Third Meditation analysis of thoughts, 1.45 where our focus will be on what he said about ideas. Let us begin with how he sorted out ideas into three distinct kinds:

> Among my ideas, some appear to be innate, some to be adventitious, and others to have been invented by me. My understanding of what a thing is, what truth is, and what thought is, seems to derive simply from my own nature. But my hearing a noise, as I do now, or seeing the sun, or feeling the fire, comes from things which are located outside me, or so I have hitherto judged. Lastly, sirens, hippogriffs and the like are my own invention. But perhaps all my ideas may be thought of as adventitious, or they may all be innate, or all made up; for as yet I have not clearly perceived their origin. (AT VII 37–38; CSM II 26)

So, tentatively, we are told that we might divide ideas into three categories: innate, adventitious, and factitious. Innate ideas, presumably, have their origin in one's mind – the ideas of thinking and truth are examples; adventitious ideas presumably have their origin in things existing "outside" the mind – the ideas of heat and the sun are examples; and factitious ideas are put together by the mind, where presumably their contents are borrowed from other ideas – the ideas of Pegasus and a lion-headed goat (a chimera) would be examples. "But the chief question at this point," he wrote, "concerns the ideas which I take to be derived from things existing outside me: what is my reason for thinking that they resemble these things?" (Ibid.).

1.46   Descartes provided several accounts that might explain his holding that his adventitious idea of the fire (next to which he is sitting), for instance, not only represents some object that exists "outside" his mind, but resembles it, too. For starters, he noted, "nature" has taught him this. What he seemed to have in mind was that his experience as a human being has "taught" him such things – he stands at some distance from the fire and he feels cold; he walks closer to the fire and he feels warmth; he puts his hand directly over the fire and feels intense heat! He repeats all this, which results in similar experiences. In this way, his experience has led him to think that the heat is a property of the fire.

1.47   These are not things that he ever really *reasoned* about. For, had his holding that the fire existed outside his mind and has certain properties such as heat were the result of reasoning, then that would have been revealed by the "natural light." And any verdict of the natural light (reason) is yet to be rendered. The natural light is different, he said, from what nature teaches (AT VII 38; CSM II 27). Instead, his views about "external" objects and their properties are the results of "lessons" taught in the course of living an ordinary life of a human being. The *Meditations* marks the attempt in his life to examine what nature has taught him by subjecting it to rational scrutiny.

1.48   A second, and perhaps more interesting, account that explains why he had been drawn into thinking that his adventitious ideas represent (and resemble) objects existing outside his mind is that such ideas "do not depend simply on me. Frequently I notice them even when I do not want to: now, for example, I feel the heat whether I want to or not, and this is why I think that this sensation or idea of heat comes to me from something other than myself. . .And the most obvious judgment for me to make is that the thing in question transmits to me its own likeness rather than something else" (Ibid.). Here, we might contrast adventitious ideas to innate or to factitious ideas, in that the latter can be summoned at will. One can easily summon the idea of oneself, or summon the idea of a triangle, or summon the idea of Pegasus. But, one cannot simply summon the adventitious (sensory) idea of heat. Instead, that idea forces itself on the mind when one gets too close to the fire, which, Descartes noted, might be an explanation of why he has held that the fire plays some role in the idea's being brought before the mind, and why he has held that what the idea presents to his mind resembles some property of the fire.

As we have seen, Descartes sometimes used phrases such as "inside my   1.49
mind" and "outside my mind." These were phrases that were commonly
used (and still are). In the Third Meditation, however, Descartes made an
effort to introduce a technical, philosophical, set of terms that better
expressed "inside" and "outside" with respect to the mind, which allowed
him to emphasize the *representational* aspect of ideas. He used the terms
"formal reality" and "objective reality." He took these to denote two distinct
though related kinds of reality, or ways of being. What we will see in the
study that follows, is that these terms can be defined thus:

> **Formal reality** is the kind of reality or being something possesses
> insofar as it is an *existent* or an *actual* thing.
> **Objective reality** is the kind of reality or being something possesses
> insofar as it *represents* something.

Insofar as Descartes exists (in that he is thinking), say, he would be said to
possess formal reality. Insofar as Pegasus does not exist, he would be said
not to possess formal reality. This is admittedly an odd way of saying such
a thing, odd to us anyway, but it was a familiar way of talking to those who
had gone to college in the seventeenth century.

Now, insofar as something *represents* something, the item doing the rep-   1.50
resenting would be said to possess objective reality. Such an item would
possess both kinds of reality. Insofar as it was an actually existing thing, it
would possess formal reality. And, insofar as it represents something, it
would possess objective reality. Consider Descartes's idea that represents
the fire. Insofar as the idea is an occurring, existent mode, it is said to possess formal reality; and insofar as it represents something (the fire in this
case), the idea is said to possess objective reality. When we look carefully at
Descartes's discussions of objective reality, he attributed it only to ideas. So,
even though a mirror or a painting is said to represent things, strictly speaking we will not say that they possess objective reality, though we could certainly employ either as working analogies in our attempt at understanding
this kind of reality (we will in fact employ a case of a mirror image in a
moment). It is just that in the end, strictly speaking, objective reality will be
limited to ideas.

Descartes continued:

> And although the reality which I am considering in my ideas is merely objec-
> tive reality, I must not on that account suppose that the same reality need not
> exist formally in the causes of my ideas, but that it is enough for it to be pre-
> sent in them objectively. For just as the objective mode of being belongs to

ideas by their very nature, so the formal mode of being belongs to the causes of ideas – or at least to the first and most important ones – by *their* very nature. And although one idea may perhaps originate from another, there cannot be an infinite regress here; eventually one must reach a primary idea, the cause of which will be like an archetype which contains formally <and in fact> all the reality <or perfection> which is present only objectively <or representatively> in the idea. (AT VII 41–42; CSM II 29)

Here, Descartes made it clear that the objective reality possessed by an idea must have an origin. Although the objective reality of some ideas could certainly come from the objective reality possessed by other ideas, ultimately objective reality must have its origin in something *real*, in something that actually exists. In other words, the objective reality of ideas ultimately must have its origin in things that possess formal reality.

1.51   Consider as a working analogy a case of Descartes standing before a mirror. There are two things in the room – Descartes and the mirror. Both are real; both exist. According to the view, then, each possesses formal reality. So far, so good. But what about the *image* of Descartes that we find on the mirror's surface? It is real, right? Well, yes, but its "reality" is not the same kind that Descartes and the mirror possess as things that exist. Instead, it is understood in terms of objective reality. Objective reality is the reality of the *image*. Notice that although we "locate" the image on the surface of the mirror, we nevertheless say that the image is "of" Descartes. It represents *him*. In light of the view that we are trying to work out, we might apply our analogy as follows. Allow the mirror's image of Descartes to be the analogue to an idea understood in terms of its objective reality, and allow the mirror to be the analogue of the mind. We locate the image on the mirror; we "locate" an idea in the mind.

1.52   Now, why might an idea be "of" Descartes, say, and not of something else? Well, ask that question about the mirror case: why is this image "of" Descartes? We say that the image is of Descartes because he is clearly playing a significant causal role in the image's "production." If Descartes was not standing in front of the mirror, there could be no mirror *image* of Descartes. The image depends on Descartes in a way that Descartes does not depend on the image. To be sure, the mirror is an important player, too, since the image is located on its surface. And, it, too, is playing a significant role, for without the mirror, there would be no mirror-image of Descartes. Even so, notice that we do not say that this image represents the mirror – it represents Descartes. Likewise, we do not say that the idea represents the *mind* – the idea represents Descartes. Descartes and the mirror must be playing different causal roles, where that difference would account for why it is that we say that the image is "of" Descartes but not the mirror.

So, why might an idea represent Descartes and not the sun? Descartes's view tells us that the objective reality possessed by, or contained in, the idea has its origin in the formal reality of Descartes, and not in the formal reality of the sun. If the objective reality of an idea did have its origin in the formal reality of the sun, then that idea would be "of" the sun, it would represent or exhibit the sun.

This causal account of the objects of thought, the ideas, would apply solely to what Descartes called in the above passage "primary ideas." A primary idea is an idea whose objective reality has its origin in the formal reality of some object. This, it seems, includes both the category of innate ideas and adventitious ideas. Factitious ideas, which the mind fabricates, use the contents of other ideas. So, their objective reality could be derived or borrowed from the objective reality of other ideas; in the way that the idea of Pegasus might borrow from the adventitious ideas of a horse and a bird (where we get the idea of wings). 1.53

Descartes applied the same causal story to cases involving only formal reality, without any reference to objective reality. So, this story must be taken by us to be important. The formal reality that a thing possesses cannot come from nothing. It, too, must have its origin in something real, in something that also possesses formal reality. If the sun exists, and so possesses formal reality, the formal reality it possesses must be traceable to the formal reality of some other thing (or things). Descartes wrote: 1.54

> Now it is manifest by the natural light that there must be at least as much <reality> in the efficient and total cause as in the effect of that cause. For where, I ask, could the effect get its reality from, if not from the cause? And how could the cause give it to the effect unless it possessed it? It follows from this both that something cannot arise from nothing, and also that what is more perfect – that is, contains in itself more reality – cannot arise from what is less perfect. And this is transparently true not only in the case of effects which possess <what the philosophers call> actual or formal reality, but also in the case of ideas, where one is considering only <what they call> objective reality. A stone, for example, which previously did not exist, cannot begin to exist unless it is produced by something which contains, either formally or eminently everything to be found in the stone; similarly, heat cannot be produced in an object which was not previously hot, except by something of at least the same order <degree or kind> of perfection as heat, and so on. But it is also true that the *idea* of heat, or of a stone, cannot exist in me unless it is put there by some cause which contains at least as much reality as I conceive to be in the heat or in the stone. For although this cause does not transfer any of its actual or formal reality to my idea, it should not on that account be supposed that it must be less real. The nature of an idea is such that of itself it requires no formal reality except what it derives

from my thought, of which it is a mode. But in order for a given idea to contain such and such objective reality, it must surely derive it from some cause which contains at least as much formal reality as there is objectively reality in the idea. For if we suppose that an idea contains something which was not in its cause, it must have got this from nothing; yet the mode of being by which a thing exists objectively <or representatively> in the intellect by way of an idea, imperfect though it may be, is certainly not nothing, and so it cannot come from nothing. (AT VII 40–41; CSM II 28–29)

In the above passage, Descartes introduced the example of a stone. If the stone now exists, given that it cannot be the cause of itself or that it cannot have come from nothing, it must be considered the effect of some cause or causes. Whatever "reality" the stone possesses, keeping in mind we are talking about formal reality in this case, was derived from its cause or causes.

1.55   Consider another example, which should make the import of his use of the notions of cause and effect clearer: the case of a pot of water sitting over a raging fire. We measure the heat of the water and let us say that we measure it to be 100 units of heat. Let us agree that the heat possessed by the water has its origin in the fire. A common understanding of causation in the period, and one that Descartes mentions, would tell us that the fire "transmits" some of its heat to the water. Given that we have measured the water's possessing 100 units of heat, and holding that whatever heat the water possesses comes from the fire, we can infer that the fire possesses at least 100 units of heat. If it had less, then the heat possessed by the water, the effect, would be greater than the heat possessed by the fire, the cause. The effect would be "more real" with respect to heat than its cause, in which case the extra heat possessed by the water must have come from nothing. But, something cannot come from nothing. That is, nothing cannot be the cause of anything. So, the effect cannot ever be "more real" than its cause.

1.56   Toward the end of the passage just quoted, as pointed out just a moment ago, Descartes had applied this causal analysis to the relationship that holds between the objective reality of ideas and the formal reality of things. If an *idea* represents a stone, whatever is the cause of the objective reality contained in this idea, assuming it is a primary idea, must possess at least as much "reality" as we find in the idea. In such a case, we must ultimately conclude that whatever objective reality is possessed by an idea, if it must have a real and existent cause, will have its origin in the formal reality of some object. And, to be crystal clear on this point, this would hold specifically for what in an earlier quoted passage he called "primary ideas" – the "level" of formal reality of the cause must be as great as the "level" of objective reality exhibited in a primary idea. About such "levels" he wrote:

Undoubtedly, the ideas which represent substances to me amount to something more, and so to speak, contain within themselves more objective reality
than the ideas which merely represent modes or accidents Again, the idea
that gives me my understanding of a supreme God, eternal, infinite, <immu-
table,> omniscient, omnipotent and the creator of all things that exist apart
from him, certainly has in it more objective reality than the ideas that represent finite substances. (AT VII 40; CSM II 28)

In this passage, we are told that not only will an idea, in possessing or con-
taining objective reality, represent something to the mind, but it will also
represent the "level" of formal reality possessed by the object.

The level of formal reality is a kind of marker for the thing's ontological 1.57
place in the cosmos. Descartes looks to have been working under the
assumption that there are at least two places (or "levels") that an item can
occupy in his ontology: *substance* or *mode*. Substances are more real than
modes. A mode depends for its existence on the existence of a substance in
a way that a substance does not depend for its existence on the existence of a
mode. An idea, which is a mode, depends for its existence on the existence
of a mind, a substance, in a way that a mind does not depend for its existence
on the existence of an idea. Think of a cow. Notice that when you were not
thinking of it, *you* still existed. The existence of your mind does not depend
on the existence of any of your ideas, including the one about the cow. But, if
your mind ceased to exist, *your* idea of the cow could never be thought again.
Its existence does depend on the existence of your mind. To be clear, this is
all talk about formal reality. On this front, Descartes made it clear that:

> The nature of an idea is such that of itself it requires no formal reality except
> what it derives from my thought, of which it is a mode. (AT VII 41; CSM II 28)

This looks to be connected to something he had said just a bit earlier in the
Third Meditation:

> In so far as the ideas are <considered> simply <as> modes of thought, there
> is no recognizable inequality among them: they all appear to come from
> within me in the same fashion. (AT VII 40; CSM II 27–28)

So, when we consider an idea in terms of its being a mode, we do not make
reference to the object it represents, but instead focus solely on its status as
mode of mind. When we do this, we consider the idea's formal reality. According
to Descartes, all ideas have the same ontological status: they are modes of a
mind. All actually existent modes possess the same level of formal reality.

1.58   Objective reality is not formal reality. That much is clear. It is a kind of representational reality – we might say that it *represents* formal being or reality to the mind. If the idea represents the sun, according to an earlier quoted passage from the Third Meditation, it will also represent the level of formal reality possessed by the sun, which is presumably that of a finite *substance*. This "level" of objective reality is associated with the level of formal reality of a finite substance. The idea of the sun's shape, on the other hand, insofar as it represents a shape, will also represent the level of formal reality possessed by this shape, which in this case is that of a *mode*. So, this idea's "level" of objective reality would be associated with (it represents) the level of formal reality of a mode.

1.59   Notice that insofar as they are actually occurring (existent) ideas, the idea of the sun and the idea of its shape, each possesses the level of formal reality of a mode. In simpler terms, they are existent modes. And, in this sense, Descartes said, there is no recognizable inequality holding between them. But, when we consider an idea's "object," we will discover that the idea of the sun, for example, will not only present an object that is in an important sense different from the object presented in the idea of shape (say, the idea of a sphere), but will also possess a greater level of objective reality than the idea of a shape. This is so since the sun is a finite substance and a shape is a mode (of body).

1.60   The causal account that Descartes developed tells us that if an idea possesses a level of objective reality associated with, say, a finite substance – that is, it represents a finite substance – it cannot ultimately have been caused by something whose level of formal reality is that of only a mode. A mode's reality is not great enough. It is "less" real than a substance. This is like the previous case of the heated water: whatever level of heat we find in the water must have its origin in something whose level of heat is at least as great. Instead, the idea that represents a finite substance must ultimately have its origin in something that possesses at least the level of formal reality of that of a finite substance. Otherwise, the effect, the idea's objective reality, would be greater than its cause. It would be like the water being hotter than the fire.

1.61   To summarize what we have learned, we now have enough on the table to support our claiming that Descartes appeared to think that there were at least two "levels" of formal reality: the level of that of a *mode*, and the level of that of a *substance*, or as he specifically qualified it at the end of this last passage, a *finite substance*. And, what is more, there are at least two correlated or associated levels of objective reality: the level of that of a mode, and the level of that of a finite substance. But a third and higher "level" is suggested by what he said about his idea of an infinite being (God). Let us explore this and clean some of this up before moving forward.

To do this, let us recount some of what we have learned about the ontol- 1.62
ogy. The level of formal reality of a finite substance is "greater" than that of a
mode, since a mode depends for its existence on a substance, but a substance
does not depend for its existence on a mode. A mode, remember, is simply a
"way of being" a substance. This looks to be a version of an Aristotelian substance–attribute ontology. For instance, "The ball is blue" is analyzed so that
what is denoted by "The ball" is the *substance* and what is denoted by "is blue
(being blue)" is the *attribute* or *property* that "modifies" the substance (the
ball). Notice that we can destroy this instance of blue without destroying the
ball – we could paint the ball red, for instance – but if we destroyed the ball,
we would also destroy this instance of blue. In this sense, the substance is
"more real" than any of its properties. We will see in the section focused on
Descartes's argument for the existence of a material world, a mind-
independent world, will have something to say about the commonsense
practice of attributing colors, like blue, to bodies, like the ball.

Focusing on mind, Descartes said that an *idea* is a mode of thinking, it is 1.63
mode of a mind. Recall from the Second Meditation that Descartes had discovered that his nature, that which defined what he was, a mind, was *thinking* or *thought*. He would go further in the Sixth Meditation, which we will
look at in a moment, to identify thinking or thought as *the* defining characteristic of mind. In the *Principles*, he would go on to characterize thinking or
thought as the mind's *principal attribute* (AT VIIIA 25; CSM I 210). Modes,
as we will also see in a moment when we look at the Sixth Meditation, are
best understood as modes of the principal attribute. So, an idea is a mode of
thinking. Additionally, again in the Second Meditation, Descartes had entertained that the defining characteristic of body was extension (in length,
breadth, and depth). Extension, he will show in the Fifth and Sixth
Meditation, is the defining characteristic of body. Later, he would claim in
the *Principles* that extension is the principal attribute of body (Ibid.). Shape,
ontologically speaking, is a mode of or "a way of being" extended; it is a way
of being an instance of extension. So, shape is best understood as a mode of
extension. Shape is to extension (body) as idea is to thinking (mind).

1.3 Clarity and Distinctness: A Model Based
on Simple Natures

Clarity and distinctness are among the most important epistemological 1.64
concepts in Descartes's philosophy, though he said remarkably little about
them. In the *Discourse*, Descartes had proposed a general rule, based on his

analysis of his intuiting the connection between "I am thinking" and "I exist." He wrote:

> ... I considered in general what is required of a proposition in order for it to be true and certain; for since I had just found one that I knew to be such, I thought that I ought also to know what this certainty consists in. I observed that there is nothing at all in the proposition "I am thinking, therefore I exist" to assure me that I am speaking the truth, except that I see very clearly that in order to think it is necessary to exist. So I decided that I could take it as a general rule that the things we conceive very clearly and very distinctly are all true. (*Discourse*, Part Four: AT VI 33; CSM I 127)

We encountered something like this in the Third Meditation. Let us recall that passage. Within the context of his discovery that not even a supremely powerful being could deceive him about the truth of "If I am thinking, I exist," he wrote:

> Do I not therefore also know what is required for my being certain about anything? In this first item of knowledge there is simply a clear and distinct perception of what I am asserting; this would not be enough to make me certain of the truth of the matter if it could ever turn out that something which I perceived with such clarity and distinctness was false. So, I now seem to be able to lay it down as a general rule that whatever I perceive very clearly and distinctly is true. (*Meditations*, Third Meditation: AT VII 35; CSM II 24)

1.65 About propositions, it seems to have been Descartes's view that they are linguistic entities used by human beings to express the contents of their ideas. Our words "declare" our thoughts (*Discourse*, Part Five: AT VI 56–59; CSM I 140–141). But, technically speaking, what constitutes the "content" of our ideas? We have already considered this question in terms of objective reality or being. And, we have also considered this question in terms of the "objects" represented or presented (or exhibited) in our ideas. But, what are such "beings," such "objects," constituted of exactly? Although not perfectly clear, Descartes proposed the view that the "elements" of our ideas are what he called "simple natures." For example, in the *Rules*, he wrote:

> We should turn to the things themselves; and we should deal with these only in so far as they are within the reach of the intellect. In that respect we divide them into absolutely simple natures and complex or composite natures. Simple natures must all be either spiritual or corporeal, or belong to each of these categories. As for composite natures, there are some which the intellect experiences as composite before it decides to determine anything about

them: but there are others which are put together by the intellect itself. . .In view of this, we divide natures of the latter sort into two further classes, *viz.* those that are deduced from natures which are the most simple and self-evident. . ., and those that presuppose others which experience shows us to be composite in reality. (*Rules*, Rule Eight: AT X 399; CSM I 32)

If the simple natures are the "inhabitants" of our ideas – they are what the mind is directly aware of in a moment of consciousness or awareness – they can be understood as either being absolutely simple, or compounded out of simples. The simplest natures, Descartes suggested, can be classified as members of one of two distinct classes: as members of the class of thinking (thinking things), or as members of the class of extension (extended things). *Thinking* or *thought* is a principal attribute, which defines the former class of simple natures; *extension* is a principal attribute, which defines the latter class. We learn from a careful study of the *Rules* that class membership is determined by the "presupposes" relation. Thus, since *shape* presupposes *extension*, or as Descartes said in the *Principles*, *extension* is what underwrites the intelligibility of *shape* (AT VIIIA 25; CSM I 210), the simple nature *shape* is a member of the class of extended things (specifically, *shape* is the name of a subclass of simple natures in the class of *extension*; where in this subclass would be the classes of *circle, triangle, quadrilateral, sphere, pyramid, cube,* and so on). The same would hold for the class of *thinking*. *Doubting*, for instance, presupposes *thinking* – that is, *thought* or *thinking* is what makes *doubting* intelligible. *Colors, sounds, smells,* and the like, would also be understood as simple natures. Interestingly, such "qualities" would find membership in the *thinking* class.

In the Second Meditation, Descartes would again mention this way of 1.66 understanding mental content. Our waking experiences, he noted, present to us all sorts of objects, typically composed out of simpler elements. The latter, of course, may not be obvious at first. But upon analysis, they can be separated out. Our imagining things, or even our dreams, are composed out of these same natures. He wrote:

For even when painters try to create sirens and satyrs with the most extraordinary bodies, they cannot give them natures which are new in all respects; they simply jumble up the limbs of different animals. Or if perhaps they manage to think up something so new that nothing remotely similar has ever been seen before – something which is therefore completely fictitious and unreal – at least the colors used in the composition must be real. By similar reasoning, although these general kinds of things – eyes, head, hands and so on – could be imaginary, it must at least be admitted that certain other even simpler and more universal things are real. These are as it were the real colors from which we form all the images in things, whether true or false, that occur in our thoughts. (AT VII 20; CSM II 14)

We could, then, translate what we have considered thus far in terms of propositions into simple nature talk. For instance, we could restate our discovery of the (necessary) truth of "If A is shaped, A is extended," as our having discovered that the simple nature shape presupposes the simple nature extension, where if A is shaped, A is extended. Can any of this help us better understand Descartes's view on clear and distinct perception? Yes!

1.67   In a careful study of the *Rules* (and some correspondence), we would learn that *clarity* is to be understood in terms of our recognizing the necessary connections between simple natures – those elements constituting the contents of our ideas. The model for this was brought out in our recognizing a necessary connection between *thinking* and *existence*. We also discovered a necessary connection between *doubting* and *thinking*, and a necessary connection between *shape* and *extension*. In light of what Descartes said in the *Discourse* passage above, we can say that when we recognize the necessary connection between the simple natures that make up an idea, this idea is *clear*. When we recognize a necessary connection to hold between *all* of the simple natures included in an idea, the idea can be said to be *maximally* clear. It cannot get any clearer than that. But there can be lesser degrees of clarity: for instance, if we recognize a necessary connection to hold between only some of the simple natures in the idea but not all. That is easy enough. So what about distinctness? How are we to understand that?

1.68   In the *Principles*, Descartes defined "clear perception" and "distinct perception." He wrote:

> I call a perception "clear" when it is present and accessible to the attentive mind – just as we say that we see something clearly when it is present to the eye's gaze and stimulates it with a sufficient degree of strength and accessibility. I call a perception "distinct" if, as well as being clear, it is so sharply separated from all other perceptions that it contains within itself only what is clear. (AT VIIIA 22; CSM I 207–208)

1.69   Descartes's first principle is made *clear* to him when he recognized a necessary connection holding between *thinking* and *existence* – he recognized that *thinking* presupposes *existence*. In line with this criterion, then, his idea of a shaped thing was also shown to be clear when he recognized the necessary connection between *shape* and *extension* – he recognized that *shape* presupposes *extension*. If an idea includes simple natures for which no necessary connection could be recognized, then the idea would be said to be *obscure* – it is maximally *unclear*. We might think of this as telling us that the connection between ideational elements is obscured from mental view. No connection is seen. Perhaps it is obscured by various jumbled elements included in the idea; or perhaps there just is no connection between them. Either way we fail to see any connection. The thing to stress is that:

Clarity = recognition of a necessary connection between simple natures in an idea,

And, its opposite:

Obscurity = no recognition of a necessary connection between simple natures in an idea.

A maximally clear idea is one for which we recognize a necessary connection to hold between *all* of the simple natures included. A maximally obscure idea is one for which we recognize *no* necessary connection to hold between any of the simple natures included in the idea. Now, if we recognize a necessary connection to hold between *some* simple natures, but not all, then we can say that the idea is clear, but not maximally clear. Such an idea can also be said to be obscure, since we recognize no necessary connection to hold between some of the simple natures that make up the idea. But because we recognize a necessary connection to hold between some of the simple natures, this idea is not maximally obscure. An idea that is more clear is less obscure, and an idea that is less clear is more obscure. "More" and "less" in this context could be understood in terms of the proportion of simple natures included in the idea that are related necessarily. The more that are related, the clearer the idea.

Consider the sensory idea of the sun. This sensory idea exhibits to you an 1.70 extended, round-shaped, yellow, hot object. As we already know, there is a necessary connection holding between the simple natures *shape* and *extension*, so that "*if the sun is round-shaped, it is extended*" is true. So, this much about the idea is clear. But in order for the idea to be maximally clear, we must see how *all* of the simple natures it contains are connected. So, let us start with the simple nature *hot*. If something is hot, *must* it be shaped or yellow or extended? Here, the focus is on *hot* as a sensed *quality*. With respect to such sensed qualities – colors, sounds, feels, smells, and tastes – Descartes, as we know, will say that although they are exhibited to you in sensory experience, it is not at all obvious that to conceive them we must conceive *extension*. This is very different from modes such as shape, size, position, and motion. Those *require* extension in order to be conceived. That is, there is a necessary connection that holds between *shape* and *extension*, between *size* and *extension*, and so on. But between *hot* and *extension*? This much seems obvious: given that minds perceive properties such as hot, cold, yellow, and the like, if there were no minds, such properties (as perceived) would not exist. This suggests that the intelligibility of *hotness* (the sensed quality), and other simple natures like it, require the conception of mind – specifically the conception of a mind that perceives *hot* and items like it. But at this point in the Third Meditation, even this connection is fuzzy. No necessary connection is perceived to hold between the presented *hot*, say, and *extension*, or *thinking*, or *shape*, or *color*, and so on. Since this is so, the sensory (adventitious) idea of the sun includes simple natures for which we recognize *no* necessary connection to hold between them and the other simple natures also included in the idea. And since we do not see a necessary connection between *all* of the simple natures that are included in this idea, it follows that the sensory idea of the sun is not maximally clear but is (to some degree or with respect to some of its content) obscure. Further, since a distinct idea includes *only* what is clear (so, a distinct idea is maximally clear), the sensory idea of the sun is not distinct. It is *confused*. The Latin word *confusio*, which Descartes used, means a *mixing together* (*con = with* and *fusio = mixed*). We might understand this to mean that a confused idea mixes together simple natures that lack a necessary connection to one another. Like *clarity* and *obscurity*, *distinctness* and *confusion* are opposites.

According to Descartes, ideas can be:

clear and *distinct*,
clear and *confused*,
obscure and *confused*,

but never:

obscure and *distinct*.

An example of a clear and distinct idea is the idea that one has that includes the simple natures *thinking* and *existence*. Here, one recognizes that there is a necessary connection between *thinking* and *existence*. An example of an obscure and confused idea is one's idea that includes *thinking* and *extension* (one's pre-philosophical idea of oneself as a *thinking body* – that is, a body with a face, limbs, that senses, thinks, and so on). To say that this idea is obscure, we mean that it is not maximally clear (we recognize a necessary connection to hold between some of the simple natures, but not all). Another example of an obscure and confused idea, discussed already, is one's sensory idea of the sun. In the Third Meditation, Descartes in fact compares his sensory idea of the sun with what he calls his astronomical idea of the sun (AT VII 39; CSM II 27). The sensory idea is obscure and confused. But the astronomical idea, which includes only simple natures associated with extension – so, size, shape, motion – is clear and distinct. He will tell us more about such ideas in the Fifth and Sixth Meditation.

But, before leaving the Third Meditation, let us now apply what we know 1.71 about Descartes's view about ideas and look carefully at his examination of his idea of the infinite being, his idea of God, and how it supported Descartes's trust in his faculty of reason.

1.4 The Idea of the Infinite Being: A Proof for God's existence

In the Third Meditation, Descartes had been working with the idea of him- 1.72 self that represented himself as a thing that thinks. In terms of formal reality, this idea possesses the level of that of a mode. What about in terms of objective reality? Well, insofar as this idea represented him as a thing, a *substance*, the *level* of objective reality of this idea is that of a substance. Descartes said: "It is true that I have the idea of substance in me in virtue of the fact that I am a substance" (AT VII 45; CSM II 31). This aligns with what was stated earlier, when Descartes noted that the idea of what a thing is, what thinking is, and so on, "seems to derive simply from my own nature" (AT VII 37; CSM II 26). Given that this idea of himself is derived from himself, in Descartes's terms we can say that the idea's objective reality is derived from the formal reality of his own mind, where in saying that, his mind is said to possess formal reality, which is to say that he, a mind, exists. "But," Descartes said, none of this would "account for my having the idea of an infinite substance, when I am finite, unless this idea proceeded from some substance which really was infinite" (AT VII 45; CSM II 31).

Descartes was aware of the commonly held view of God as the kingly 1.73 individual who had long hair and a beard, who wore a long flowing robe, who ruled the universe from a throne in Heaven, and so on. But this is not how Descartes conceived God in his philosophical work. "By the word 'God'," he wrote, "I understand a substance that is infinite, <eternal,

immutable>, independent, supremely intelligent, supremely powerful, and which created both myself and everything else (if anything else there be) that exists" (AT VII 45; CSM II 31). And insofar as the idea of God represents an infinite substance, its level of objective reality is immeasurably greater than that which represents a finite substance. So, instead of two levels of objective reality, as suggested in a passage considered earlier, we learn that there are *three* levels of objective reality:

> *Infinite substance*
> *Finite substance*
> *Mode*

As you would expect, the level of reality of an infinite substance is greater than that of a finite substance, and the level of reality of a finite substance is greater than that of a mode. And, as you would also expect, the levels of reality are expressions of ontological dependence: a mode depends ontologically on a finite substance, and a finite substance depends ontologically on an infinite substance. The infinite substance depends on no other thing – it is self-sufficient. In Part One, Article 51 of the *Principles*, Descartes would make it clear that the term "substance," strictly speaking, only applied to God, to an infinite substance that depended on nothing. He wrote:

> By *substance* we can understand nothing other than a thing which exists in such a way as to depend on no other thing for its existence. And there is only one substance which can be understood to depend on no other thing whatsoever, namely God. (AT VIIIA 24; CSM I 210)

He would go on to say that we could use the word "substance" in a qualified sense, if we wanted to use it to refer to finite things. Specifically, in this qualified sense, we can refer to finite things as *substances* which do not depend on other finite things for their existence, but only depend on God, or the infinite substance, for their existence. For Descartes, as he would make clear in the next article, Article 52, there were only two kinds of finite substance: *mind* and *body* (AT VIIIA 25; CSM I 210). In this and the following article (Article 53), he would also claim that we identify each kind by way of its principal attribute. As we know from earlier discussions, the principal attribute of mind is *thought* or *thinking*, and the principal attribute of body is *extension* (in length, breadth, and depth).

1.74   Specifically concerning ideas, recall, the three levels of objective reality are to be understood as telling us that an idea that represents a mode has the level of objective reality associated with the level of formal reality of a mode, an idea that represents a finite substance has the level of objective reality associated with the level of formal reality of a finite substance, and an idea that represents an infinite substance has the level of objective reality associated with the level of formal reality of an infinite substance.

Descartes considered whether the idea of the infinite being was an idea   1.75 that he could have constructed out of the idea he had of himself. In this way, it would be like the idea of Pegasus; an idea made from other ideas. Thinking back to his tripartite division of ideas introduced earlier (innate, adventitious, and factitious), if the idea of God was like this, it would be a factitious idea. How might the construction go? Here is how Descartes entertained such a construction: He comes to know one thing (that he exists so long as he thinks), and then comes to know another (that he is at the very least a thing that thinks). So, on Monday he knows one thing, on Tuesday he knows a second thing, on Wednesday a third, and so on. The idea of an infinite knower, then, might be constructed by extrapolating, where each day he is a "greater" knower than the day before. Why is this not an acceptable account of how he acquired the idea of the infinite being? Here is Descartes's answer:

> First, though it is true that there is a gradual increase in my knowledge, and that I have many potentialities which are not yet actual, this is all quite irrelevant to the idea of God, which contains absolutely nothing that is potential; indeed, this gradual increase in knowledge is itself the surest sign of imperfection. What is more, even if my knowledge always increases more and more, I recognize that it will never actually be infinite, since it will never reach the point where it is not capable of a further increase; God, on the other hand, I take to be actually infinite, so that nothing can be added to his perfection. (AT VII 47; CSM II 32)

An idea of God that Descartes might construct from the idea of himself (the latter, remember, is an idea of a finite substance) would be an idea of a *potentially* infinite being. A potentially infinite being is not an actually infinite being; just like a potentially moving object is not an actually moving object. In fact, a potentially moving object is actually *not* moving (well, if A is a potential mover in respect to B, then A is not actually moving in respect to B; though A and B *could* be actually moving in respect to C, where C ≠ B. But, let us put that aside). Likewise, a potentially infinite being is actually not infinite. So, his constructed idea of a potentially infinite being is not an idea of an actually infinite being. And yet, Descartes says, he has an idea of an *actually* infinite being. That is what he is calling "the idea of God." Now, if he does have an idea of an actually infinite being, then he cannot be its origin, for the level of formal reality that he possesses, which is that of a finite substance, is simply not great enough to cause the level of objective reality possessed by his idea of an actually infinite being. At best, Descartes can be the origin of the idea of a potentially infinite being.

1.76   But, is there another way he could have come by the idea of the infinite? What about this: The idea is simply a *negative* idea – that is, it is the negation of the finite? No doubt the logical or grammatical relationship between "finite" and "infinite" is no different from other paired opposites, such as "moral" and "immoral." In cases like the latter, we take "moral" to be the *positive* stem and then add to it the *negative* prefix, "im," so that "immoral" is simply the negation of "moral." We might think, then, that we take "finite" to be the positive stem and then add to it the negative prefix, so that "infinite" is simply the negation of "finite." So, it is not that we have an idea of some *thing* that is infinite, but rather we have simply produced a linguistic entity, the *term* "infinite," which correlates to no idea we have. So, "infinite" is simply a negative construction from our idea of a finite being.

1.77   But, Descartes will argue that this account would not work in the end. Inspecting his idea of finite being, Descartes found that there are at least two ideational components that made it up: (i) limitless *being* and (ii) some *limitation*. Here, limitless being is identical to infinite being. It is boundless being. What Descartes discovered was that the idea of the finite is actually constructed out of the idea of the infinite *and* the introduction of some limitation. So, unlike "moral" and "immoral," "infinite" is actually expressing the *positive* stem and "finite" is its negation! As Descartes put it: "I must not think that, just as my conceptions of rest and darkness are arrived at by negating movement and light, so my perception of the infinite is arrived at not by means of a true idea but merely by negating the finite" (AT VII 45; CSM II 31). In fact, the infinite, he said, "is in some way prior to" the finite (Ibid.). Using a term we learned earlier, finite being *presupposes* infinite being. As Descartes puts it in a 1649 letter to his friend Claude Clerselier:

> I say that the notion I have of the infinite is in me before that of the finite because, by the mere fact that I conceive being, or that which is, without thinking whether it is finite or infinite, what I conceive is infinite being; but in order to conceive a finite being, I have to take away something from this general notion of being, which must accordingly be there first. (AT V 356; CSMK III 377)

To conceive being without limitation is to conceive the infinite. The idea of finite being is the idea of *limited* being. Descartes's point was that the idea of finite being presupposes the idea of infinite being. To limit x, you first have to have x. A limitation of x is a limitation imposed *on* x. The finite is a limiting of the infinite. For example – mathematically, we form a finite line segment from limiting a line, the latter being "endless," extending infinitely in both directions. The "limit" here is where we "cut out" a segment of line. The line segment no longer extends infinitely in both directions. Putting this in Descartes's terms, we construct the finite line segment out of the boundless infinite line by introducing two limitations (one at each "end"). If we think of the line as "being," we might think of the limitation as "non-being." A line segment (being) is "bounded" by regions of non-line (nonbeing) (Figure 1.2).

The unbounded line

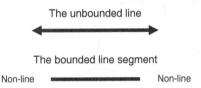

The bounded line segment

Non-line   Non-line

Figure 1.2 The Finite Presupposes the Infinite.

We do not construct the boundless, infinite, line by setting bounded line segments side by side. That would never amount to an infinite line. Instead, we construct the bounded, finite, line segment from the boundless, infinite, one. The boundless, infinite, line is presupposed in the bounded, finite, line segment. Similarly, Descartes claimed that the idea of the infinite is not constructed out of our idea of finite being. Instead, the idea of the finite is constructed out of the idea of the infinite. The idea of infinite being is presupposed in the idea of a finite being. This is a sense in which the finite *depends* on the infinite being!

If it is true that the finite depends on, or presupposes, the infinite, Descartes has a reason to think that he, in being a finite being, depends on the infinite, on God. In other words, he has a reason to now hold that ultimately, and this would be true for any finite being in fact, the infinite being is presupposed, or in metaphysical speak, the infinite is ultimately the origin of the finite – or, in theological speak, the infinite being is creator of the finite. This line of reasoning alone, suggested Descartes, provided the following argument for God's existence:

1.78

> Altogether then, it must be concluded that the mere fact that I exist and have within me an idea of a most perfect being, that is, God, provides a very clear proof that God indeed exists. (AT VII 51; CSM II 35)

This argument looks to go as follows: the idea that Descartes has of himself, an idea that represents him as a finite thing, presupposes the idea of an infinite being. So, if he has such an idea of himself (and he does), he *ipso facto* (by that very fact) has an idea of the infinite, too. The "presupposes" language tells us that in every conceivable world in which a finite being exits, an infinite being exists, too. Moreover, given what was said about the various levels of reality, the "presupposes" language also expresses the notion that Descartes (understood as a finite being) ontologically depends on the infinite being: he depends for his existence on the infinite being in a way that the infinite being does not depend on Descartes for its existence. Thus, if he (Descartes) exists, then so does the infinite being. Here is the nutshell version of the argument:

> *If I (qua finite being) exist, then God (qua infinite being) exists.*
> *I exist (qua finite being).*
> *Therefore, God (qua infinite being) exists.*

Premise (1) was established in the Third Meditation; premise (2) was established in the Second Meditation. Together they yield (3).

1.79   Although what has been said might apply, say, to talk about the beginning of the universe, that was long ago. Surely, Descartes does not *now* depend for his existence on God, right? Well, not so fast. In the Third Meditation, Descartes would go on to write:

> For a lifespan can be divided into countless parts, each completely independent of the others, so that it does not follow from the fact that I existed a little while ago that I must exist now, unless there is some cause which as it were creates me afresh at this moment – that is, which preserves me. For it is quite clear to anyone who attentively considers the nature of time that the same power and action are needed to preserve anything at each individual moment of its duration as would be required to create that thing anew if it were not yet in existence. Hence the distinction between preservation and creation is only a conceptual one, and this is one of the things that are evident by the natural light. (AT VII 49; CSM II 33)

So, Descartes's mind, in being a finite being, has a "beginning" point in time. Prior to that temporal moment, prior to the act of the creation of his mind, we might agree that Descartes's mind did not exist. But, surely, once his mind had been created, from that point of time forward the "creator" would no longer be needed. Not so, says Descartes in the above passage. If we analyzed something's existence over some duration of time – let us say it exists over the duration t_1 to t_3 – Descartes claims that the power required to sustain or to preserve this thing over this duration of time would be identical to the power required to create it anew at every moment – at t_1, then at t_2, then at t_3. There is nothing about Descartes's own existence at t_2 that guarantees his existence at t_3. Thus, if Descartes is said to exist over the duration measured by t_2 and t_3, something other than Descartes is responsible for that – namely, God. To be sure, we might identify several underlying finite beings that are responsible for his continued existence (such as his body, the earth, an atmosphere, the sun, and so on). But each of those are finite beings, and cannot in principle be the causes of themselves. Ultimately, if we stuck to the story that included only finite beings, all possible causes of Descartes's existing over time would be finite. As he said in an earlier quoted passage about objective reality, such things cannot go back forever. At some point, if any finite being is real at all, and subsequently we claim that all of the finite beings that make this possible are real, nothing could be real unless at bottom there existed something that itself is not caused (and so, is not finite). There must be in place at any given moment something that sustains or supports every existing finite being – a being that has no beginning or end, an infinite being. Thus, if Descartes's mind exists *now*, then ultimately this is so because there exists an infinite being.

As interesting as the above arguments are, they are warm-up to Descartes's 1.80 *main* argument for the existence of God. The main argument for God's existence, at least in the Third Meditation, turns on the fact that the level of objective reality in the idea of God, that is, the idea of an actually infinite being, requires a cause other than Descartes's own mind. This argument hinges specifically on the notion of a primary idea and the connection between objective and formal reality. We have everything we need to make sense of this main argument, where we can then move on to considering why it is that the infinite being cannot be a deceiver.

From our earlier discussion, we can formulate two working causal–rep- 1.81 resentational principles:

The objective reality of a primary idea has its origin in the formal reality of some thing or mode.

And,

The *level* of formal reality possessed by this thing or mode (from which the idea derives its objective reality) is at least as great as the level of objective reality in the idea.

Descartes noted that the level of objective reality possessed by the idea of God is immeasurably greater than the level of objective reality possessed by any idea that represents finite being. Concerning the latter, since Descartes's mind possesses a level of formal reality of that of a finite substance, it possesses a level of formal reality sufficient to account for the level of objective reality possessed by the idea of himself (the idea that represents him as a finite substance). But the level of formal reality that he possesses (insofar as he is a finite substance) is not sufficient to account for the level of objective reality possessed by the idea of God. It is simply too weak to be the origin of this level of objective reality. Since Descartes cannot be the origin of this idea's objective reality – in other words, he cannot fabricate its content – it looks to be a primary idea (either innate or adventitious). According to the first causal–representational principle, since this idea is a primary idea, its objective reality will have its origin in (it will be derived from) the formal reality of some object. And, according to the second causal–representational principle, the thing from which a primary idea derives its objective reality must possess a level of formal reality that is at least as great as the level of objective reality possessed by the idea. So, if the level of objective reality possessed by the idea of God is associated with the *infinite*, then the cause (or origin) of this objective reality must possess a level of formal reality that is at least as great. Therefore, the cause (or origin) of the idea of God must possess at least a level of formal reality that is infinite. Since Descartes's mind is finite, the origin of his idea of God cannot be himself. The origin must be some being other than himself that possesses an infinite level of formal reality. And, since formal reality is simply another way of expressing existence, to say that the cause of this objective reality possesses formal reality is to say that it *exists*. Thus, God, or the infinite being, *exists*. The cause (or origin) of the idea of God must be something that exists and is infinite. So, applying this to you, given that you have an idea of God (an idea of an actual infinity), "from what has been said it must be concluded that God necessarily exists" (AT VII 45; CSM II 31). This is Descartes's main argument in the Third Meditation for the existence of God.

1.5 Why God, Creator of Descartes's Mind, Cannot be Understood as Being a Deceiver

1.82 Why must God be benevolent? Why cannot God be evil? Descartes reasoned that if God is the origin of his faculty of reason, and supposing that God is all powerful and God *cannot* be a deceiver, then whenever Descartes used this faculty appropriately, this faculty could never go wrong. It could go wrong only if God intended it to go wrong. But, if God's intentions are those of a benevolent being, intending wrongdoing must be ruled out. And, if God is all powerful, God could certainly do whatever God intended to do. To be sure, one could misuse the faculty of reason, in which case going wrong would certainly be possible. But that would not be due to any fault in the design. Instead, it would be the fault of the one employing the faculty. This is basically Descartes's line of reasoning in the Fourth Meditation, when considering how it is that error in judgment is possible.

The upshot is this: if Descartes's faculty of reason compelled him to 1.83 assent to, say, "If I am thinking, I exist," and God is the author of that compulsion, Descartes can trust this compulsion, he can trust his faculty of reason, the one that God designed. If Descartes cannot conceive a case in which "I am thinking" is true and "I exist" is false, then that would also tell Descartes that it is impossible that "If I am thinking, I exist" is false. Whatever his faculty of reason tells him is true *is* true. If anything like "If I am thinking, I exist," which he understood with such clarity, *could* turn out to be false, God would be to blame for having provided Descartes with such a lousy faculty. And given that God could have suited him with a reliable faculty but did not, God must be taken as being nothing short of a deceiver (or as an underachiever of some sort). So, why cannot God be a deceiver?

An analysis of the concept of *deception*, Descartes suggested, would show 1.84 us that deception is a complex idea composed of two items: *being* and *nonbeing* (privation). Now, we have seen this sort of analysis before: in Descartes's analysis of his idea of finite being. Let us keep that in mind, for there looks to be a connection between the idea of the finite and the idea of deception. Very likely borrowing from Augustine, Descartes identified the metaphysical concepts of being and nonbeing with the epistemic concepts of *truth* (being) and *falsity* (nonbeing). We saw that already supported by what he said in a letter to Clerselier. But, Descartes will also associate being and nonbeing with the *moral* concepts of *good* (being) and *evil* (nonbeing). On this view, evil is not something that is "real," but is simply the absence of being, the absence of what is "real." (So, on this view, God is not cast as having *created* evil, since evil is not anything at all, and so it is not something that is created.)

Suppose that Jones aims at deceiving Smith. How is this to be under- 1.85 stood? On Descartes's view, Jones will succeed at deceiving Smith if she can convince Smith that there is something (being) when in fact there is nothing (nonbeing), or if she convinces Smith that there is nothing (nonbeing) when in fact there is something (being). For example, Jones takes a gold coin and appears to place it in her right hand. She closes her right hand tightly. Smith sees Jones do this. He believes that the coin is there, in Jones' closed right hand. But through sleight of hand, Jones actually retained the coin in her left hand the entire time. Her closed right hand is actually empty. Jones succeeds at deceiving Smith by getting him to believe that there is a gold coin (being) in her right hand, when in fact there is no gold coin (non-being) there.

1.86   Recall that the idea of God, the idea of an actual infinity, is an idea of boundless being. The idea contains *being* only – there is no limitation or privation. Putting things together in terms of being, truth, and goodness, God *is* being, truth, and goodness. By contrast, and this is important, insofar as no limit or privation is associated with the infinite (as Descartes understood it), God simply cannot be understood in terms of nonbeing, falsity, or evil. Since the concept of deception requires both being and nonbeing for its formulation, and the idea of God includes only the first of these, *being*, then the concept of deception cannot apply to God. In other words, we cannot conceive of God as being a deceiver. For, to do that we would have to impose some element of limitation or privation. But as soon as we did that, we would render the idea an idea of *finite* being. It would no longer be the idea of God. In fact, the idea of an infinite being who was a deceiver is an *internal contradiction*. This insight is important to Descartes's view. For if God is conceived as being infinitely powerful (omnipotent), say, then God cannot be conceived as being a deceiver. The very idea of a deceitful infinitely powerful being is a contradiction, no different from the idea of a square-circle, or from a contradiction discussed earlier, when noting that the supremely powerful evil being, assuming there was such a being, could not deceive you, because in order to do so, it would have to make it so that you exist and do not exist at the same time. Why is this important? Well, recall that the supremely powerful evil being was cast as an *infinitely* powerful, *deceitful* being. According to Descartes's analysis, the idea of a supremely powerful evil being is shown to be a contradiction. Such a being is *not* possible: it *cannot* be conceived. So, although Descartes initially raised the concern about a supremely powerful evil being in the First Meditation, by the close of the Third Meditation, he demonstrated that that concern was ill-formed. For, since a supremely powerful evil being is akin to a square-circle, it is not a possibility (that is, it is not conceivable!). Descartes suggests to the reader that we were just confused when raising this issue initially in the First Meditation. But, philosophizing in an orderly and proper way has cleared this up. If Descartes has shown that God exists, is no deceiver, and is the origin of his mind, he can now dispense with the skeptical concern, as slight as it was, that a deceiver created his mind and its faculty of reason. When used properly, the faculty of reason can be trusted!

A supremely powerful evil being, then, was really not something that should 1.87 have ever worried us. As noted earlier, Descartes would admit that his initial worry looked to have been based on a rather serious confusion. But, luckily, philosophy straightened all of that out. And, if that story was really the only thing holding us back from trusting our faculty of reason, and we have dismissed that story as a story that cannot even be told (it is self-contradictory), we have no other reasons for doubting the reliability or trustworthiness of our faculty of reason. As was just affirmed, reason can be trusted.

So, here is a summary of what we should have learned in the Third and 1.88 Fourth Meditations: God exists, God is no deceiver, and God is the origin of Descartes's faculty of reason. How did Descartes establish this last claim? He showed that all finite beings, including his own mind, will ultimately have their origin in the Infinite being, namely, in God. Now, Descartes had recognized that his faculty of reason sometimes compelled him to assent to the truth of a clear and distinct idea. Were it the case that an idea to which one was compelled to assent (a clear and distinct idea) was in fact false, then God, who authored the compulsion to assent, would be a deceiver. But God cannot be a deceiver. So, it cannot ever turn out that an idea to which one is compelled to assent is false. It would appear, then, that all of those propositions that are classified as eternal truths, the ones that compel our assent to affirming their truth, which includes his first principle and all mathematical propositions, are true.

The conclusion just drawn, including the "truth rule" that whatever he 1.89 clearly and distinctly perceives is true, expresses what Descartes would claim toward the close of Part Four of the *Discourse*:

> For in the first place, what I took just now as a rule, namely that everything we conceive very clearly and very distinctly is true, is assured only for the reasons that God is or exists, that he is a perfect being, and that everything in us comes from him. It follows that our ideas or notions, being real things and coming from God, cannot be anything but true, in every respect in which they are clear and distinct. Thus, if we frequently have ideas containing some falsity, this can happen only because there is something confused and obscure in them, for in that respect they participate in nothingness, that is, they are in us in this confused state only because we are not wholly perfect. And it is evident that it is no less contradictory that falsity or imperfection should proceed from God than that truth or perfection should proceed from nothingness. But if we did not know that everything real and true within us comes from a perfect and infinite being then, however clear and distinct our ideas were, we would have no reason to be sure that they had the perfection of being true. (AT VI 38–39; CSM I 130)

1.6 The Problem of the External World Continued: The Case for a Material World

1.90 Descartes's proof for the existence of the material world is offered in the Sixth Meditation. There are two stages of the proof. In the first stage, we find what is sometimes referred to as the "Real Distinction Proof." This establishes the possibility that mind and body can exist separately or independently of one another. It is in the Fifth Meditation that Descartes worked out some of the details of the nature of body, which allowed him in the Sixth Meditation to draw a real distinction between body and mind. We will focus primarily on the Sixth Meditation in what follows. In the second stage, we find the proof of the existence of body (or the material world). Let us look at each stage. This will bring our examination of Descartes to a close.

1.6.1 The Real Distinction Proof: Descartes's Mind–Body Dualism

1.91 In the Synopsis of the *Meditations*, Descartes summarized the results of the Second, Fourth, and Sixth Meditations. He wrote:

> The inference to be drawn from these results is that all the things that we clearly and distinctly conceive of as different substances (as we do in the case of mind and body) are in fact substances which are really distinct one from the other; and this conclusion is drawn [ultimately] in the Sixth Meditation. (AT VII 13; CSM II 9)

Several paragraphs later, still in the Synopsis, specifically concerning the Sixth Meditation, Descartes would write:

> ... the mind is proved to be really distinct from the body, but is shown, notwithstanding, to be so closely joined to it that the mind and the body make up a kind of unit.... (AT VII 15; CSM II 11)

The "unit" that he is talking about here is the human being. The human being is composed of both a mind and a body. As he would show in the Sixth Meditation, they worked together by divine institution. Even so, the metaphysics shows that what makes up this "unit," namely *mind* and *body*, are nevertheless ontologically independent entities – they *can* exist independently of one another.

1.92   Descartes held that we can conceive of the nature of mind independently of the nature of body, and vice versa. In the Sixth Meditation, he wrote:

First, I know that everything which I clearly and distinctly understand is capable of being created by God so as to correspond exactly with my understanding of it. Hence the fact that I can clearly and distinctly understand one thing apart from another is enough to make me certain that the two things are distinct, since they are capable of being separated, at least by God . . . on the one hand I have a clear and distinct idea of myself, in so far as I am simply a thinking, non-extended thing; and on the other hand I have a distinct idea of body, in so far as this is simply an extended, non-thinking thing. And accordingly, it is certain that I am really distinct from my body, and can exist without it. (AT VII 78; CSM II 54)

The two ideas – the idea of mind and the idea of body – are cast by Descartes as being *distinct* ideas. We now know that an idea is distinct whenever it includes or contains only what is clear. And, we know that an idea is clear whenever we recognize a necessary connection to hold between the simple natures in the idea. Since a distinct idea includes only what is clear, then a distinct idea is *maximally* clear. This means that a necessary connection is recognized to hold between *all* of the simple natures constituting the idea's content. So, the idea of mind and the idea of body as described in the above passage is each maximally clear. This line of reasoning is not surprisingly related to the notion of *presupposition*, which we will now discover is importantly related to what Descartes says about *abstraction* and *exclusion*. Let us pause to work this out before moving forward.

Recall we said that *shape presupposes extension* in the sense that our con- 1.93 ceiving *shape* required our conceiving *extension*. We engage in the mental activity of *exclusion* when we focus on one ideational element and remove or separate out the others, where post-removal the ideational element, the one on which we are focusing, remains intelligible. Sometimes Descartes says that the way we go about removing or separating out the other elements is by *negating* them. If we were to exclude, remove, or separate out the simple nature *extension* from our idea of *shape*, we would render *shape* unintelligible. What this reveals is that in every conceivable world in which B is shaped, B is extended. Were we to negate *extension*, we would also negate *shape*. Once we negate (remove or separate out) *extension*, *shape* will not remain as an intelligible item. Even so, we can focus on *shape* in our idea, *ignoring* the fact that it is *extended*. Ignoring is not the same as negating or removing. When we focus on some simple nature in an idea and ignore others, we are engaged in the mental activity of *abstraction*. So, in focusing on *shape* while simply ignoring the fact that it is extended, we produce an abstract idea – the abstract idea of shape. We can abstract *shape* from *extension* by focusing on shape (as given in the idea) and ignoring extension, but we cannot exclude extension from the idea of shape.

Doing so (removing or excluding extension) would immediately render shape, that on which we are focused, unintelligible.

1.94   Now, two things are "really distinct," Descartes says, if we can exclude them. In line with what he will later say in the *Principles* (AT VIIIA 28; CSM I 213), we can define *real distinction* as follows:

> **A is *really distinct* from B if, and only if, we can conceive A (or its nature) independently of our conceiving B (or its nature), and vice versa.**

The paradigm case is the case of mind and body. We can conceive of the nature of mind, which is *thinking*, independently of our conceiving of the nature of body, which is *extension*, and vice versa. Using the *exclusion* language, we say that we can exclude the simple nature *extension* from our idea of mind and the simple nature *thinking* from our idea of body. Showing that mind and body are really distinct from one another is the first stage of the proof of the material world.

1.95   The second stage of the proof begins by again analyzing the idea of body (the idea of corporeal substance). In the *Meditations*, Descartes would note that the level of objective reality contained in the idea of body could have its origin in the formal reality of the mind. This was unlike the result of our analysis of the idea of God. In that case we reasoned that the level of objective reality contained in this idea was too great to have its origin in a being whose level of formal reality was only that of a finite substance. In this new analysis of the idea of body Descartes no longer concerns himself with the *level* of objective reality contained in the idea, but instead focuses on the fact that this idea exhibits to the mind an *extended* thing. This simple nature, we now know, can be understood independently of the nature of mind. Its independence is emphasized in Descartes's noticing that his ideas of bodies, especially those that constitute sensory experience, are "produced without my cooperation and often even against my will" (AT VII 79; CSM II 55). What is more, the shapes, sizes, and motions that he perceives in bodies are modes whose very intelligibility requires the conception of extension (the simple nature). "But it is clear," he wrote, "that these other faculties (the capacity to be shaped, sized, etc.), if they exist, must be in a corporeal substance and not an intellectual one; for the clear and distinct conception of them includes extension, but does not include any intellectual act whatsoever" (AT VII 79; CSM II 55). So, there must be some *other* substance, he claimed, a substance other than his mind, that was the origin of the objective reality of the (primary) ideas of bodies.

1.96   This theme was briefly entertained back in the Third Meditation. There, Descartes had asked what it was about his sensory ideas of bodies that led him to believe that they have their origin in things existing "outside" his mind. He answered:

> . . . I know by experience that these ideas do not depend on my will, and hence that they do not depend simply on me. Frequently I notice them even when I do not want to: now, for example, I feel the heat of the fire whether I want to or not, and this is why I think that this sensation or idea of heat comes to me from something other than myself, namely the heat of the fire by which I am sitting. (AT VII 38; CSM II 26)

The trouble, he said, is that his thinking that such ideas have their origin in bodies existing independently of his mind looked to be based on a "spontaneous impulse," something that may be simply the product of human nature. That these ideas have their origin in a *material* reality was not revealed by reason or by the "natural light." In the Third Meditation, he was not in a position to trust this spontaneous impulse. This led him to conclude in the Third Meditation:

> All these considerations are enough to establish that it is not reliable judgment but merely some blind impulse that has made me believe up till now that there exist things distinct from myself which transmit to me ideas or images of themselves through the sense organs or in some other way. (AT VII 39; CSM II 27)

The question of this impulse reemerged in the Sixth Meditation. Descartes 1.97 now thought that he was in a better position to assess its veracity. This would begin by considering that there are only four possible causes (origins) of the idea of body:

his mind,
some finite mind other than his,
God,
Body.

Since the ideas of bodies appear to come to him even against his willing them, it follows, Descartes says, that his mind cannot be their origin. For, if he were their origin, he would know it. But, if it *were* his mind, or some other finite mind, or even God, and minds are essentially non-extended, then the ideas of bodies would represent to him their causes as having a property that they in fact do not possess – as least not formally. At best, his mind, or some other finite mind, or God would possess extension eminently. We should pause here and get clear about this formal/eminent distinction.

1.98   As with many of the philosophical distinctions we find in Descartes's work, this was another that was taught in the schools. We already know about the formal reality/objective reality distinction. The formal–eminent distinction is different, though it does employ the term "formal." The distinction is discussed in some detail in Aquinas' work. It has to do with two ways in which we think about the possession of properties. To be said to possess a property formally, two criterions would have to be met. We can define formal possession this way:

> A *formally* possesses property P if, and only if, A can give P to other things, and "A is P" is true.

Take, for example, the hot fire. We can say that the fire formally possesses heat, since the fire can give heat to other things, and "The fire is hot" is true. By contrast, eminent possession can be defined thus:

> A *eminently* possesses property P if, and only if, A can give P to other things, and "A is P" is false.

Consider a charred log sitting in the firepit. The fire "caused" the log to blacken. In this sense, the fire is understood as having given the property *black* to the wood log. Even so, we know that "The fire is black" is false. Given that the fire can give to other things the property *black*, and yet "The fire is black" is false, we say that the fire possesses black *eminently*.

1.99   Returning to Descartes's consideration of the possible causes of his ideas of bodies, ideas that represent to him essentially *extended* things, he noted that whatever is the cause must possess extension either formally or eminently. We now know what that would mean. How does this distinction inform his analysis? Let us look.

1.100   Descartes claimed that his ideas of bodies represent to him objects that are *essentially* extended. That is, his ideas represent bodies as things possessing extension *formally*. So, whatever is their cause, it would have to be true that they are extended. If his mind, or some other finite mind, or God *were* the cause (origin) of your ideas of body, then these ideas would misrepresent their object (the cause or origin of the ideas). For, they would misrepresent an essentially non-extended thing as though it were an essentially extended thing! Descartes reasoned:

> But since God is not a deceiver, it is quite clear that he does not transmit the ideas to me either directly from himself, or indirectly, via some creature

which contains the objective reality of the ideas not formally but only eminently. For God has given me no faculty at all for recognizing any such source for these ideas; on the contrary, he has given me a great propensity to believe that they are produced by corporeal things. So, I do not see how God could be understood to be anything but a deceiver if the ideas were transmitted from a source other than corporal things. It follows that corporeal things exist. (AT VII 79–80; CSM II 55)

The "great propensity to believe" that his ideas of bodies originate in bodies, a propensity given to him by God, turns out to be that spontaneous or blind impulse he considered back in the Third Meditation. Back then, he was not in a position to assess its veracity, so he put little stock in it. But now that he has discovered that God exists, is no deceiver, and is the origin of his mind, which includes that great propensity to believe that his ideas of bodies originate in bodies, that impulse *can* be trusted. For, were God to give him this impulse, and yet it compelled him to believe something that was false, then God would be a deceiver. But, God is not a deceiver. So, it follows that this impulse, which God gave him, compels him to believe something that is true. Specifically, now using Descartes's technical terminology, the impulse compels him to believe that the objective reality of the idea of body has its origin in the formal reality of body – that is, in the formal reality of a *corporeal* substance. And, since saying that *a thing possesses formal reality* is identical to saying that *it exits*, then in saying that body possesses formal reality, which is the origin of the objective reality contained in his idea of body, this is no different than saying that body exists (or that bodies exist). This is Descartes's proof for the existence of the material world, a world that exists independently of the mind.

We can now apply a way of casting a distinction between "internal to the 1.101 mind" and "external to the mind," which was briefly introduced in our Introduction. A thing is said to be *internal* to a mind if, and only if, it depends on this mind for its existence. A thing is said to be *external* to a mind if, and only if, it does not depend on this mind for its existence. Casting the distinction this way allows us to avoid thinking of the mind as a kind of box, which has an inside and an outside. The mind, at least according to Descartes, is *not* extended, and so it is not like the box, which is extended. To think of the internal/external distinction in this "boxy" sense, if talking about the mind, we would be speaking metaphorically at best. When Descartes claims that bodies exist *external* to his mind, he is not speaking metaphorically. What he is claiming is that bodies do not depend on his mind for their existence.

Reference

Husserl, Edmund. (1960) *Cartesian Meditations*, translated by Dorion Cairns, The Hague: Martinus Nijhoff Publishers (Seventh Impression, 1982), pp. 15–16.

Readings

Primary Descartes Readings

Descartes, René. (1637) *Discourse on the Method.* https://earlymoderntexts.com/assets/pdfs/descartes1637.pdf.
Descartes, René. (c.1628) *Rules for the Direction of the Mind.* https://learning.hccs.edu/faculty/robert.tierney/phil1301-3/substantive-course-materials/unit-iii/descartes-rules-for-the-direction-of-the-mind/view.
Descartes, René. (1641) *Meditations on First Philosophy Objections and Replies to the Meditations.* https://www.earlymoderntexts.com/assets/pdfs/descartes1641.pdf; https://www.earlymoderntexts.com/assets/pdfs/descartes1642_3.pdf.
Descartes, René. (1644) *Principles of Philosophy.* https://www.earlymoderntexts.com/assets/pdfs/descartes1644part1.pdf.

Secondary Readings

Newman, Lex. (2016). Descartes' Epistemology, *The Stanford Encyclopedia of Philosophy*, Edward N. Zalta (ed.) https://plato.stanford.edu/entries/descartes-epistemology/.
Smith, Kurt. (2020). Descartes' Life and Works, *The Stanford Encyclopedia of Philosophy*, Edward N. Zalta (ed.) https://plato.stanford.edu/entries/descartes-works/.
Smith, Kurt (2021) Descartes' Theory of Ideas, *The Stanford Encyclopedia of Philosophy*, Edward N. Zalta (ed.) https://plato.stanford.edu/entries/descartes-ideas/.

2

THOMAS HOBBES

Thomas Hobbes was born 5 April 1588; raised in the town of Malemesbury, 2.1
England. Around 1602, at about 14 years old, he entered college at Oxford.
He graduated in 1608, after which he went to work for the Cavendish fam-
ily. Around the 1620s, Hobbes looks to have also worked for Francis Bacon.
During the 1630s, he traveled Europe and crossed paths the Marin Mersenne
in Paris. His first significant philosophical works came in the 1640s, when
he published *Elements of Law* and *De Cive* (*Concerning the Citizen*), both
works in political philosophy. Also around this time, by way of Mersenne,
Hobbes wrote what would become the Third Set of Objections to Descasrtes's
Meditations. This exchange revealed some of Hobbes's views on metaphysics and epistemology. His relatively long stay in Paris appears to have been
prompted by the English Civil Wars. After he had returned to England
(1651), Hobbes published what some take to be his masterpiece, *Leviathan*
(1651). In the mid to late 1650s, he completed two works, *De Corpore*
(*Concerning Body*; 1655) and *De Homine* (*Concerning Man*; 1658), that
together with *De Cive* would form a kind of philosophical trilogy. Hobbes
died 4 December 1679, at one of the homes of the Cavendish family.

2.1 Hobbes's Materialism

Hobbes and Descartes were contemporaries. They even met in person once. 2.2
Due to the efforts of Friar Marin Mersenne (1588–1648), who served as
editor of the *Meditations*, history has been treated to a focused written
exchange between the two, Hobbes authoring what would become the
Third Set of Objections, which was appended to the *Meditations*.

This Is Modern Philosophy: An Introduction, First Edition. Kurt Smith.
© 2023 John Wiley & Sons, Inc. Published 2023 by John Wiley & Sons, Inc.

2.3   When reading the Third Set of Objections and Replies, we can detect some tension between Hobbes and Descartes. As we know, Descartes was a dualist – the view that there are exactly two kinds of finite substance that inhabit or make up the cosmos: mind and body. Descartes took the mind's principal attribute, its defining characteristic, to be *thought* or *thinking*. If a thing is a mind, it thinks; and, if a thing thinks, it is a mind. Independently of this kind of thing was body, its principal attribute being *extension* in length, breadth, and depth. If a thing is a body, it is extended; and, if a thing is extended, it is a body. Descartes's *real distinction* argument, discussed in the previous chapter on Descartes, had concluded that mind and body *can* exist independently of one another, since the nature of each could be conceived independently of the other. It was in terms of *conceptual* independence that Descartes grounded his claim about the *ontological* independence of mind and body.

2.4   It was in terms of ontological independence that the distinction between "internal" and "external" could be understood: we said that something was *internal to* the mind if, and only if, its existence depended on the mind; whereas something was *external to* the mind if, and only if, its existence did not depend on the mind. Since, as real distinction showed, body does not depend on the mind for its existence – that is, body is ontologically *independent* of mind – it followed that if body exists, it is *external to* the mind. The Sixth Meditation proof for the existence of body, then, was Descartes's proof for the existence of an external world. Even so, as was also noted in the previous chapter, Descartes's argument for the existence of God, which he had made before making the proof for the existence of body, was an argument that concluded that at least one thing other than Descartes's mind existed – specifically, something that did not depend for its existence on Descartes's mind. This, as was also suggested in the last chapter, might count as a proof for the existence of an external world – a world that exists independently of one's mind.

2.5   Hobbes was a materialist. *Materialism* tells us that the only kind of stand-alone substance that inhabits or makes up the cosmos is corporeal or bodily. Insofar as Hobbes held that only *one* kind of substance existed, his view was an instance of *monism* (*mono* = one). We can contrast this to Descartes's *dualism* (*dual* = two). It was no surprise, then, that Hobbes disagreed with Descartes about the claim that there was an independently existing mental substance. On Hobbes's view, if there are minds, they are bodily, or they ultimately depend for their existence on the existence of body. Either way, minds would not be stand-alone substances.

2.2 Hobbes's View of Mind

In the Third Set of Objections, Hobbes tells Descartes that a mind is "noth-   2.6
ing more than motion occurring in various parts of an organic body" (AT
VII 178; CSM II 126). So, a mind, strictly speaking, was not a *body* – that is,
a mind was not a corporeal *substance* (or material *thing*). Instead, a mind, in
being identified in terms of *motion*, was nothing more than a *mode* of body;
it was a property or characteristic of a body. In Cartesian terms, since a
mode depends for its existence on the existence of the substance of which it
is a mode, a mind, in being a certain collection of motions, depended for its
existence on the existence of the body of which it is a mode. This would
mean that no mind could exist independently of a corporeal (extended)
substance.

Even so, Hobbes would also say in his exchange with Descartes that he   2.7
believed in the existence of "invisible and immaterial creatures who serve
God" (AT VII 180; CSM II 127), suggesting that perhaps there were stand-
alone beings that are incorporeal after all. But his saying this is probably
best understood within the context of his recognizing the limitations of our
conceiving or *imagining* such things. For, his point to Descartes seemed to
be that even supposing that there were such beings, human beings could
only conceive or imagine them *as* bodily – as a flame, say, or as a child with
wings (AT VII 179; CSM II 126). The mind cannot be *imagined* as something immaterial. Nothing could. It would turn out that Hobbes's peculiar
remark to Descartes about his belief in the possibility of immaterial beings
was disingenuous or if held, short-lived, for he would go on to suggest in
later writings, as made clear by Geoffrey Gorham, that even God (and
presumably any creature serving God) was corporeal (2013).

In identifying a mind as a certain set of motions that are present in a   2.8
living thing, a host of questions arise, an obvious one being: *which*
motions present in a living organism constitute a mind? Though not
perfectly clear, Hobbes's answer begins by assuming the existence of a
living organism and bodies that are not identical with this organism
that are nevertheless spatially related to it. The *motions* of those bodies
not identical with the living organism are conveyed by way of various
media, for example light and air, which are themselves constituted of
very tiny corpuscles or "particles." The motions of air particles, for
example, are transferred to the particles that form the surface of the living organism. Those particles on the surface begin to move, transferring
the motions to other particles located ever deeper in the organism *via*

systems of particles that constitute the organism's sensory organs. In the case of human beings, these motions ultimately reach the particles that constitute the human being's *brain* and *heart*. Hobbes does more than to suggest that it is the motions of the particles constituting these two organs that account for what he is referring to as this organism's *mind* – specifically, the mind of a human being.

2.9   According to Hobbes, the motions of the matter constituting the brain form what he calls a *phantasm*. The term "phantasm" comes from the ancient Greek language of Aristotle, which means "something appearing." This *appearing* or *seeming* is what he calls "fancy." (There is clearly a connection between the notions of *fancy, fantasy, phantasm,* and so on.) Although in his exchange with Descartes, Hobbes had used the word "idea," which is also derived from ancient Greek, in later writings, he mostly used "phantasm." Here, we will read Hobbes as having taken "idea" and "phantasm" to be synonymous. Even though the account of the phantasm locates it in the brain, at which point one might think that the account is complete, the motions of the particles constituting the heart play an important role. According to Hobbes, the motions of the matter constituting the heart generate an *impulse*, which, for lack of a better word, informs the phantasm in the brain, giving to the phantasm a directedness *outward*, away from the organism (*Leviathan*, Part I, Chapter I, paragraph 4). With the addition of this impulse, a phantasm can be understood to be something like an *image*; specifically, it is *about* or it *refers to* whatever it is that caused the motions that now inform the matter constituting the brain of the organism. For example, let us say that the motions of the particles constituting a fire next to which someone is sitting are communicated through air particles to the particles constituting the surface of the organism's body. These motions are in turn communicated through the organism's sensory organ systems, where they reach the brain and heart. A phantasm is formed in the brain which is informed by an impulse generated by the heart, which directs the phantasm outward (or back toward the source of the motions), away from the organism, the phantasm now given as a representation of the "external" object – in our example, the fire next to which this someone is sitting: for instance, perhaps it represents (or presents) the fire as being hot.

2.10   There are several important questions worth highlighting that Hobbes does not address in any detail in his discussions of phantasms. For instance, he never says exactly what "sees" or is "aware of" the idea or phantasm located in the brain. It is not as though there is an eye or some self (whose eye it is) that hovers over the surface of the brain looking at the image in or on the brain. So, for what or for whom is the occurring motions in the brain an image? To whom does it *seem* that the fire is hot? Where exactly is the *perceiver* in all of this who perceives the phantasm? Is the perceiver motion, too? If so, when we say that the mind perceives a phantasm, are we saying that motion *perceives* motion? What could "perceives" mean here? Further, when one sees a red rose, the *red*, like the *heat* felt when sitting next to the fire, the *quale* as it is called in contemporary philosophy of mind, might be taken as being distinct in kind from the motions occurring in the brain. Hobbes commits himself to the view that the only thing that motion can produce is motion (*Leviathan*, Part I, Chapter I, paragraph 4). The quale red that appears certainly does not appear as motion – it appears as a determinate color. Descartes, for instance, thought that motion could be understood as conveying or as transferring the material "information" that can, in the right (divinely inspired) conditions, serve to help "produce" (occasion) the *quale* red in the mind, but even for Descartes what was not being transferred was the *quale*. The red – that is, the *quale* – is not being transferred from the rose, through the material medium we call light (a system of particles), through a sensory organ system, and then to the brain. What was being transferred (or communicated) was motion. If a *quale* is fundamentally different from a motion, as Descartes had noted in the *Principles*, where he says that there is not any conceptual or logical (that is, necessary) relation between motions and what it is like, say, to see *red* or to feel *heat* (*Principles*, Part IV, Article 198), we might ask Hobbes: what is the ontological status of *qualia*? If we think of *qualia* as constituting the *contents* of our phantasms, Hobbes would still have some explaining to do. Of course, given his commitment to the claim that motion produces only motion, he may have thought it nonsense to speak about phantasmal content, for his materialism may have ruled out such talk. Even so, he does speak of the "subject" of experience, the object of which someone is aware, which he identified as body, to which we attribute "accidents" or properties. This appears to be content-talk. In any event, Hobbes does not say very much about such issues.

In his reply to the Third Objections, Descartes had gleaned from Hobbes's remarks that Hobbes had taken ideas to be solely corporeal – so, the ideas (phantasms) themselves were corporeal and what they "represented" (or referred to) were corporeal substances. Descartes writes: 2.11

> Here my critic wants the term "idea" to be taken to refer simply to the images of material things which are depicted in the corporeal imagination; and if this is granted, it is easy for him to prove that there can be no proper idea of an angel or of God. But I make it quite clear in several places throughout the book, and in this passage in particular, that I am taking the word "idea" to refer to whatever is immediately perceived by the mind. (AT VII 181; CSM II 127)

2.12   In *De Corpore* (*Concerning Body*: 1655), written several years after his
exchange with Descartes, Hobbes would provide an analysis of the phantasms of *space, time, body,* and *motion,* which he offered as his account of
the possibility of a human being's *intelligible* experience of the material
world. Suppose that a phantasm of a red rose is produced in the brain by
way of an act of sensing. Like all sensory-produced phantasms, this one will
be of a *particular* object. This object will be given as existing at some
moment and at some distance from the perceiver; it will be given as the
bearer of certain properties, and the like. The phantasms of space, body,
motion, and time are *primitive,* so to speak, in the sense that they can be
discovered (through analysis) as informing any occurring phantasm produced *via* the act of sensing, including the aforementioned occurring phantasm of the red rose.

2.13   Body was characterized by Hobbes as follows:

> A BODY *is that which having no dependence upon our Thought is coinci-
> dent or coextended with some part of Space.* (*De Corpore,* Part 2, Chapter
> VIII, p. 75)

Here, Hobbes suggests that a body presupposes space. A body, Hobbes says,
is coincident or coextended with some part of space. Notice that, contrary to
Descartes's view, a body for Hobbes is not identical with space. Instead, the
suggestion here is that space is prior: space provides the "place" in which a
body exists. Space accounts for the possibility of a body's occupying a place.
Since what we are really talking about are phantasms, we might more accurately say that the phantasm of body presupposes the phantasm of space.

2.14   Hobbes says in the above definition that a body has no dependence on
thought. Understanding this will be a bit tricky. For, if he is a materialist,
what can he mean by "thought" exactly? Presumably, an occurring phantasm is an example of a thought. As we know, he had told Descartes that the
mind, to which the word "thought" is typically associated, is motion (or
motions) occurring in a living organism. Thus, one way to read Hobbes is
to emphasize that thought, if it is anything, is ultimately motion, in which
case it would then be taken as a mode of a body. Since "phantasm" is referring to these motions, too, we might take the two words, "phantasm" and
"mind," to be synonymous, as we did with "phantasm" and "idea," but the
word "mind" had a wider reference for Hobbes, which included reference to
various *capacities* and occurring *processes* such as sensing, imagining,
remembering, reconning or reasoning, and so on. Reasoning, for instance,
is neither identical with the process of producing a phantasm in the brain

nor with the phantasm drawn, but presumably is instead an *activity* of the mind that can make *use* of an occurring phantasm for some end. So, we might (and in this chapter we will) interpret Hobbes as holding that among the various capacities and processes that fall under the umbrella of the notion of *mind* is the process of generating phantasms, and we should also include the phantasms themselves, but a mind is more than just this or that process or more than a particular occurring phantasm. To keep our reading of Hobbes as clear as possible, we will limit "thought" to referring to any of the *actually* occurring processes that fall under the umbrella notion of *mind*, including any *actually* occurring phantasms generated in the brain. For our purpose, then, the most general word is "mind," which covers capacities as well as occurring processes and occurring phantasms, then there is "thought," which covers actually occurring processes and actually occurring phantasms, and then there is "phantasm" (and "idea"), which covers actually occurring image-like drawings in the brain. In the end, of course, when interpreting Hobbes, what we are really talking about when talking about mind and its capacities and active processes and occurring phantasms is motion. Understood this way, as motion, the existence of thought will depend on a body, since motion is a mode of body, but a body (the corporeal *substance*) will not depend for its existence on thought (on one of its modes). Emphasizing this asymmetrical ontological dependence relation between a substance and its modes, as we have done here, allows us a way of identifying at least one sense in which a body does not depend on our *thought*, the latter understood as a motion (or some collection of motions) in a living organism.

As noted earlier, body presupposes space, or, perhaps more accurately, the *phantasm* of body presupposes the *phantasm* of space. Either way, the logic here is that space is a necessary condition for body, which is to say: *If there is a body, there is space.* Hobbes defines "space" as follows: 2.15

> SPACE is the Phantasme of a Thing existing without the Mind Simply; that is to say, that Phantasme, in which we consider no other Accident, but onely that it appears without us. (*De corpore*, Part 2, Chapter VII, Section 2)

The peculiar phrases "without the mind simply" and "appears without us" are significant, for they are expressing an important feature of actually occurring phantasms – this feature a *form* that every phantasm takes. Here, the phantasm of space is responsible for a phantasm's being directed outward, away from the organism, which, as was said, is based on an impulse given to the phantasm by way of the heart. This is the feature that ultimately gives to an occurring phantasm in the brain its image-like character, which is the sense in which a phantasm can be taken to refer to or to represent an object that is "outside" or "external to" the organism. To contemporary philosophers of mind, what Hobbes says about this *directedness* or *aboutness* feature may look like a very early account of what they call *intentionality* – an essential feature of consciousness. It is that feature that accounts for a mind's being *aware of* something.

2.16   Concerning motion, Hobbes writes:

> MOTION, *is a continual relinquishing of one Place, and acquiring of another*; and that Place which is relinquished is commonly called the *Terminus a quo*, as that which is acquired is called the *Terminus ad quem*; I say a continual Relinquishing, because no Body, how little soever, can totally and at once go out of its former Place into onother, so, but that some part of it will be in a part of Place which is common to both, namely, to the relinquished and the acquired Places. (*De corpore*, Part 2, Chapter VIII, Sec. 10, p. 79)

Motion is defined as a body's relinquishing some initially occupied place and its acquiring another. The place initially occupied by a body Hobbes calls the "*terminus a quo*," and the place toward which or into which this body moves he calls the "*terminus ad quem*." Motion is never instantaneous. That is, a body could never instantaneously and completely exit its *terminus a quo* and occupy a *terminus ad quem*. The exit and entry are always in reciprocal proportion to one another. As a body relinquishes its initial place and acquires its new place, it occupies less and less of the former and proportionally more and more of the latter. This is an essential characteristic of all motion.

2.17   Time is derivative of motion; it is the measure of motion. In terms of phantasms, the phantasm of time presupposes the phantasm of motion, which in turn presupposes the phantasms of body and space. An *instant* of time for Hobbes is simply an occurring motion that is too small to be measured, and hence cannot have a number assigned to it when "computing." Motion "at an instant" is called an *endeavor*. "I define *endeavour*," Hobbes writes, "to be motion made in less space and time then can be given; that is, less then can be determined or assigned by exposition or number" (*De Corpore*, Part 3, Chapter XV, Sec. 2, p. 151). So, even *at* an instant motion occurs *in* or *over* that instant of time. An instant is simply an artifact of a system of measure; it is a *limit* inherent in any attempt to measure (divide) motion. It is important to keep in mind that at an instant motion is not "frozen," so to speak. If a body is in motion, even "at an instant" it still is exiting a *terminus a quo* and entering a *terminus ad quem*. It is just that this exiting and entering is not measurable (divisible) by way of the relative system of measure.

Hobbes's view suggests that even if we were to engineer a machine that   2.18
could now measure a short duration of motion that was up until now not
(physically) measurable, there would still be some even shorter duration of
motion that would now escape measure. This even shorter, unmeasurable
duration would now be our new instant. Time is "exposed" (i.e. made intelligible) he says by imagining an object moving uniformly over a line (*De
Corpore*, Part 2, Chapter XII, Sec. 4, pp. 103–104). For Hobbes, then, there
are no *metaphysical* temporal atoms – that is, no temporal instants that could
not in principle be divided (by way of measuring). Time, like motion, is a
continuum. As with points and lines, when we say that between any two
points on the line is another point, we say with instants and time, between
any two instants of time is another instant. Even so, as just noted, we could
say that there are *artificial* temporal atoms, but this would mean only that
there are tiny spans of motion that our system of measure cannot currently
measure. In this sense, in terms of the systems of measure, there is no instant
between two contiguous instants, but instead an instant stands for some artificial quantum of time (motion). The upshot of all this is that Hobbes looks
to hold that both *past* and *future*, which are temporal references to *terminus
a quo* and *terminus ad quem*, respectively, are in play even *at* an instant. For,
a motion, even one that is currently unmeasurable (an endeavor), requires
us to conceive it in terms of *past* and *future*, since motion essentially is *continual* movement from a *terminus a quo* to a *terminus ad quem*.

We can find lurking in Hobbes's account of motion two possible argu-   2.19
ments for the existence of an external world, a world that exists independently of a mind. The arguments are suggested in what he says about *cause*
and *effect*, and about *power* and *act*, concepts he casts in terms of motion.
Let us take a brief look at this material before bringing this chapter to a
close. Interestingly, we will find some of this view resurrected by Mary
Shepherd, whose view is considered in Chapter 6.

2.3 Concept-Pairs

Let us consider the concept-pairs *agent* and *patient*, and *cause* and *effect*.   2.20
Hobbes writes: "As when one body by putting forwards another body generates motion in it, it is called the agent, and the body in which motion is so
generated, is called the patient" (*De Corpore*, Part 2, Chapter IX, Sec. 1,
p. 87). The agent is called the "cause" and the patient the "effect." Hobbes
reworks the then familiar Aristotelian conceptions of causes. For instance,
the aggregate of accidents (i.e. corporeal properties) possessed by the agent,
"required for the production of the effect, is called the *efficient cause*"

(*De Corpore*, Chapter IX, Sec. 4, p. 88). The aggregate of accidents in the patient required for its being affected by an agent is called the *material cause* (Ibid.). Each by itself, the efficient and material cause, is only a "partial cause." It is only when both are together "joyned" that they constitute what Hobbes calls the "entire cause" (Ibid.). Here, the entire cause is such that the efficient cause (the aggregate of the accidents of the agent) and the material cause (the aggregate of the accidents of the patient) are joined "in the same instant" (*De Corpore*, Part 2, Chapter IX, Sec. 6, p. 89). What is being caused or produced in the patient, of course, is motion or a change in motion (*De Corpore*, Part 2, Chapter IX, Sec. 9, p. 91). So, in plain terms, it appears that what Hobbes has in mind is that the agent possesses the *ability* to produce motion in a patient, and the patient possesses the *ability* to be moved by some agent.

2.21   In fact, Hobbes immediately turns to recasting cause and effect in exactly these terms. "Correspondent to *cause* and *effect*," he writes, "are *power* and *act*; nay, those and these are the same things" (*De Corpore*, Part 2, Chapter X, Sec. 1, p. 93). Considering the cause: "For whenever any agent has all those accidents which are necessarily requisite for the production of some effect in the patient, then we say that agent has *power* to produce that effect, if it be applied to a patient" (Ibid.). The accidents possessed by the agent, he says, constitute "the power of the agent," or the "active power," where "the *power of the agent*, and the *efficient cause* are the same thing" (Ibid.). But there is more: ". . . that *cause* is so called in respect to the effect already produced, and *power* in respect to the same effect to be produced hereafter, so that cause respects the past, power the future time" (Ibid.). We can understand this as follows: When an effect is being produced, which would be in the context of talk of the entire cause, we refer to the agent as *cause*. However, so long as an effect is not being produced, then that agent which we take to be a possible future cause we call a *power*.

2.22   Something similar will hold when talking about effects. The patient possesses some aggregate of accidents that determine its ability to be affected by some agent. Hobbes writes: "it is the *power* of that patient to produce that effect, if it be applied to a fitting agent," which he goes on to call its "passive power," equating this with material cause (*De Corpore*, Part 2, Chapter X, Sec. 1, pp. 93–94). When the powers of the agent and patient are "joyned together" (*De Corpore*, Part 2, Chapter X, Sec. 3, p. 94), they constitute what Hobbes calls a "plenary power," which he says "is the same thing with entire cause" (Ibid.). Cause and effect are to power and act as entire cause is to plenary power. Hobbes tells us more: "as the accident (i.e., motion) produced in respect of the cause [is] called an *effect*, so in respect of the power it is called an *act*" (Ibid.). So, whenever there is an entire cause, the patient is called the effect. However, whenever we consider plenary power, a patient that has yet to be affected by an agent is, with respect to the agent, an act (if we take a power, a future cause, as something like a potentiality, then when this does produce an effect, the effect is this potentiality made actual. Thus, the future effect can be understood in terms of its being the actualization of the potentiality.) So, future causes are called *powers* and future effects are called *acts*; and similarly, future entire causes are called *plenary powers*.

Hobbes suggests that there are no causes without effects and vice versa   2.23 (*De Corpore*, Part 2, Chapter X, Sec. 2, p. 94). They can only be understood properly, as cause and effect, within the conceptual scheme of *entire cause*. The entire cause marks the "moment" at which the agent is acting on the patient, or, in other words, at the very "moment" the effect is being produced. As we will see shortly, the claim that *only within the context of entire cause can a cause and effect be properly conceived* will play an important role in the argument for the existence of an external world.

To best understand this, we might start by comparing what Hobbes says   2.24 to cases more familiar to us. For example, the conceptual relation between cause and effect looks to be very much like the relation between the concepts *inside* and *outside,* or between the concepts *concave* and *convex*. The relations between such concepts establish certain constraints – for instance, there is no inside without outside, and vice versa; there is no concave without convex, and vice versa. As referred to earlier, they are what we might call "concept-pairs," where the possibility of talking about one (*inside*) entails the possibility of our talking about the other (*outside*). Likewise, in every case in which it makes sense to talk about an *effect*, it makes sense to talk about its *cause*, and vice versa. This will not mean that we *know* what the cause of some effect is. Rather, it simply tells us that if we identify something as an effect, we *ipso facto* (by that very fact) take there to be some cause. Similarly, if we identify something as a cause, we *ipso facto* take there to be some effect. Neither can be understood (as *cause* or *effect*) without the other.

Hobbes, as also suggested above, looks to provide a way for talking about   2.25 agents and patients when they are not technically speaking causes and effects (they are not at the moment joined, constituting an entire cause). Here, Hobbes allows the natural philosopher a way of conceiving a *future* cause that has yet to "join" with a *future* patient – it is considered to be a power. And he allows the natural philosopher a way of conceiving a *future* effect that has yet to join with a *future* agent – it is considered to be an act. The two, *power* and *act*, are also concept-pairs. They are understood within the context of the conceptual scheme of a *plenary power*. The point to stress here is that even though we consider an agent as a possible future cause, when considering it as such, *agent* is conceptually paired with *patient*, so that in our conceiving something as an *agent*, we are, whether directly or indirectly, conceiving something else as *patient*. The two – *agent* and *patient* – always go together. Likewise, when conceiving something as a possible future *cause*, we are *ipso facto*, whether directly or indirectly, conceiving something else as a possible future *effect*. The two – *cause* and *effect* – always go together.

2.26   Hobbes says, "all active power consists of motion" (*De corpore*, Part 2, Chapter X, Sec. 6, p. 96). Since it is conceptually impossible to conceive of the agent's active power in complete isolation from the conception of a patient's passive power, then when we are talking about the active power of the agent, which Hobbes says is a motion, we are either explicitly or implicitly engaged in talking about the passive power of the patient. Although not perfectly clear, Hobbes seems to think that the passive power of the patient is also a motion. He writes, ". . . power is not a certain accident which differs from all acts, but is indeed an act, namely motion, which is therefore called power . . ." (*De Corpore*, Part 2, Chapter X, Sec. 6, p. 96). Given that "the effect is produced at the same instant in which the cause is entire . . ." (*De Corpore*, Part 2, Chapter X, Sec. 2, p. 94), it is reasonable to take Hobbes as thinking that there is really only one motion in play, just conceived from different points of view. This way of understating things is different from the way we have thus far considered the matter. Let us take a look.

2.27   Consider two related events: A moves B and B moves C. There are two ways to think about them. First, in the way conceived thus far, which seems to be the most natural way: A is moving and then A contacts B, and as a result B moves. B is now moving and then B contacts C, and as a result C moves. The focus here is on A, B, and C, on *what* is moving, and on *what* causes motion to come about in another thing (in another *what*). Consider the case of A moves B: from the agent's (A's) point of view, A's motion is a cause; from the patient's (B's) point of view, B's motion is an effect. Here, it is reasonable to think that we are talking about two distinct motions – A's and B's. Now, consider the case of B moves C: B's motion is now the cause and C's motion is the effect. As in the previous case, we seem to be talking about two distinct motions: B's and C's. Taken all together, then, we appear to be talking about three distinct motions: A's motion, B's motion, and C's motion. Since here we are focused on the bodies in play, on A, B, and C, let us call this way of understanding things the *substantive* account – our focus is on *substances*, on the *things* that move. On this way of thinking about the matter, there will be as many motions are there are things.

2.28   But there seems to be a second way of understanding the matter: there are not really three distinct motions (with respect to A, B, and C), but only *one* motion. The one motion is shared, so to speak, between them. So, on this way of understanding the matter, there will not be as many motions as there are things. This second way of interpreting Hobbes is supported by what he says after identifying active and passive powers (the relevant aggregates of accidents) as motions. He claims that an act is also a power by telling us that it is a power because "another act shall be produced by it afterwards" (*De Corpore*, Part 2, Chapter X, Sec. 6, p. 96). The example he gives is helpful:

> For example, if of three bodies the first put forwards the second, and this the third, the motion of the second in respect to the first which produceth it, is the act of the second body, but in respect to the third, it is the active power of the same second body. (*De Corpore*, Part 2, Chapter X, Sec. 6, p. 96)

So, return to our case of bodies A, B, and C. A moves B and B moves C. To get a sense of this second way of understanding things, we will want to start by focusing on what Hobbes says about body B, the second body in the causal chain. Considering A moves B, A's motion is the *cause*, and B's motion is the effect. And when we consider B moves C, as before, B's motion is now the cause, and C's motion is the effect. Thus far, this all looks familiar. But now let us focus on Hobbes's assessment of B's motion as provided in his example, for he casts it in two lights. In light of A, B's motion is an effect, but in light of C, B's motion, *the very same* motion that we just cast as an effect with respect to A, is now a cause. The point to stress here is that we are talking about *one* motion (B's) from two different points of view. This analysis would conclude the same if we applied it to an examination of the cause of A's motion or the effect of C's. For instance, let X's motion be the cause of A's, and, as before, let A's motion be the cause of B's. Now A is the second object considered in the chain, and with respect to X, A's motion is an effect, whereas with respect to B, A's motion, *the very same* motion that we just cast as an effect with respect to X, is now, with respect to B, a cause. This analysis if applied to C, or any other body for that matter, would yield the same result. This second way of understanding the matter arises when we consider a motion "between" two bodies. Thus far, we have considered the motion of a single body, starting with B. We concluded that from one point of view (in B's relation to A), B's motion is an effect, from another point of view (in B's relation to C), B's motion is a cause. But could we not say the same if we considered the motion as it stands "between" A and B? When considering A moves B, the motion of A is the cause, whereas when considering B, the motion of B is the effect. But is not this, as before, *one and the same* motion, just considered from two points of view? Could we not take A and B to be the *terminus a quo* and *terminus ad quem*, respectively, of a single motion? This same analysis would yield the same for B and C: only one motion between the two. But it would also hold with respect to all three. On this view, there are three things, but only one motion.

2.29   We might have expected something like this, of course, given that Hobbes's view is that motion is "transferred" from one body to another, or, in light of our example, the view is that one and the same motion is "transferred" from A to B to C. For lack of a better name, we might call this second way of understanding things the *modal* account – our focus is on the *mode*, which in this case is motion. It would be important to keep the two accounts straight – the substantive and modal accounts – otherwise we would run the risk of reifying the mode. That is, we would run the risk of thinking about motion, a mode, as though it were a stand-alone substance, able to exist independently of bodies A, B, and C.

2.30   It is not clear which of the above interpretations best illustrates Hobbes's view. This may not matter, however, since the arguments for the existence of an external world are lurking in both. To keep this chapter focused, however, in what remains we will examine what earlier was characterized as the more natural way of understanding the matter. But before we ferret out the argument (in support of the claim that there exists a world external to or independently of a mind), it will be helpful to bring to light one more claim that Hobbes makes about motion.

2.4 A Body Cannot be the Origin of Its Own Motion

2.31 Hobbes clearly rejected the view that a body could move itself. If a body moves, it is the direct result of some other body, which is moving, and which comes into contact with the resting body. In our example earlier, C, for instance, cannot move unless it is moved by some other body, B, which is moving. But, of course, B cannot move unless it is moved by some other body, A, which is moving, and so on. Here is Hobbes's argument for holding that a body cannot move itself but requires some other body already in motion:

> *Whatsoever is at Rest, will alwayes be a Rest, unless there be some other Body besides it, which by endeavouring to get into its Place by motion, suffers it no longer to remain at Rest.* For suppose that some Finite Body exist, and be at Rest, and that all Space besides be Empty; if now this Body begin to be Moved, it will certainly be Moved some way; Seeing therefore there was nothing in that Body which did not dispose it to Rest, the reason why it is Moved this way is in something out of it; and in like manner, if it had been Moved any other way, the reason of Motion that way had also been in something out of it; but seeing it was supposed that Nothing is out of it, the reason of its Motion one way would be the same with the reason of its Motion every other way; wherefore it would be Moved alike all wayes at once; which is impossible. (*De Corpore*, Part 2, Chapter VIII, Sec. 19, pp. 83–84)

Here, Hobbes imagines a case of a body at rest. It is just this body, all by itself, no other body anywhere near it. The space surrounding this body is empty. To be sure, he says, we could imagine that this body begins moving, and if we did, we will have imagined it moving in some direction. If we imagine that it moves, and there are no other bodies around, we must imagine that the *reason* it moves arises from something inherent its own nature, for it is the only thing being considered. Let us call the reason for its moving in direction1, for instance, reason R1. Fine. But, we can also just as easily imagine that this body moves in some other direction, direction2, say, which is not identical to direction1. Let reason R2 be the reason it moves in direction2. Clearly, since direction2 is not identical to direction1, it is assumed that R2 is not identical to R1. We could multiply the possible directions and reasons indefinitely, but we only need the two introduced here to make Hobbes's point, which is: if we consider R1 and R2, Hobbes says that both will have the same cognitive weight – or, put differently, neither reason is greater (or more likely to be true) than the other. We have just as much reason to think that the body will move in direction1 as we do to think that it will move in direction2. Cognitively speaking, we are sort of stuck, much like Buridan's donkey. Unless some new condition arises, such as that of a second body in motion entering the picture, we have no reason that is great enough to justify our thinking that our original hypothetical body at rest will move in any one direction over the others. Until one reason outweighs the others, all reasons will weigh equally. This is another way of saying that until a second body enters the picture, and its interaction with our body at rest gives to one of our reasons more weight than the others, our body at rest, conceptually speaking, will simply remain at rest. Of course, if a moving body enters the picture and collides with our hypothetical body at rest, as just noted, this might give more cognitive weight to R2, say, which is the reason to think that the body at rest will now move in direction2, and not in the others. If the moving body collides with our resting body at a different location (on the resting body's surface), there might be more cognitive weight given to R1, in which case we would expect the body to move in direction1. But, according to Hobbes, a body at rest will remain at rest unless contacted by another body, where this other body will be in motion. Interestingly enough, this same line of reasoning can show that, conceptually speaking, a body in motion will remain in motion unless contacted by another body. This is a good example of how someone like Hobbes who many take to hold a form of empiricism looks to also hold some form of rationalism. For, as made clear here, the claims about a body's remaining at rest or remaining in motion, which would emerge as fundamental "rules" in Modern physics, are not derived from observation but instead from an inspection of the concept of body.

Hobbes's view, then, is that a body at rest will remain at rest, unless it is 2.32 moved by some other body. His thought experiment more than suggests that a body at rest can move itself is inconceivable, which translates into its being taken as impossible.

2.5 A Proof for the Existence of an External World

2.33   At this point it will be helpful to remind ourselves that in a cases like that of A moves B and B moves C, Hobbes says that B's motion, for instance, which is the effect of A's, can be understood only in light of its place in the conceptual scheme of entire cause. The same goes for B moves C. Let us begin with the case of B moves C. In light of this case, Hobbes seems to be saying that C's motion is "produced" at that instant in which the cause is *entire*. Thus, when we claim that C begins to move, that will ultimately require, whether directly or indirectly, a reference to B, whose motion is cause, and likewise when we claim that B begins to move. That will ultimately require a reference to A, since A is cause.

2.34   So, return to Hobbes's claim that a mind is a specific (collection of) motion in a living organism (specifically, the human being). We will limit our analysis to the act of *sensing*. Our hypothetical human being will be Mary. Let C be the matter constituting Mary's brain (and heart). And, let C's *motions* be coextensive with what Hobbes might refer to as Mary's *mind*. Let B be the matter constituting some facet of Mary's sensory system (that is, some sensory organ system). In the case in which Mary *senses*, C's motions are caused by B's. Lastly, suppose that A is the matter constituting some object not identical with Mary's body. B's motions are caused by A's. So, we have the cases of A moves B and B moves C – the motions attributed to C coextensive with Mary's *mind*.

2.35   Here is the argument that seems to be lurking in all of this. First, assume that C begins to move. C's motions are coextensive with Mary's mind. Since C's beginning to move cannot have been caused by some nonexistent thing, for the simple reason that nonexistent objects are not the sorts of things that *can* move, and C cannot be the origin of is its own motion, it will follow that something must be the cause of C's motions. It must be something not identical with C. So, it is necessary that at the very moment C begins to move, which must be conceived under the scheme of entire cause, there exists some object not identical with C that is the cause of C's motions. Call this B. This line of reasoning concludes that necessarily when C begins to move, there exists at least one body other than C, namely B, which causes C to move. Since, C's motions are coextensive with Mary's mind, it follows necessarily that if Mary's mind exists, at least one body not identical to Mary's mind exists. At least at the "moment" in which the cause is entire (when the effect is being produced).

Since this other body must be other than C, then when Mary's mind exists, there exists at least one thing independent of Mary's mind. That is, there exists a world *external to* Mary's mind. Of course, earlier we identified B as the matter constituting Mary's sensory organs. Does this change the conclusion? Not at all. The sense of "external" at work here is not extended to what is "outside" Mary's body – though we could limit it to mean this. Rather, for our purpose, it has been limited to C, to Mary's *mind*. Of course, if we want "external" to mean something like "external to Mary's body," we could easily apply the line of reasoning to B. The same analysis would show that necessarily when B begins to move, there exists at least one body not identical to B, which is the cause of B's beginning to move. We earlier referred to this as A. But even supposing that A is part of Mary's body, at some point, if we kept this up, and given that Mary's body does not extend indefinitely in three dimensions, eventually we will arrive at a body that is not identical with Mary's, and so in principle we would satisfy this more *materialistic* sense of "external" – a world of bodies that exist external to Mary's body. That is, we would have proven that there exists a material world independent of Mary's mind.

Reference

Gorham, Geoffrey (2013) The theological foundation of hobbesian physics: a defence of corporeal God, *British Journal of the History of Philosophy*, 21, 2, 240–261.

Readings

Primary Hobbes Readings

Hobbes, Thomas. (1651) *Leviathan*. http://files.libertyfund.org/files/869/0161_Bk.pdf.
Hobbes, Thomas. (1655) *De Corpore*. https://archive.org/details/english workstho21hobbgoog/page/n8/mode/2up.
Hobbes, Thomas. (1641) Third Set of Objections to Descartes's *Meditations*. http://people.tamu.edu/~sdaniel/Hobbes%20Objections%20III.pdf.

Secondary Reading

Duncan, Stewart. (2021) Thomas Hobbes, in *Stanford Encyclopedia of Philosophy*. https://plato.stanford.edu/entries/hobbes/.

3

GEORGE BERKELEY

3.1 Berkeley (pronounced *Bark-lay*) was born in Kilkenny, Ireland, on 12 March 1685. He entered Kilkenny College in 1696, and Trinity College in 1700. He graduated with a Masters in 1707, remaining at Trinity as a tutor and lecturer. In 1721, he took Holy Orders in the Church of Ireland, earning a doctorate in divinity. He was made Dean of Dromore, and then in 1724, Dean of Derry. These positions were associated with cathedrals of the Church of Ireland. In 1728, he moved to North America, settling in Newport, Rhode Island, and returned to England in 1732. He was made Bishop of Cloyne (in Ireland) in 1734. In 1752, he moved to Oxford, England. Berkeley died at Oxford, 14 January 1753, and is buried in Christ Church Chapel. He is famous in philosophy for defending a form of idealism, which he refers to as *immaterialism*.

3.1 Berkeley's Rejection of a Material World

3.2 Berkeley believed that there is no *material* world – a world of extended space filled with extended impenetrable bodies clanking about, a world that according to Descartes and others existed independently of the mind. It is important to stress that Berkeley did not *doubt* that there was a material world. He was not a skeptic. He had good reasons for rejecting the claim that there was a material world. Even so, he did not reject the idea of there being a world that existed independent of one's mind. On his view, there is a reality that exists independently of one's mind (that is, independently of the finite human mind). So, there is an *external* reality, where by "external" it is meant that it exists independently of one's mind (it does not depend on the human mind), it is just that it was not a *material* one. For Berkeley, the world is immaterial,

This Is Modern Philosophy: An Introduction, First Edition. Kurt Smith.
© 2023 John Wiley & Sons, Inc. Published 2023 by John Wiley & Sons, Inc.

constituted entirely of minds and their ideas. This was very different from the sort of view held by Descartes or Hobbes. Descartes's view, recall, said that there are two kinds of things in the world, minds and bodies. He was a meta-physical dualist (*dual* = *two*). In holding that there is only one kind of thing in the world, namely *mind*, Berkeley was a metaphysical *monist* (*mono* = *one*). Hobbes, like Berkeley, was also a monist, but instead of the fundamental sub-stances being minds, Hobbes was a materialist and held that the fundamental substances were bodies.

In two of Berkeley's works, he made his case for the rejection of the exist-ence of a material world. The first was published in 1710, titled *Principles of Human Knowledge*; the second in 1713, titled *Three Dialogues Between Hylas and Philonous*. In this chapter, we will focus mostly on the *Principles of Human Knowledge* (hereafter *PHK*).[1] We will appeal to what he said in the *Three Dialogues* when doing so will illuminate his view in *PHK*. There are a few interesting and helpful items related to the *Three Dialogues* that we should consider before turning to our study of *PHK*.   3.3

3.1.1 Three Dialogues *Between Hylas and Philonous (1713)*

Berkeley wrote the *Three Dialogues* after having published *PHK*. They lay out in a very straightforward fashion the philosophical view established in *PHK*. The dialogues are in the style of a play, and should remind you of Plato's dialogues. The discussions take place between two friends, Hylas and Philonous. Their names are revealing. "Hylas" is based on the ancient Greek word for matter (*hyle*); "Philonous" on the ancient Greek word that means something like *lover of mind* (*philos* = lover, *nous* = mind). As his name indicates, Hylas believes that in addition to minds there exist bodies, or, more generally, a material reality; whereas Philonous, as his name sug-gests, believes that only minds and their ideas exist. He rejects the existence of anything that might be called a *material* world. Insofar as Hylas holds that there are two kinds of things in the world, minds and bodies, he is, like Descartes, a *dualist*. Of course, it may be possible to read Hylas' view as expressing a form of materialism, but the texts better support reading him as a dualist. By contrast, Philonous is a *monist*: he holds that there exists only one kind of thing, namely mind (or immaterial being). As you would have learned in reading the Introduction of this book, this sort of   3.4

---

[1] I shall be using the *First Dialogue* and *Principles of Human Knowledge* texts found in *George Berkeley: Principles of Human Knowledge and Three Dialogues*, Roger Woolhouse (ed.), London: Penguin Books, 1988.

philosophical view is called *Idealism* (Berkeley refers to it as *Immaterialism*). Philonous represents Berkeley's view in the *Three Dialogues*, while Hylas represents something close to Descartes's or Locke's view.

3.5   Berkeley anticipated that people would find his view odd, for it is commonsensical to believe that ordinary objects exist independently of the human mind. Hylas says that the sort of view for which Philonous (i.e. Berkeley) advocates, namely that only minds and their ideas exist, is extravagant, fantastical, irresponsible, and repugnant to commonsense. Philonous disagrees. He points out to Hylas that Hylas' view – that a *material* reality exists independently of the mind – does not actually originate from commonsense at all but is instead a piece of obscure metaphysics, introduced by philosophers in support of commonsense. Commonsense only requires the belief that ordinary objects of the senses (apples, trees, stones, rivers, and the like) continue to exist when no longer perceived by him, you, me, and perceivers like us. Nothing in commonsense requires such things to be *material*. That they are commonly held to be material is the result of philosophers having forced onto folks the view. Matter is not a commonsensical notion; it is a philosophical invention. What is more, once properly analyzed, says Philonous, this notion proves to be more extravagant and even more repugnant to commonsense than his view. What emerges between Hylas and Philonous is a tentative agreement: the better view will be the one that better supports and better aligns with commonsense – the view dealing with *ordinary* objects, the objects of commonsense (such as apples, trees, etc.).

3.6   Berkeley introduced several arguments aimed at defeating the view that a material reality exists independently of minds. We will focus on several of them. The first will be based on a rejection of Descartes's notion of exclusion. This argument is supported by the principle that no one can conceive a contradiction. This principle comes into play again in Berkeley's analysis of the idea of a material substrate. Another argument will be based on the view that objects are collections of ideas, and that ideas exist only "in" minds. Lastly, we will look at the arguments against the idea of a material substrate, which will require us to consider a now-famous distinction between primary and secondary qualities. Let us briefly look at them in this order, paying attention to how they are related.

3.2 Abstraction versus Exclusion

3.7   Berkeley thought that there was a problem with how abstract ideas were cast by previous philosophers. He noted that in the *Essay Concerning Human Understanding* (1689), Locke had wrongly cast abstract ideas as being "general" ideas – ideas, we might say, that presumably represent a *kind* as opposed to representing a *particular thing*. According to Locke, the general abstract idea of a triangle, for example, could be constructed by first considering an idea of a particular triangle and then by removing any of the particular and specious features included in the idea. So, start with the idea of a particular triangle whose sides measure 3, 4, and 5 units of length, respectively. Remove the particulars – here, the particular assignments of 3, 4, and 5. What would remain is an idea of a triangle whose sides are each unequal with the others, though they are not unequal by any *particular* ratio. This would presumably be an idea of a species of triangle, namely the idea of a scalene triangle. But we can go further. Remove the specifics – here, the specific relation holding between the sides; so remove whatever represents each side's being unequal to the others. Thus, the sides are no longer represented specifically as each being unequal to the others (so, it is no longer represented specifically as scalene). But, specifically speaking, the sides are also not represented so that two of the three sides are equal (it is not represented as isosceles), and they are also not represented so that each side is equal with the others (it is not represented as equilateral). And yet, suggested Locke, since no specific triangle is represented, and so the idea does not rule out any specific kind of triangle, all three possible relations are represented. This would presumably be the general abstract idea of a triangle, which represents a kind of shape, or generally speaking, *triangularity* – so it does not represent specifically scalene, isosceles, or equilateral, and yet in not representing any specific triangle, represents all three. According to Locke, the content of this general abstract idea in fact represents all possible particular triangles.

Berkeley argued that if the above is what was meant by a *general abstract idea*, then Locke's view advocated for the impossible – it advocated for nothing short of an idea whose content is internally contradictory. No triangle can meet the criteria presumably represented in the idea. In what intelligible sense, Berkeley asked, could you conceive of a triangle whose sides were neither equal nor unequal, and yet both equal and unequal, whose angles were "*neither oblique, nor rectangle, equilateral, equicrural, nor scalenon, but all and none of these at once?*" (*PHK*, Introduction, Article 13). Even so, there is hope for what we might call *abstract* ideas, once we have jettisoned Locke's problematic account of *generality*. Like Descartes, Berkeley seems to adopt the view that we can form an abstract idea by focusing attention on an element included in a complex idea while ignoring all the other elements in the idea (*PHK*, Introduction, Articles 7 and 8). Thus, he wrote, we can make the abstract idea of color by considering a complex idea of, say, an apple, and then by focusing on a particular ideational element, in this case, we focus on the color, while ignoring the rest. Berkeley wrote:

3.8

For example, there is perceived by sight an object extended, coloured, and moved: this mixed or compound idea the mind resolving into its simple, constituent parts, and viewing each by itself, exclusive of the rest, does frame the abstract ideas of extension, colour, and motion. Not that it is possible for colour or motion to exist without extension: but only that the mind can frame to itself by *abstraction* the idea of colour exclusive of extension, and of motion exclusive of both colour and extension. (*PHK*, Introduction, Article 7)

Recall that Descartes had held that there was a difference between *abstraction* and *exclusion*. Here, unfortunately, Berkeley muddies the water a bit when using the word "exclusive" in his discussion about abstraction. As we will see, he does not mean by "exclusive" what Descartes had meant by "exclusion." According to Descartes, again recall, we abstract by focusing on one ideational element while *ignoring* the rest; by contrast, we exclude by focusing on one ideational element while *negating* the rest, that is, we in effect *remove* the latter from the idea. Shape, recall, can be abstracted from extension, but it cannot be excluded from extension. To exclude extension from shape, Descartes said, rendered shape unintelligible (*Principles of Philosophy*, Part I, Article 53: AT VIIIA 25; CSM I 210). The salient example of exclusion for Descartes involved the ideas of mind and body. We can exclude the simple nature *thought* from the idea of body and the simple nature *extension* from the idea of mind. The two, the natures of mind and body, can be conceived completely independently of one another. In light of the passage quoted above, and now casting what Berkeley says in Descartes's terms, Berkeley said that *colors* and *shapes* and *motions* cannot be excluded from *extension*, but that they can be abstracted from it.

3.9   This notion of abstraction allowed Berkeley to repair some of what he thought Locke had wrongly claimed. Locke's general abstract idea of a triangle, recall, was an idea that reportedly represented a three-sided figure whose sides were neither equal nor unequal and yet both, whose angles were neither obtuse nor oblique nor right and yet all three at once, and so on. Berkeley's remedy begins with our thinking of a particular triangle, such as the 3, 4, 5 triangle, and then with our focusing on the fact that it is three-sided, say, while *ignoring* the particular ratio of 3, 4, and 5 (in the figure below, this is represented by *greying* the numerals). In doing this, we produce an abstract idea of a three-sided figure.

Particular triangle   Abstracted triangle

We can then, when reasoning about geometrical figures, *assign* this 3.10
abstract idea the *role* of standing for all ideas of three-sided figures. Berkeley
will insist, however, that this idea is *still* the idea of the particular triangle
whose sides are 3, 4, and 5, but in ignoring the particulars and in *assigning*
it the *role* of standing for other ideas of particular triangles, we produce an
idea that can replace Locke's misguided general abstract idea. Berkeley,
then, reclaimed a sense in which an idea is "general," where its being such
was cast in terms of the *role* it is assigned (as standing for other ideas), the
notion of *generality* no longer cast in terms of an idea's content.

Berkeley's view on abstraction ushers in the first of several arguments 3.11
aimed at rejecting any claim that asserts the existence of a material world –
that is, a material world that exists independently of a mind. This first argument looks to be aimed directly at Descartes's claim, established in the Sixth
Meditation, that mind and body are *really distinct*. Berkeley will reject
Descartes's claim that mind and body are really distinct. Let us quickly
rehearse Descartes's claim before discussing Berkeley's argument against it.

As we saw in Chapter 1 of this book, in the Sixth Meditation, Descartes 3.12
analyzed his ideas of mind and body. He concluded:

> [O]n the one hand I have a clear and distinct idea of myself, in so far as I am
> simply a thinking, non-extended thing; and on the other hand I have a
> distinct idea of body, in so far as this is simply an extended, non-thinking
> thing. And accordingly, it is certain that I am really distinct from my body,
> and can exist without it. (AT VII 78; CSM II 54)

Just before this, Descartes reminded us that "the fact that I can clearly and
distinctly understand one thing apart from another is enough to make me
certain that the two things are distinct, since they are capable of being separated, at least by God" (Ibid.). All of this aligns perfectly with what he later
would say in the *Principles* when defining what he calls *real distinction* (AT
VIIIA 28; CSM I 213). Descartes's view was that if we can conceive (the
nature of) mind independently of (the nature of) body, and vice versa, then
mind and body are really distinct. By being able to conceive one independently of the other, and vice versa, Descartes was claiming that we can
exclude one from the other: we can exclude the simple nature *thinking* from
the idea of body, and we can exclude the simple nature *extension* from the
idea of mind. It follows, and this is the import of showing real distinction,
that mind and body *can* exist independently of one another. And, as the
Sixth Meditation unfolded, Descartes showed that not only can they exist
independently of one another but that they *do* exist independently of one
another.

3.13   The above view formed the basis of Descartes's dualism, the metaphysical view that there are two basic kinds of things in the universe – minds and bodies. Here is the import of all of this relative to our discussion. Suppose that you leave your classroom and go home. You no longer perceive the classroom or any of the objects that inhabit it – for example, its tables and chairs. There is no doubt that *perceiving* the tables and chairs is an act of your mind. It is an act that your mind performs. Now, you believe that even though you no longer perceive the tables and chairs in the classroom, they nevertheless continue to exist. Right? What reason might you have for thinking that the tables and chairs in the classroom still exist – that is, exist independently of your perceiving them? Descartes had an answer, which was forged from his metaphysics: since the tables and chairs are bodies, and bodies can and do exist independently of minds (mind and body are really distinct), then the tables and chairs can and do exist even when you are no longer perceiving them. You have a reason for thinking that such things exist independently of your mind. This is the metaphysical view that supports your commonsense belief that ordinary objects such as apples, tables, chairs, and so on, exist independently of your mind. Notice, however, that thinking that these objects are specifically *material* is an artifact of a metaphysical thesis, and is not an inherent component of commonsense.

3.14   We can now construct a simple version of Berkeley's argument:

1. *A body (e.g., an apple, a stone, a chair, etc.) can exist independently of its being perceived only if mind and body are really distinct.*
2. *Mind and body are not really distinct.*
3. *Therefore, a body (e.g., an apple, a stone, a chair, etc.) cannot exist independently of its being perceived.*

For lack of a better name let us call this the *Anti-Exclusion Argument*. Premise 1 is a version of Descartes's claim found in the Sixth Meditation. Premise 2 expresses Berkeley's rejection of Descartes's claim that mind and body are really distinct; it is the denial of the consequent of Premise 1. Premise 2 denies that the nature of mind can be excluded from the idea of body and that the nature or body can be excluded from the idea of mind. This argument takes the valid form of Modus Tollens. So, if the premises are true, the conclusion is too! Let us look at Berkeley's reasons for holding Premise 2.

3.15   Return to the question: *What reason do you have for thinking that the tables and chairs in the classroom exist when no longer perceived by you?* We know Descartes's answer: we are justified in thinking that they exist when not perceived because bodies and minds are really distinct. Let us say that you are at home and recall the tables and chairs in the classroom. This is not an act of sensing, of course, since you are not actually seeing the tables and chairs, but it is nevertheless an act of your mind – it is an act of imagining. As it was for Descartes, for Berkeley, both sensing and imagining are understood to be acts of the mind. Both are acts of *perception*. And even though you are not sensing the tables and chairs at the moment, you can nevertheless imagine or conceive them sitting there in the room. They are there all by themselves. As you imagine this, you emphasize that they are there all by themselves, which suggests, of course, that no one is there to perceive them. So, why does not that count as a ground for believing that they *can* exist when not perceived? Here is why it cannot count. Admittedly, said Berkeley, you can focus on the tables and chairs as they are presented to you in your imagination and ignore the fact that *they are being perceived by you*. By doing this, you have simply produced an abstract idea; you have produced an abstract idea of tables and chairs in a classroom. You can easily produce the more abstract idea of bodies in the classroom, by ignoring that they are tables and chairs. Berkeley had no problem with that. But you cannot *exclude* from your perceiving the tables and chairs the fact that they are being perceived by you. Doing so results in a contradiction: you would be claiming that you are perceiving tables and chairs that are not being perceived by you (*PHK*, Part I, Articles 11–23). So, if like Descartes you believe that there is a material world that exists independently of your mind based on the claim that you can conceive body completely independently of mind (and vice versa), you have made a big mistake. The mistake you will have made is similar to the mistake you would have made had you taken *shape*, for example, to exist (or to be able to exist) independently of *extension*. You can focus on *shape* and ignore *extension*, thus making an abstract idea of *shape*, but you cannot exclude *extension* from the idea of *shape*. Likewise, you can focus on your idea of the tables and chairs and ignore the fact that they are being perceived by you, thus making an abstract idea of the tables and chairs, but you cannot *exclude* from the occurring idea of these tables and chairs the fact that they are being perceived by you. So, according to Berkeley, if you believe that the tables and chairs can exist independently of their being perceived, you have wrongly taken yourself to have shown this by way of exclusion when in fact all you have done is produced an abstract idea.

Here is another way to get a sense of what Berkeley is up to. Consider 3.16 these two claims:

(Active Voice) *You perceive x.*
(Passive Voice)   *x is perceived by you.*

In every possible world in which the first is true, the second is true, too, and vice versa. They are simply two ways of expressing the same event or the same fact. Even so, in the first, *you* are the subject, whereas in the second, *x* is the subject. They emphasize different elements that constitute this fact. But this difference in emphasis has no bearing on their truth. Both are made true by the very same fact. Even so, in connection to active and passive constructions, Plato brings to light an interesting asymmetry between such propositions. In the *Euthyphro*, for instance, Socrates asks which is the proper *grammatical* order of these sorts of propositions. That is, he asks whether one is in some sense *prior* to the other. So, he asks, which of the following is correct?

A.   *You perceive x* because *x is perceived by you.*
B.   *x is perceived by you* because *you perceive x.*

Socrates and Euthyphro agree that (B) is the correct answer. The proposition put in the active voice is taken to be *prior* in some sense to the one put in the passive voice. So, the active and passive formulations are not identical in every way. Even so, the *fact* that makes the proposition put in the active voice true is ultimately the same fact that makes the one put in the passive voice true.

3.17   Now, imagine those tables and chairs. Since imagining is a kind of perception, then when we say that you imagine the tables and chairs, we are saying that you perceive them. Put in the active voice: *You perceive these tables and chairs.* Berkeley assumed that when you say that you can imagine things that can (and do) exist independently of your mind, the "things" to which you are referring are the very things that you are imagining, like those tables and chairs. So, let us say that someone asks whether you believe that those tables and chairs in the classroom can exist independently of your perceiving them, and you answer: "Yes, I believe that *they* can exist independently of my perceiving them. I am in fact imagining *them* right now, just sitting there in the classroom unperceived by any mind." But wait! You are imagining *them*. In other words, you are perceiving *them*. So, the above claim put in the active voice is true: *You perceive the tables and chairs.* But in every world in which this is true, its passive alternative is too. So, this is true:

These tables and chairs are perceived by you.

But your claim is that these very tables and chairs, the ones that you are imagining at this very moment, exist *unperceived* by any mind. This is the import of your claiming that you can imagine things that exist independently of any and all minds. So, according to you, these tables and chairs, the ones that you are imagining, are *not* perceived by you – in fact, they are not perceived by anyone: presumably you are imagining that they are not being perceived by anyone. If this is the case, you look to hold the following two claims:

These tables and chairs are perceived by you

and

These tables and chairs are not perceived by you.

The conjunction of these two claims forms a contradiction. So, now put more generally: although you can *focus* on body in your idea (of body) and ignore the fact that it is something that is at the moment being conceived (perceived) by you, thus making an abstract idea of body, you cannot actually *exclude* from your idea of body the fact that it is something being conceived (or perceived) by you. To do so would result in producing the sort of contradiction just produced in the table and chair case. The point is that if you cannot in fact conceive body independently of mind (of the mind's activity), body and mind are not really distinct. This line of reasoning works to establish Premise 2 of the Anti-Exclusion Argument. Thus, if Hylas, who held a view similar to Descartes's, held Premise 1, and now is convinced about Premise 2, given that the argument is valid (and it is!), he must now hold the argument's conclusion, namely that *a body (e.g., an apple, a stone, a chair, etc.) cannot exist independently of its being perceived.* Of course, you'll see that Hylas resisted this argument. So, Philonous moves to making other supporting arguments. Let us consider one of those.

3.3 Objects are Collections of Ideas

In *PHK*, Part I, Article 1, Berkeley said that an apple, for example, is a collec- 3.18
tion of *ideas.* The name "apple," he claimed, is something we simply assign to this collection of ideas. The word refers to or picks out this collection of ideas. Other sensible objects such as stones, trees, books, and so on, are also just collections of ideas. We will look more closely at this claim in a moment. But first let us work out the other important elements of the argument.

3.19   In *PHK*, Part I, Article 2, Berkeley would go a bit further and introduced the notion of the thing that perceives ideas – namely, a *mind*. A mind is not an idea, but is that which perceives ideas. The mind is the metaphysical bearer of ideas. Berkeley had a specific take on the "bearing" relation: a mind is the bearer of ideas in the sense that it *perceives* them. This is the sense in which ideas depend for their being or their existence on a mind. No ideas exist independently of their being perceived; ideas are not just floating around unperceived in the cosmos waiting to be perceived. "The existence of an idea," Berkeley would say at the close of Article 2, "consists in being perceived."

3.20   For Berkeley, *being* and *existing* are coextensive with *being perceived*. At the close of *PHK*, Part I, Article 3, he would make his now-famous claim about sensible objects such as apples, stones, trees, and so on: "Their *esse* is *percipi*," which is to say that their *being* is nothing other than their *being perceived*. Although Berkeley referred to the *being* of objects, he pretty clearly was focusing (in these three articles) on the *existence* of objects. Now, when talking about the *being* of the apple, philosophers, in following Aristotle, would likely take you to be talking about its color, shape, taste, and so on – that is, they would very likely take you to be talking about whatever it is that makes something an apple. But, Berkeley was interested in something more than the nature or essence (the being) of the apple: he is interested in an account of the *existence* of this apple. Not only is the being of the apple – its color, shape, taste, and so on – constituted of ideas, but the *existence* of the apple is understood in terms of those very ideas now perceived by some mind. In other words, to talk about the existence of the apple is to talk about the fact that the apple is something *perceived*. The argument at this early point in *PHK* is:

1.   *An object (e.g., an apple, a stone, a chair, etc.) is solely a collection of ideas.*
2.   *The existence of an idea consists in its being perceived.*
3.   *Therefore, the existence of an object (e.g., an apple, a stone, a chair, etc.) consists in its being perceived.*

For lack of a better name, let us call this the *Objects-are-Collections-of-Ideas Argument*. Berkeley anticipates critics of the Objects-are-Collections-of-Ideas Argument. He says:

> It is indeed an opinion strangely prevailing amongst men, that houses, mountains, rivers, and in a word all sensible objects have an existence natural or

real, distinct from their being perceived by the understanding. But with however great an assurance and acquiescence this principle may be entertained in the world; yet whoever shall find in his heart to call it in question, may, if I mistake not, perceive it to involve a manifest contradiction. For what are the forementioned objects but the things we perceive by sense, and what do we perceive besides our own ideas or sensations; and is it not plainly repugnant that any one of these or any combination of them should exist unperceived? (PHK, Part I, Article 4)

If someone did hold that houses, mountains, rivers (and we could add apples, stones, etc.) can (and do) exist independently of their being perceived, Berkeley suggested that it is due to their having wrongly applied the doctrine of abstract ideas (*PHK*, Part I, Article 5). We looked at this very criticism in the previous section. Rhetorically, he asked: "For can there be a nicer strain of abstraction than to distinguish the existence of sensible objects from their being perceived, so as to conceive them existing unperceived?" (*Ibid.*) As noted in the earlier discussion of the Anti-Exclusion Argument, you can focus on a house, for example, the object being perceived (where "house" refers to this collection of ideas), and ignore the fact that it is being perceived, and so produce the abstract idea of a house, but you cannot exclude or separate from this idea the fact that it is being perceived. According to the Objects-are-Collections-of-Ideas Argument just introduced, you cannot exclude from your idea of the house the fact that it is being perceived because the house is an idea (or a collection of ideas), and the existence of ideas consists in their being perceived. In this way the Anti-Exclusion Argument and the Objects-are-Collections-of-Ideas Argument are related.

Focusing now on the Objects-are-Collections-of-Ideas Argument, and 3.21 yet keeping in mind the Anti-Exclusion Argument, it would seem that Berkeley was arguing that those who deny the conclusion of the Objects-are-Collections-of-Ideas Argument, namely that *the existence of an object (e.g., an apple, a stone, a chair, etc.) consists in its being perceived*, do so based on a misunderstanding of the doctrine of abstract ideas.

Here are some further important philosophical insights. Since the 3.22 Objects-are-Collections-of-Ideas Argument is valid (recall that the Anti-Exclusion Argument was also valid), if one thinks that the conclusion is false, one must think that at least one of its premises is false, too. For, in being valid, the argument cannot have all true premises and a false conclusion. So, if one rejects the conclusion of a valid argument, one is in turn committed to rejecting at least one of the argument's premises. If an argument is valid and yet has at least one false premise, philosophers say that it is *unsound*. For, to be sound an argument must be valid and all of its premises must be actually true. So, the critic of Berkeley's argument would be essentially claiming that his argument is unsound. Berkeley did more than to suggest that the premise that most philosophers would be prepared to reject was Premise 1. Their denying Premise 1 would not only be based on a misunderstanding of the doctrine of abstract ideas, but also would be based on their holding a problematic idea of *matter* or *material substance*. Since we have already looked at Berkeley's view on abstraction, let us now look at what he took to be the problematic ideas of material substance employed by philosophers such as Descartes, Hobbes, and Locke.

3.3.1 The Problematic Ideas of Matter or Material Substance

3.23   Berkeley accepted the fact that people commonly believe that apples, stones, mountains, rivers, and so on – in short, ordinary objects – exist independently of their being perceived. And, he was cognizant of how people would respond to his proposal that *to be is to be perceived*. No doubt they would argue: Since admittedly ideas exist only when perceived, it follows that if apples, stones, and so on, can and do exist independently of their being perceived, they cannot be *solely* collections of ideas. In fact, they must be something *more* than ideas. So, according to what is commonly held, Premise 1 of the Objects-are-Collections-of-Ideas Argument, namely that *an object (e.g., an apple, a stone, etc.) is solely a collection of ideas*, has got to be false. The disagreement with Berkeley would in part be based on one's thinking that ordinary objects have a life, so to speak, outside of or independently of the mind. According to commonsense, even if there were no minds, the world of ordinary objects could nevertheless exist.

3.24   Later in *PHK*, Berkeley admitted that Premise 1 of the Objects-are-Collections-of-Ideas Argument would no doubt rub folks the wrong way. Be that as it may, he reassured readers, the premise was nevertheless true. In Part I, Article 38, for instance, Berkeley wrote:

> But, you say, it sounds very harsh to say we eat and drink ideas, and are clothed with ideas. I acknowledge it does so, the word *idea* not being used in common discourse to signify the several combinations of sensible qualities, which are called *things*: and it is certain that any expression which varies from the familiar use of language, will seem harsh and ridiculous. But this does not concern the truth of the proposition, which in other words is no more than to say that we are fed and clothed with those things which we perceive immediately by our senses. The hardness or softness, the colour,

taste, warmth, figure, and such like qualities, which combined together constitute the several sorts of victuals and apparel, have been shown to exist only in the mind that perceives them; and this is all that is meant by calling them *ideas*; which word, if it was as ordinarily used as *thing*, would sound no harsher nor more ridiculous than it. I am not for disputing about the propriety, but the truth of the expression. If therefore you agree with me that we eat and drink, and are clad with the immediate objects of sense which cannot exist unperceived or without the mind, I shall readily grant it is more proper or conformable to custom, that they should be called things rather than ideas.

According to Berkeley, you have become acquainted with the *thing* you call an "apple" by way of seeing, touching, tasting, and so on. You learned "thing-talk" from your parents and from others. Even so, seeing, touching, tasting, hearing, and smelling are all informed by ideas. That is, your seeing the apple is nothing more nor less than your mind's perceiving the idea of red, the idea of a certain shape; your tasting the apple is nothing more nor less than your mind's perceiving the idea of sweet, and so on. If there is no mind, then there are no ideas of red, shape, sweet, and so on. To be sure, the apple is an ordinary object, but if you think about it more carefully, in being an object of the senses, the apple is, strictly speaking, just a certain collection of ideas. So, in ordinary-speak it is fine to call the apple a *thing*, but, as Berkeley said in the above passage, this *thing* was really just a collection of ideas. So, he was willing to continue calling the apple a *thing*, but he conditioned that on your willingness to accept his analysis that showed, in being an object of the senses, that the apple was nothing more nor less than a certain collection of ideas.

Berkeley entertained several ideas of matter that philosophers had   3.25
employed in their reasoning about a world that exists independently of the mind. Each idea is problematic. Consider again the sensory idea of an apple. If any idea is an idea of an ordinary object, it is this one. Now, the apple is given to you in sensory experience as being red, as having a certain shape, as being smooth (if you touch it), as being sweet (if you bite it), and so on. Berkeley insisted on the following: What you perceive, in perceiving the apple, is an *idea* of red, an *idea* of smooth, an *idea* of sweet, and so on. The apple, as noted just a moment ago, the "object" given to you in experience, is simply this collection of ideas. If you think that the apple is more than this, then you think that there is more to it than what is seen, touched, tasted, and the like. The first problematic idea of matter comes to the fore when we analyze an idea like the sensory idea of the apple. *Matter* or *material substance*, according to philosophers who believed that bodies existed

independently of minds, is that which underlies the shape, the red, the smooth, and so on. It is in Aristotelian terms the *substance* or *substratum* that supports or underlies these properties ("sub" + "stance" = "standing under"). Such properties depend for their being (their existence) on this material substance. The substratum basically "unifies" these properties into a single thing or unity. If no material substance, then no properties; but also, if no material substance, then no *thing*. Substances are special in the ontology (the theory of being), since the existence of a substance requires nothing other than itself (even so, according to many early modern philosophers, all finite substances do depend on God, the infinite substance; so they are substantial only in the sense that they do not depend on one another). All of this should be familiar, since we encountered it in our studies of Descartes and Hobbes.

3.26   Now, if an apple is an example of a *material substance*, it can exist independently of any other finite thing, including any mind. Being a material substance is the "something more" that many think accounts for the apple's being able to exist independently of its being red and so on, but more importantly, it is the "something more" that many think accounts for its being able to exist independently of its being perceived. On Berkeley's view, an analysis of the idea of the apple reveals that once all of the sensed qualities have been stripped away, what is left is nothing at all. That is, take away the perceived redness, shape, sweetness, and so on, and at some point in the analysis nothing remains in your idea. If this remaining idea of nothing is the alleged idea of matter or material substance, the idea is empty! So, what do the words "matter" or "material substance" refer to here? To what does "unity" refer? For, if "material substance" is meaningless (because the idea signified by these words is empty), and yet the unity of the apple is understood in terms of "material substance" (the material substance is what unifies all the properties into a single thing), then "unity" looks to be equally meaningless. (Berkeley in fact made a case against the meaningfulness of "unity" in *PHK*, Part I, Article 13.) So, what exactly do philosophers think exists independently of its being perceived? Nothing? According to Berkeley, they have made a pretty big mistake if they take this nothing to be a something.

3.27   The above analysis is based on the important notion of a *sensible object*. This notion is directly related to Berkeley's establishing Premise 1 of the Objects-are-Collections-of-Ideas Argument, namely that *an object (e.g., an apple, a stone, etc.) is solely a collection of ideas*. This, recall, is the premise that philosophers would very likely reject. A sensible object, not surprisingly, is initially cast by Berkeley, plainly and simply, as an object of the senses – that is, an object that can be seen, heard, felt, tasted, and smelled.

An apple is a sensible object. But what does that mean exactly? To answer this, Berkeley draws a distinction between what he called *mediate* and *immediate* perception. This was also done very clearly in the *First Dialogue*. So, we might appeal to this as we go.

Let us first consider mediate perception. The term "mediate" in this con-   3.28
text refers to something's *mediating*. That is, something standing between the perceiver, so to speak, and the object perceived. So, "mediate" here might best be read to mean something like "standing between" or "standing in the middle." Berkeley would sometimes cast this in adverbial form, so that instead of saying that *Smith's perception of x is mediate*, we would say that *Smith mediately perceives x*. Where P is a perceiver, and *x* and *y* are objects of perception (and $y \neq x$), we can define *mediate* perception thus:

P *mediately* perceives *x* if, and only if, P perceives *x* by way of perceiving *y*.

Object *y* stands between P and *x*. So, P never directly perceives *x*, but indirectly perceives *x* by way of directly perceiving *y*. Insofar as *y* is directly perceived, then, where nothing stands between it and P, *y* is said to be *immediately* perceived. "Immediate" (*im* + *mediate*) is the negation of "mediate," and might best be taken to mean something like "nothing standing between" or "nothing standing in the middle." So, *y* stands between P and *x*, whereas nothing stands between P and *y*. And so, P immediately perceives *y*, but mediately perceives *x*.

As just noted, the distinction between mediate and immediate percep-   3.29
tion takes front and center in the *First Dialogue*. Philonous provides a few cases for study. He says to Hylas:

> In reading a book, what I immediately perceive are the letters, but mediately, or by means of these, are suggested to my mind the notions of God, virtue, etc. Now, that the letters are truly sensible things, or perceived by sense, there is no doubt: but I would know whether you take the things suggested by them to be so too.

Hylas agrees that the letters are sensed things: they are immediately perceived. So, nothing stands between them and you, the perceiver. They are what you are directly aware of. But the *story*, which in this example includes talk of God, virtue, and what not, is not a sensed thing: the story is not immediately perceived. Instead, it is only suggested to the mind by way of your sensing the letters – by way of your immediately perceiving the letters. The letters stand between you, the perceiver, and the story. Philonous replies: "It seems then, that by *sensible things* you mean those only which can be perceived immediately by sense." Hylas accepts this.

3.30   Philonous offers another case. He asks:

> Does it not follow from this, that though I see one part of the sky red, and
> another blue, and that my reason does thence evidently conclude there must
> be some cause of that diversity of colors, yet that cause cannot be said to be a
> sensible thing, or perceived by the sense of seeing?

Here, in the context of their discussion, Philonous is very likely describing
the sunrise (for they began their discussion in a garden just before dawn).
As the sun rises, part of the sky appears red while part of it appears blue. We
see the colors. Since they appear directly to us – that is, nothing seems to
stand between us and them – they are said to be immediately perceived. So,
they count as sensible things. But, we also believe that the *appearance* of
these colors has a cause. For instance, we may believe that it is the angle of
the earth's surface to the sun, along with various characteristics of the earth's
atmosphere, that accounts for a breaking apart of the light emitted by the
sun. The various light waves (or, according to seventeenth-century philosophers, motions of fine particles) then reach our eyes, which in turn some-
how produce in us the experience of red and blue. But the bit about light
waves or motions of fine particles is like the earlier case of the story about
God and virtue. We do not actually *see* the fine particles or their motions.
Instead, what we *see* is red and blue. Like God and virtue in the earlier case,
the causes of the colors we see are only suggested to the mind by way of
what we see. To put this in stricter terms, the red and blue are immediately
perceived, whereas the motions of fine particles (the alleged causes of the
appearance of these colors) are mediately perceived. We perceive these
motions by way of perceiving colors. The colors stand in perception between
us and these motions. It should be clear that this is perfectly analogous to
the reading case: the letters are to the story as the colors are to that which
allegedly causes them to appear (the motions of particles).

3.31   Mediate perception is an odd kind of *perception* – for, it is not really anything like sensory perception. For instance, we do not *see* any story; we do
not *see* any motions of fine particles. Philonous says that these things are
only *suggested* to us when we immediately perceive things like letters or
colors. Hylas agrees. In response to Philonous, Hylas says:

> . . . I tell you once for all, that by *sensible things* I mean those only which are
> perceived by sense, and that in truth the senses perceive nothing which they
> do not perceive immediately: for they make no inferences. The deducing
> therefore of causes of occasions from effects and appearances, which alone
> are perceived by sense, entirely relates to reason.

So, mediate perception is a bit more interesting than initially thought. It is actually not perception proper, if by that we mean *sensory* perception. Mediate perception is intellectual, not strictly sensory. Although Philonous initially says that what is mediately perceived is simply *suggested to* the mind, he later says that what is mediately perceived is *concluded by reason*. Hylas agrees with this last bit and says that what is mediately perceived is *deduced by* or is *inferred by* the mind. Both agree that mediate perception, though based on what is immediately perceived, is really a function of reason.

A sensible thing, like the apple, is that which is immediately perceived. 3.32
The exchange between Philonous and Hylas results in revealing the first problematic idea of matter (mentioned earlier):

Philonous: This point then is agreed between us, that sensible things are those only which are immediately perceived by sense. You will further inform me, whether we immediately perceive by sight anything beside light, and colours, and figures: or by hearing, anything but sounds: by the palate, anything besides tastes: by the smell, beside odours: or by the touch, more than tangible qualities.
Hylas: We do not.
Philonous: It seems therefore, that if you take away all sensible qualities, there remains nothing sensible.

The import of this exchange challenges the earlier claim that matter is that which underlies qualities such as red, smooth, sweet, and so on. If we strip away these sensible qualities, nothing remains in the idea of the apple. There is no "thing" there! So, if this *nothing* is ultimately what one is referring to when speaking about matter or material substance, one is referring to nothing at all (or, to be clearer, one is not referring to anything). If we *do* have an idea of matter or material substance, it would seem that it is something gained by way of mediate perception. That is, material substance is something that is deduced by or is inferred by the mind when immediately perceiving objects such as apples, stones, and so on. But matter or material substance is not something that we immediately perceive. In short, matter or material substance is not a sensible thing.

The view that material substance is inferred by the mind is affirmed in 3.33
Part I, Section 18 of *PHK*:

But though it were possible that solid, figured, movable substances may exist without the mind, corresponding to the ideas we have of bodies, yet how is it possible for us to know this? Either we must know it by sense, or by reason. As for our senses, by them we have the knowledge only of our sensations, ideas, or those things that are immediately perceived by sense, call them what you will: but they do not inform us that things exist without the mind, or unperceived, like to those which are perceived. This the materialists themselves acknowledge. It remains therefore that if we have any knowledge at all of external things, it must be by reason, inferring their existence from what is immediately perceived by sense.

The following line of reasoning is suggested: given that ordinary objects such as the apple is a sensible thing, and that matter or material substance is not a sensible thing, it follows that ordinary objects like apples are not *material* things – that is, they are not *material substances*.

3.34   Although Hylas has agreed with Philonous that the idea of matter is inferred by reason – it is an object of mediate perception – he is just not ready to accept Philonous' conclusion. Hylas will not give up the view that the idea of matter is a sensory idea. For surely, he thinks, some of what we immediately perceive *are* features actually possessed by mind-independent bodies. Like what? Well, in light of Descartes and Locke, Hylas thinks that what are sometimes called "primary qualities" are items immediately perceived that are actual properties of bodies – properties such as extension, shape, size, motion, and the like. So, if Hylas is right, the sensory idea of matter is not empty after all. Hylas suspects that his initial agreement with Philonous about matter's being mediately perceived arose from his allowing Philonous to strip away too much from the sensory idea when performing the analysis. But even though Hylas will make a nice attempt to recover his initial view about the idea of matter (as being sensory), he will fail. Let us look at his attempt at repairing his view before getting to the idea of material substance that is allegedly inferred by reason.

3.3.2 Ideas of Primary and Secondary Qualities

3.35   Versions of the primary quality and secondary quality distinction can be found discussed in work spanning the entire modern period. In both the *Meditations* and the *Principles*, for example, Descartes sorted the modes of substances into two groups: those that presuppose thinking and those that presuppose extension. Recall that the notion of presupposition was understood in terms of *intelligibility*. In Chapter 1, we adopted a view akin to: *A presupposes B if, and only if, conceiving A requires the conceiving of B.* The example on which we focused was that of the mode *shape*. *Shape* presupposes *extension*, we said, since conceiving *shape* requires the conceiving of *extension*. It is impossible to conceive something that was shaped but not extended. The very intelligibility of *shape* depends on *extension*. The principal attribute of body, Descartes said, is extension (in length, breadth, and depth). This was his way of saying that extension is the essence or the nature of body. All modes of body, Descartes argued, presuppose extension. Likewise, all modes of mind presuppose thinking or thought. And, as you also know from Chapter 1, for Descartes the principal attribute of mind is thinking or thought. Thinking is the nature of mind. *Doubt*, for instance, presupposes *thinking*. That is, conceiving *doubt* (or conceiving what doubting is) requires the conceiving of *thinking*. It is impossible to conceive of someone who was doubting something but was not thinking. The very intelligibility of *doubting* depends on *thinking*. So, in the way that shape is understood to be a mode of extension, doubt is understood to be a mode of thinking. Thus, there are two distinct groups of modes or properties: the properties of body (those that presuppose extension) and the properties of mind (those that presuppose thought).

Descartes was keen on emphasizing that the modes of body, namely size, shape, motion, and position, are expressible *mathematically* – they specifically constituted the subject-matter of geometry. In the Sixth Meditation, about bodies, Descartes wrote: 3.36

> They may not all exist in a way that exactly corresponds with my sensory grasp of them, for in many cases the grasp of the senses is very obscure and confused. But at least they possess all the properties which I clearly and distinctly understand, that is, all those which, viewed in general terms, are comprised within the subject-matter of pure mathematics. (AT VII 80; CSM II 55)

Bodies possess shape, size, and so on, which, as just noted, are mathematically expressible. But there are lots of other properties that do not fall within the domain of mathematics – for example, the "qualities" of colors, sounds, feels, tastes, and so on. To be sure, we can recast the latter in terms of shape, size, and motion, as we do when conceiving color or sound in terms of the motions of tiny particles (which together produce "activity" like waves in the ocean), but in doing that, we no longer have in mind the particular *quality* that we sense – the color or the sound. The quality has been replaced in our account as motions of tiny bodies with various shapes, sizes, and the like, where now all we have before the mind are ideas of tiny bodies moving about. What is more, these sensed qualities – the colors, the sounds, and so on – are not *necessary* (conceptually speaking) to body – that is, when conceiving a body we need not conceive it as being colored or as being hot or cold or as being smelly. By contrast, when conceiving a (finite) body, we *must* conceive it as being sized and as being shaped, as being in motion or at rest, and the like. And, as just noted, the conceiving of size, shape, and so on, requires the conceiving of body (an *extended* something) insofar as they presuppose extension. Descartes would go further in Part IV of the *Principles*, arguing that although the two groups of properties appear to be correlated – for instance, certain motions of tiny bodies look to effect one's sensory organs which in turn occasion or give rise to sensory ideas such as the idea of red, or blue, or cold, or hot – there was no intelligible way to understand *how* they are related outside of the brute correlation (AT VIIIA 322; CSM I 285). That is, although we may discover that when one's body comes into contact with fast-moving tiny particles (like those we think are involved in combustion) and ultimately give rise to the sensory idea of heat, there is no way for us to understand how these *motions* and the occurring ideational quality *heat*, say, are related, for they are not *conceptually* related, at least they are not related like shape and extension are – they are simply correlated. And so, there is no way to understand how the one could come from the other. Discovery of the brute correlation is as good as it gets for us.

3.37   Descartes argued that although the ideas that exhibit to us the qualities heat, color, odor, and so on, are occasioned by our body's interactions with other bodies, these qualities are not themselves *in* or are not themselves properties *of* those bodies. The only properties of bodies are those that conceptually presuppose extension. In a very early work titled *The World* (1629–1633), Descartes says that when a man makes sound by moving air particles with his lungs and mouth, the idea of *sound* that arises in the mind as a result is very different from the correlated physical events (AT IX 5; CSM I 82). He says:

> Most philosophers maintain that sound is nothing but a certain vibration of air which strikes our ears. Thus, if the sense of hearing transmitted to our mind the true image of its object then, instead of making us conceive the sound, it would have to make us conceive the motion of the parts of the air which is then vibrating against our ears. (AT IX 5; CSM I 82)

The implication here is that the idea of sound – that is, the idea that presents a certain quality – is a *false* image of the events that occasion the idea; in this case, the motions of the tiny air particles hitting the eardrums. In the Sixth Meditation, he again would claim that although our sensory ideas – like the ideas of colors, sounds, and smells – do not *resemble* any of the properties in bodies responsible for occasioning these ideas in the mind, the differences found in our ideas of colors, sounds, and the like, do *correspond* to actual differences among the properties of bodies – differences in their sizes, shapes, and motions.

About these sensible qualities (such as colors, heat, sounds), Descartes   3.38
claimed in Part I, Articles 66–70 of the *Principles* that we cannot conceive
what they would even be like "outside" the mind (AT VIIIA 32–36; CSM I
216–218). As Berkeley would later put it, we cannot conceive what they
would be like unperceived. Their being perceived is essential to what they
are. In Part IV of *Description of the Human Body* (circa 1647), Descartes
hypothesized a correlation between certain *ratios* of motions of tiny bodies
and the sensible quality *color*:

> The material, as I said, is composed of many small balls which are in mutual
> contact; and we have sensory awareness of two kinds of motion which these
> balls have. One is the motion by which they approach our eyes in a straight
> line, which gives us the sensation of light; and the other is the motion whereby
> they turn about their own centers as they approach us. If the speed at which
> they turn is much smaller than that of their rectilinear motion, the body from
> which they come appears *blue* to us; while if the turning speed is much
> greater than that of their rectilinear motion, the body appears *red* to us. (AT
> IX 255–256; CSM I 424)

Even though your sensory awareness is *of* or is *about* a ratio of motions,
neither the motions nor their ratio are exhibited directly to you in the experience. Rather, what is exhibited directly or immediately to you is the quality *blue* or *red*. In Berkeley's terminology, we might say that the motions and
their ratios are mediately perceived, whereas the *red* and *blue* are immediately perceived. In *Comments on a Certain Broadsheet* (1648), Descartes
wrote that the motions of bodies do not actually ever "transmit" anything of
themselves to the mind (AT VIIIB 359; CSM I 304). This is so because a
mind is not extended. Motion can only modify an extended thing (a body).
So, how is it exactly that motions give rise to ideas of colors, sounds, and
odors? Descartes's answer was that God wills the correlation – end of story.
There is no explanation to be made outside of that. Since bodies do not possess qualities such as color, and it is also true that such qualities begin and
end in the mind, Descartes said that it follows that they are *innate* – that is,
the mind possesses an inherent faculty or capacity for producing them.
And like Berkeley's view later on, Descartes's view was that the life of the
sensible qualities begins and ends in the mind.

In the *Essay*, Locke also had drawn a distinction between ideas of proper-   3.39
ties that *must* be in bodies and those that need not be in bodies. Like
Descartes, Locke held that the properties that are in bodies are those that
are conceptually necessary in our conceiving body, whereas the properties
that are only in a mind are those that are not necessary in our conceiving
body. When comparing the ideas of both sorts of property, Locke was

among the first in the period to specifically identify one group as ideas of *primary qualities*, and the other group as ideas of *secondary qualities*. In Book II, Chapter VIII of the *Essay*, Locke wrote that primary qualities

> are utterly inseparable from the body, in what estate soever it be; and such as in all the alterations and changes it suffers, all the force can be used upon it, it constantly finds in every particle of matter which has bulk enough to be perceived; and the mind finds inseparable from every particle of matter, though less than to make itself singly be perceived by our senses: v.g. [for example] take a grain of wheat, divide it into two parts: each part has still solidity, extension, figure, and mobility; divide it again, and it retains still the same qualities; and so on divide it on, till the parts become insensible; they must retain still each of them all those qualities. (*Essay*, Book II, Chapter VIII, p. 112)

Here, the inseparability of *primary qualities* and *body* is understood in terms of the mind's finding them to be inseparable. So, the point about inseparability is at the very least a conceptual one (as with Hobbes, we find here an empiricist who also trades in a form of rationalism). When the mind conceives a body, it must conceive it as being extended, as having some bulk, as having some size, as having some shape, and so on. Even if a body were divided into tiny bodies and those divided into tinier bodies, he says, where the latter were now so small that they were no longer sensible, these insensible bodies would nevertheless be extended, be bulky, be shaped, and the like. They *must* have these properties even though insensible, since our conceiving them as bodies (even though insensible) requires it. Our imagining these insensible *bodies* amounts to our imagining things that are *extended*, *bulky*, and *shaped*. It is inconceivable that something be a body but lack *these* qualities. But in being *insensible*, which is not to be confused with their simply not being sensed at the moment, we no longer conceive them as being colored or smelly. In saying that they are insensible, Locke was saying that they *cannot* be seen or smelled. It is impossible to sense them. And since only something sensed is colored or smelly, and these tiny bodies cannot be sensed, it follows that they cannot be colored or smelly – or at least it will no longer make sense to say that they are colored or smelly. This line of reasoning established at the very least the claim that even though insensible bodies must be shaped, sized, and so on, they need not be colored or smelly. In short, if you conceive of a body, you must conceive it as being extended, as having some shape or other, and so on. By contrast, if you conceive of a body, you need not conceive it as having a color, as being hot or cold, as being smelly, and so on. This reveals at least one important difference between what Locke called *primary qualities* (such as size and shape), which are necessary for what it is to be a body, and those qualities that are not necessary for what it is to be a body (such as colors and smells).

But it is a bit more complicated than this. For Locke recognized at least 3.40 three sorts of item in his discussion. First, he said that there are *primary qualities*; second, that there are *secondary qualities*; and third, that there are *ideas* of both sorts of quality. As noted in the previous paragraph, primary qualities are those that a body *must* possess – they must be extended, bulky, shaped, sized, and the like. Locke claimed that primary qualities can "produce simple ideas in us, viz. [ideas of] solidity, extension, figure, motion or rest, and number" (*Essay*, Book II, Chapter VIII, Section 9). Secondary qualities are understood to be *powers* that bodies possess in virtue of their possessing various primary qualities. Unlike primary qualities, which can produce in a mind ideas of extension, bulk, shape, and so on, secondary qualities can produce in a mind ideas of sensible qualities such as color, sound, smell, and the like (*Essay*, Book II, Chapter VIII, Section 10 – in Sections 13 and 14 he refers to the sensible qualities as *sensations*). This looks similar to Descartes's remarks about how the various ratios of the motions of tiny particles produce in the mind the sensory ideas of blue or red. And, like Descartes, Locke seems to have also thought that these ideas, though exhibiting directly to the mind colors and the like, are nevertheless *about* or are *of* the secondary qualities located in bodies; these ideas are about or are of the various *powers* that bodies possess.

This, then, seems to be Locke's view: the idea of red is understood as 3.41 *representing* to the mind some configuration of primary qualities in a body, the configuration constituting the power that this body possesses to produce in the mind this very idea (the idea of red). So, although the idea immediately *presents* what we are calling the quality *red*, it nevertheless *represents* some configuration of primary qualities in a body, where this configuration constitutes a power or what Locke called a *secondary quality*. Given what Berkeley said in the *First Dialogue* about the sunrise, the colors red and blue, and the motion of light, we might venture a guess as to how Berkeley would put this: the *red* is immediately perceived, whereas the configuration of primary qualities, the *secondary quality* (which "causes" in your mind the idea of red), is only mediately perceived.

According to Locke, ideas of primary qualities not only represent pri- 3.42 mary qualities that are possessed by bodies, but also *resemble* them. So, in seeing a marble, the shape exhibited to you in the idea (a sphere in this case) resembles the shape that this marble in fact possesses. This is not the case for ideas of secondary qualities. As just noted, although ideas of secondary qualities represent the various secondary qualities possessed by bodies (where a secondary quality is a *power* a body possesses to produce certain ideas in your mind), what is exhibited to the mind does not *resemble* those powers. The *red* exhibited to you in your sensory experience of this same marble, for instance, certainly does not resemble a ratio of motions of the tiny particles that constitute the marble. So, although the *shape* exhibited to you in your idea of the marble resembles the primary quality – namely, its being spherical – the *color* exhibited to you in your idea of the marble does not resemble the secondary quality – namely, the configuration of primary qualities possessed by the marble. Both ideas represent, but only the idea of the primary quality resembles what it represents.

3.43   Locke introduced several experiment-like cases to help support his point, two of which Philonous will introduce in Berkeley's *First Dialogue* – though, as we will see shortly, Philonous (i.e. Berkeley) ultimately draws from them a very different conclusion. Here is one such case. Imagine that you are standing at some distance from a fire. You feel the warmth of the fire. In other words, the sensory idea of heat is brought before the mind. A commonsensical take on this, Locke suggested, is your believing that the fire possesses this very quality – the *heat* – as it is presented to you in your experience. So, you think that the heat, the quality that you directly experience, is in (or is a property of) the fire. But now suppose that you get a bit too close to the fire, where now you feel pain. In other words, the sensory idea of pain is now brought before the mind. Here, again in line with what is commonly held, you believe that the pain is in *you*. But wait! Supposedly the very same fire that produced in you the idea of heat is now producing in you the idea of pain. So, why think that the heat is in the fire but that the pain is not? Locke suggested that since you believe that the pain is in the mind (it is in you), and only in the mind, you should be philosophically consistent and also say that the heat is too. But how do you manage this without sounding nutty?

3.44   Here's how.

3.45   What is in the fire is not the heat – that is, it is not the quality heat that is exhibited to you – but instead is some configuration of primary qualities that produces in your mind the sensory idea of heat. On Locke's view, then, there is a sense in which the "heat" is a certain configuration of primary qualities which are not in the mind but actually reside in a body, and another sense in which the "heat" is a sensible quality, an artifact of the mind. The same account can be applied in the case of the sensory idea of pain. So, both the heat and the pain are in you (your mind) as artifacts of sensory experience, and at the same time refer to some configuration of primary qualities found in what we are calling "the fire" (for the case of heat) or "one's own body" (for the cases of pain). In fact, it may be the very same configuration that ultimately produces both ideas, where the differences between the qualities heat and pain are determined instead by the differences in the configuration of the primary qualities that constitute your sensory organs. Since these organs are themselves bodies, they too must possess primary qualities. And given that they play an important role in the production of your sensory ideas, they too possess secondary qualities – powers to produce in you the ideas of heat, pain, and the like. The origin of the difference in the ideas of yellow and heat, for instance, may turn out to be simply the differences in secondary qualities that the eyes and related portions of the brain possess versus those that the skin and related portions of the brain possess. So, neither the *yellow*, nor the *heat*, nor the *pain* resembles any property that a body actually possesses. This suggests the following argument: If sensed qualities are not "in" any body, and yet are "in" the mind, and there are only two kinds of things in the cosmos, namely body and mind, then the sensed qualities must be *solely* "in" the mind. (Here, "in" means that they depend on the mind for their existence.)

Here is how Locke put the matter: 3.46

> ... I think it easy to draw this observation, that the ideas of primary qualities of bodies are resemblances of them, and their patterns do really exist in the bodies themselves, but the ideas produced in us by these secondary qualities have no resemblance to them at all. There is nothing like our ideas existing in the bodies themselves. They are, in the bodies we denominate from them, only a power to produce those sensations in us; and what is sweet, blue, or warm in idea is but the certain bulk, figure, and motion of the insensible parts, in the bodies themselves, which we call so. (*Essay*, Book II, Chapter VIII, Section 15)

And, here is the experiment-like case about the fire, discussed just a moment ago, in Locke's own words:

> Flame is denominated hot and light . . .. Which qualities are commonly thought to be the same in those bodies that those ideas are in us, the one the perfect resemblance of the other, as they are in a mirror, and it would by most men be judged very extravagant if one should say otherwise. And yet he that will consider that the same fire that, at one distance produces in us the sensation of warmth, does, at a nearer approach, produce in us the far different sensation of pain, ought to bethink himself what reason he has to say that his idea of warmth, which was produced in him by the fire, is actually in the fire; and his idea of pain, which the same fire produced in him the same way, is not in the fire. (*Essay*, Book II, Chapter VIII, Section 16)

Locke does more than to suggest that the qualities of heat and pain are "in" the mind, whereas the primary and secondary qualities, which produce the ideas of heat and pain, are "outside" the mind, and are in fact genuine properties of bodies. It should be clear by now that we are taking "inside the mind" and "outside the mind" to mean "depends for its being or existence on the mind" and "doesn't depend for its being or existence on the mind," respectively. So, the qualities hot, cold, red, blue, and the like, are inside the mind insofar as they depend for their being or existence on the mind (that perceives them). No minds, no sensible qualities. Likewise, the primary qualities such as extension, bulk, shape, size, motion, and so on, and the secondary qualities, which are various configurations of primary qualities, are outside the mind insofar as they do not depend for their being or existence on the mind. Instead, they depend for their being or existence on a body – or, as we referred to it earlier, a material substance. So, if no body, then no shapes, sizes, and the like. But if no mind, bodies and their primary qualities *could* nevertheless remain. In principle, they could exist whether or not minds did. As you no doubt surmised, this view (i.e. Locke's view) is very similar to Descartes's.

3.47   Here is a second case. This one includes the mention of *manna*, which is a kind of bread mentioned in the Old Testament of the *Bible*:

> The particular bulk, number, figure, and motion of the part of fire or snow are really in them, whether anyone's senses perceive them or no; and therefore they may be called real qualities, because they really exist in those bodies. But light, heat, whiteness, or coldness, are no more really in them than sickness or pain is in manna. Take away the sensation of them; let not the eyes see light or colours, nor the ears hear sounds; let the palate not taste, nor the nose smell, and all colours, tastes, odours, and sounds, as they are such particular ideas, vanish and cease, and are reduced to their causes, i.e. bulk, figure, and motion of parts. (*Essay*, Book II, Chapter VIII, Section 17)

The sensed qualities are dependent on sensory experience. They cease to be or cease to exist if we destroy our ability to sense. It is worth mentioning that in an extended discussion of manna (Section 18), Locke had introduced the notion of another kind of power (we might call it a *tertiary* quality so as to keep it separate from talk of secondary qualities) that bodies have, namely a power that bodies have to effect other bodies. The manna, for example, is said to have the power to produce healing in human bodies. The sun, to use another example, is said to have the power to melt wax. These are different powers from those that can produce ideas in a mind. So, secondary qualities are powers that bodies possess which allow them to effect minds, whereas tertiary qualities are powers that bodies possess which allow them to effect other bodies. Let us stay focused on primary and secondary qualities and leave behind the topic of tertiary qualities.

Here is another case, this one focused on porphyry, which is a kind of 3.48
stone:

> Let us consider the red and white colours in porphyry. Hinder light but from
> striking on it, and its colours vanish; it no longer produces any such ideas in
> us; upon the return of light it produces these appearances on us again. Can
> anyone think any real alterations are made in the porphyry by the presence
> or absence of light, and that those idea of whiteness and redness are really in
> porphyry in the light, when it is plain it has no colour in the dark? In has,
> indeed, such a configuration of particles, both night and day, as are apt, by
> the rays of light rebounding from some parts of that hard stone, to produce
> in us the idea of redness, and from others the idea of whiteness; but whiteness
> or redness are not in it at any time, but such a texture that has the power to
> produce such a sensation in us. (*Essay*, Book II, Chapter VIII, Section 19)

And, here is one last case. This one would emphasize the relative nature of 3.49
sensing ordinary objects. As we will see shortly, Berkeley will in fact employ
the first case (about fire) and this last case (which is about water). Locke
wrote:

> Ideas being thus distinguished and understood, we may be able to give an
> account how the same water, at the same time, may produce the idea of cold
> by one hand and of heat by the other, whereas it is impossible that the same
> water, if those ideas were really in it, should at the same time be both hot and
> cold. For, if the sensation of heat and cold be nothing but the increase or
> diminution of the motion of the minute parts of our bodies, caused by the
> corpuscles of any other body, it is easy to be understood that, if that motion
> be greater in one hand than in the other, if a body be applied to the two
> hands, which has in its minute particles a great motion than in those of one
> of the hands, and a less than in those of the other, it will increase the motion
> of the one hand and lessen it in the other, and so cause the different sensa-
> tions of heat and cold that depend thereon. (*Essay*, Book II, Chapter VIII,
> Section 21)

Imagine that you stick your right hand into the oven and your left into the
freezer. You keep them there for some period of time. Now, you take them
out and plunge them into a bucket of room temperature water. To your
right hand the water feels cold; to your left the water feels hot. Assuming
that hot and cold are opposites, and that nothing can possess opposite
properties at one and the same moment, then the *water* cannot possess both
the hot and the cold. Since hot and cold are qualities presented directly to
the mind, they are at the very least inhabitants of the *mind*. To say that they

are "inhabitants" of the mind is not to say that the *mind* is both hot and cold. For, it would be equally impossible for the mind to possess contrary properties. Rather, in taking hot and cold to be ideas, we only commit ourselves to saying that the ideas of hot and cold are brought before the mind. And, to make this even clearer, we should note that the *hot* is associated with the left hand, whereas the *cold* is associated with the right. The right hand is not identical to the left. There is nothing contradictory in thinking that the right hand works to produce the idea of cold while the left works to produce the idea of hot. But there would be a contradiction in thinking that one and the same body possessed both hot and cold at the same time. The thing to stress here is that hot and cold are not properties of the *water* – the body that you are now sensing.

3.50   Locke suggested that although hot and cold do not *resemble* anything in the bodies now under discussion (i.e. properties in the water, properties in the right and left hands, and properties in the brain), they nevertheless *represent* something. What exactly? Well, in this case, according to Locke, they represent certain *ratios* of motion. The idea of cold represents a ratio of motion: the ratio between the motion of the particles constituting the water and the motions of the particles constituting your right hand. Remember that your right hand has been in the oven for a while, which resulted in increasing the (speed of the) motions of the particles constituting your right hand. The idea of hot represents a ratio of motion: the ratio between the motion of the particles constituting the water and the motions of the particles constituting your left hand. Remember that your left hand has been in the freezer for a while, which resulted in decreasing the (speed of the) motions of the particles constituting your left hand. The differences in ratios – motion of right hand particles to motion of water particles versus motion of left hand particles to motion of water particles – are represented in your correlated sensory ideas of cold and hot. What is "in" the water, that is, what is a property of the water, where the water is understood to be a collection of particles, is *motion*. And what is "in" your right and left hands, where they too are understood to be collections of particles, are motions. Some of the motions are "faster" or "slower" relative to others. There is nothing contradictory in thinking this.

3.51   The theme of these experiment-like cases should be clear: primary qualities are actually in bodies, and they can be understood to exist independently of their being perceived by any mind, whereas the *sensations* that are produced in the mind by way of certain configurations of these primary qualities (these configurations being the secondary qualities) are not actually in bodies. Bodies can in fact be conceived without having to conceive them as having any of these sensations or sensory qualities – heat, cold, color, and the like.

Berkeley agreed with Descartes and Locke that the sensible qualities are   3.52
not properties of anything that exists independently of the mind. But Berkeley rejected the view that the primary qualities really do exist in bodies, where bodies are understood to be things capable of existing independently of the mind. Not surprisingly, a version of Descartes's and Locke's views is expressed by Hylas in the *First Dialogue*:

> I frankly admit, Philonous, that it is in vain to stand out any longer. Colours, sounds, tastes, in a word, all those termed *secondary qualities*, have certainly no existence without the mind. But by this acknowledgement I must not be supposed to derogate anything from the reality of matter or external objects, seeing it is no more than several philosophers maintain, who nevertheless are the furthest imaginable from denying matter. For the clearer understanding of this, you must know sensible qualities are by philosophers divided into *primary* and *secondary*. The former are extension, figure, solidity, gravity, motion, and rest. And these they hold exist really in bodies. The latter are those above enumerated; or briefly, all sensible qualities beside the primary, which they assert are only so many sensations or ideas existing nowhere but in the mind. But all this, I doubt not, you are already apprised of. For my part, I have been a long time sensible there was such an opinion current among philosophers, but was never thoroughly convinced of its truth till now.

This needs to be cleaned up a bit. As you know, according to the earlier discussion of Locke, Locke held that primary qualities and secondary qualities are in bodies. The former are those very properties that define the nature of body, whereas the latter are simply certain configurations of primary qualities that constitute powers to produce various ideas in a mind. We have ideas of these two kinds of quality. Ideas of primary qualities not only represent the qualities that are in bodies, but resemble them as well. Locke, in a kind of rationalist move, argues that resemblance is guaranteed by what is necessary in conceiving bodies: when conceiving a body, we need not conceive it as having color, for instance, but we *must* conceive it as being extended, as having some size, some shape, and so on. Ideas of secondary qualities, although representing various configurations of primary qualities or powers, do not resemble those powers. What is directly presented to the mind when sensing a secondary quality is a *sensation* or a *sensible quality* (the two terms are taken to be equivalent here) – sensations such as hot, cold, color, sound, and the like. Hylas, though a bit sloppily, is basically saying that he agrees with the view that the sensible qualities – hot, cold, color, sound, etc. – are only in the mind, and do not exist in anything "outside" the mind – that is, they depend on the mind for their existence. But he also thinks that the primary qualities – extension, shape, size, etc. – really do exist in bodies, where bodies are taken to be things that exist independently of any mind. So, if there were no minds, there would be no sensible qualities. But, if there were no minds, bodies and their primary qualities could nevertheless exist.

3.53   Hylas asserts his agreement with philosophers like Descartes and Locke after Philonous had walked him through versions of Locke's fire (heat and pain) and water (hot and cold) cases. Hylas had agreed with Philonous, for instance, that both the heat and the pain are simply items immediately perceived by a mind. (Here, Philonous diverges from Locke by identifying the idea of pain with the idea of an intense degree of heat – Locke, recall, had taken the two ideas to be different.) And Hylas also had agreed with the view that one and the same body, namely the water, cannot possess contrary properties – hot and cold in this case. So, those items, the hot and the cold, are not properties of the water, but are only items immediately perceived by a mind. Even so, in line with Descartes and Locke, Hylas draws the line at primary qualities. According to Hylas (and to Descartes and Locke), those are genuine properties of bodies, where bodies are understood as things that can (and do) exist independently of the mind. How could Philonous think otherwise? Hylas' attempt at reclaiming ideas of primary qualities is part of his attempt at reclaiming his initial view that the idea of matter or material substance is sensory. It is not an empty idea, as Philonous had tried to show. The sensory idea of a material substance is the idea of a body with all of the sensible qualities stripped away: it is an idea of an extended thing with a shape, a size, is in motion or at rest, and so on. This sounds a lot like Descartes and Locke.

3.54   Philonous (who recall is expressing Berkeley's view) argues that, just like the sensible qualities, the primary qualities are not in anything that exists independently of the mind. They are just as much in a mind (remember that by "A is in B" we mean that A depends for its being or its existence on B) as are the sensible qualities. To get crystal clear about this, let us quickly go over some of the details of the arguments against sensible qualities being in anything existing independently of a mind, and then see how they are similar to the arguments against the view that primary qualities exist in mind-independent things.

3.55   The first argument, which was akin to Locke's fire case, emphasizes that the quality heat is a quality that is only in a mind. The quality is in the mind in the sense that it is directly or immediately perceived by the mind. No minds, no perceptions of heat; no perceptions of heat, no quality heat. So, no minds, no quality heat. Philonous begins this argument by taking the ideas of heat that are initially presumed to be "produced" by the fire to be ideas of different degrees or intensities of heat. According to Philonous, then, the idea of heat that is produced in the mind when standing at some distance from the fire presents a degree or intensity of heat that is lesser than that which is presented in the idea produced in the mind when standing too close to the fire. The latter, the idea of the greater intensity of heat, is, in this case, taken to be an idea of *pain*. This is worth repeating: the idea of this great intensity of heat is taken to be identical with an idea of pain. The point is that both ideas, the ideas of lesser and greater intensities of heat, are ideas of the same quality – namely *heat*; the idea of pain is identical with the idea of the greater heat. Now, ordinarily, a perceiver will say that the lesser degree of heat that she perceives is in the fire (a body), and can exist independently of the mind. But, this same perceiver will also say that the pain she perceives is in the mind, which is to say that the greater degree of heat is in the mind. Philonous gives us three options:

Option 1: The lesser heat is in the fire but the greater heat (the pain) is in the mind.
Option 2: Both the lesser and greater heat are in the fire.
Option 3: Both the lesser and greater heat are in the mind.

Even though Option 1 looks to express commonsense, when examined we discover that we have no good reasons to choose it, that is, outside of its simply appearing to be a piece of commonsense. And there are other reasons for rejecting Option 1. For instance, we cannot justify splitting (perceptions of) *heat* up this way – some degrees of it are in the fire whereas others are in the mind? So, Option 1 is out. Now, if we choose Option 2, we are basically saying that the pain (identical with the greater degree of heat) is in the fire. And we agreed along with Philonous and Hylas that that sounded nutty. No one believes that fire has feelings like pain (or that it has feelings at all!). So, Option 2 is out. If we choose Option 3, which is the option that Philonous wants us to choose, we are saying that the heat, whether it is a little heat or a great heat, is simply and solely in the mind, the one that is perceiving the heat.

Option 3 does not commit us to the view that the *mind* is hot. Rather, 3.56 since we are talking about ideas of heat, the view is that the mind is *aware of* the heat – the heat is the immediate *object* of awareness (philosophers call this an intentional object: it is that at which the mind is directed when engaged in an act of perceiving). An idea can be "of" *x* without itself being *x*, in the same way that a photograph can be of the Empire State Building without itself being the Empire State Building. Recall that Descartes held a similar view. The point is that the idea of heat can have heat as its object without the idea itself being hot. So, when a mind perceives the heat by way of an idea, the idea presents the object, *heat*, to the mind, but for all that the mind is not itself hot (though there are philosophers of the period who would think that when perceiving hot or blue that the mind is hot or blue – Nicolas Malebranche (1638–1715), for example, held a view like this). This is analogous to what we have said about photographs. When you perceive the Empire State Building by way of a photograph, the photograph presents to you the object, the Empire State Building, and no one thinks that the photograph is the Empire State Building. Likewise, when perceiving the Empire State Building, no one, including yourself, would hold that *you* are the Empire State Building. Similarly, we say that the mind can perceive or be aware of heat without itself being hot. Hylas ultimately chooses Option 3. Even so, as we already know, he still holds that those minute bodies in motion are "outside" the mind, and these are what "produce" the ideas of heat in the mind.

3.57   The second argument that Philonous employs concerning sensible qualities is about a bucket of room temperature water (the same sort of case that Locke had earlier introduced). We stick one hand into the oven and the other into the freezer and then after some time place them into the bucket of room temperature water. To the hand that has been in the oven, the water feels cool, and to the hand that has been in the freezer, the water feels warm. Cool (cold) and warm (hot) are taken to be opposites here. Both Philonous and Hylas agree that one and the same thing cannot possess contrary or opposite properties at one and the same time. So, presumably it would be acceptable to say that something was cold at one moment and then hot at another, but it is a contradiction (it would be impossible) to say that something was both hot and cold at the same moment. So, strictly speaking, the *water* cannot be both hot and cold at the same time. These qualities – hot and cold—instead arise in your *perception* of the water. That is, although the water cannot itself be both hot and cold at the same time, it might *appear* hot from the point of view of your left hand, say, and cold from the point of view of your right. These "points of view" are ultimately perceptions in a mind. Hylas agrees. But, as in the fire case, he wants to say that even though such qualities are mind-dependent, what is "producing" them in the mind is not. The system of little bodies in motion that constitute what we are calling "the water" is effecting the motions of the little bodies that constitute your right and left hands, which in turn is effecting portions of your brain, which in turn is "producing" the ideas of hot and cold in the mind. In this case, Philonous gives us two options:

Option 1: The qualities hot and cold are in the water.
Option 2: The qualities hot and cold are in the mind.

If we choose Option 1, then we violate the principle that one and the same thing cannot possess contrary or opposite properties at one and the same time. Since we do not want to violate this principle, we cannot choose Option 1. So, Option 1 is out. So, it looks like Option 2 is the only choice. Keep in mind that in choosing Option 2 we are not saying that the *mind* is hot and cold, for that would be equally impossible. Instead, what we are saying is that the mind perceives hot and cold, where it is in respect to the left hand that it perceives the water as hot and in respect to the right that it perceives the water as cold.

You might think that we can say that the hot and the cold need not be 3.58 attributed to the water, or to the mind, but instead can be attributed to the hands. But there are problems lurking with this. For instance, the right hand, recall, has been placed in the oven. So, if anything it would presumably be hot, right? But the experiment has it that you place your right hand into the water and as a result you are aware of (you perceive) what we are calling *cold*. Now, you are not saying that you feel your *right hand* as being cold. Rather, you are saying that you feel the *water* as being cold. However, if you want to "locate" the cold in the right hand, then you would be saying that it is both hot and cold (remember, it is "hot" since it has been in the oven for a while – for, if you felt the right hand with your left, you would say that from the point of view of your left hand that your right hand feels hot). And since *nothing* can possess opposite properties, then your right hand cannot possess them either. Therefore, for the same reason that you cannot "locate" these qualities in the water, you cannot "locate" the qualities hot and cold in your hands. Instead, Option 2 is your only choice. But Hylas has no trouble in accepting that such qualities exist only in a mind that perceives them. His contention is that the primary qualities, which are ultimately responsible for "producing" in the mind ideas of qualities such as hot and cold, are actually in bodies; where bodies can (and do) exist independently of minds.

Philonous offers several arguments aimed at rejecting the claim that pri- 3.59 mary qualities are in bodies, arguments that are in fact very similar to the ones he had offered when discussing the sensible qualities (heat and pain, hot and cold). Let us consider two. The first deals with the primary quality *shape* and the second with the primary quality *size*.

You look at the table in front of you. Let us say that you are asked to draw 3.60 the shape of its top as it appears from your point of view. It looks like this:

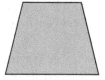

Now, someone else sitting in the room is also asked to draw the table as it appears from her point of view. It looks like this:

These are clearly different shapes. The table cannot have two different shapes at one and the same time, right? So, which shape is the table's shape? It cannot be *both*. So neither? How many possible points of view are there in the room? An indefinite number? If so, there would be an indefinite number of shapes that one could draw! Which one of those is the table's *real* shape? You hover over the table and look down and say, "*That* shape is the real shape – the rectangular shape that appears to me now." But why think that that is the *real* shape of the table? It is just one out of an indefinite number of shapes that can appear to you. What reason justifies your bias for preferring *this* shape as it appears from the point of view of hovering over the table? (This may remind you of the sort of line of reasoning that Hobbes employed when securing why it is that a body at rest must remain at rest.) You might accept the view that none of the shapes that appear to you (or to any mind) are the *real* or *actual* shape of the table. But now you would be stuck with the view that the real shape is a shape that never appears to anyone; it is a shape that no one sees or imagines. In fact, the real shape of the table is a shape that no one can *ever* see or can *ever* imagine!

3.61   So what is the real shape of the table? You immediately think of the table as having a rectangular shape. But wait – that is one of the indefinitely many *seen* or *imagined* shapes! The view that you are now stuck with, remember, says that the real shape is a shape that no one can ever see or imagine. So, Philonous again asks, "what shape do you have in mind when talking about the *real* shape of the table?" Philonous is keen to point out that your view will force you to say that you have got *nothing* in mind when talking about the real shapes of things – if by "real shape" you mean a shape that exists independently of its being perceived by a mind. Since the *only* shape you are aware of is the one that appears as an object of perception (whether sensing or imagining), the primary quality *shape* looks to depend on the mind, just like the sensible qualities *color, sound, taste,* and so on.

Philonous then considers the primary quality *size*. His thought experiment 3.62
is similar to those already discussed. Let us say that you look at a mite. It
appears to you to be a pretty small thing – and its legs even smaller. So, the
size of the mite's legs appears to you to be very tiny. But, Philonous adds, consider now that on one of those tiny legs there lives an even tinier mite. To this
tinier mite, the leg appears enormous. That is, from its point of view, the size
of the leg is very great! Well, which is it? Is the size tiny or great? It cannot be
both. Just like with the shape case discussed just a moment ago, there are only
the *apparent* sizes (the sizes that appear when either sensing or imagining). If
you believe that the mite's leg has a size, a "real" size, a size that is distinct from
an apparent size, it will be a size that never appears to anyone. So, like the
shape case, you would hold that the real or actual size of an object is a size that
no one can ever see or imagine – that is, it is a size that no one can ever perceive. So, what size do you have in mind when you say that a body has a *real*
size, a size that not only is not ever perceived by a mind but *cannot ever* be
perceived by a mind? Philonous will again bring it to light that you really have
no idea of such a thing. The primary quality *size* is as much a mind-dependent
quality as is *shape, color, sound, taste,* and the like. It is inconceivable that
there be a size "out there" that exists independently of the mind.

Hylas still holds out. He is willing to grant that perhaps these modes – 3.63
shape, size, etc. – are mind-dependent, but extension, he insists, which is
the essence or nature of body, is certainly not mind-dependent. We might
imagine that Hylas was thinking that Descartes was right in giving extension a special status in his ontology – for, unlike shape and size, recall,
which Descartes took to be *modes*, extension was taken to be an *attribute*,
and a *principal attribute* at that. Hylas might refer us back to Descartes, who
had argued that extension can be conceived independently of mind: mind
and body are really distinct. But, Philonous might ask, what does Descartes
have in mind when saying that *extension* exists independently of its being
perceived? Clearly, when Descartes or Hylas conceives of extension, just
like anyone else, they conceive at the very least something that has some
length (size). You cannot conceive, let alone see or imagine, a *sizeless* extension. And, we have already established that size is a mind-dependent quality: we cannot conceive it as something existing independently of a mind.
So, what about this strange sort of extension that allegedly exists independently of its having a size that can be conceived? This is the point in the
dialogue at which Hylas is forced to return to the earlier view, initially
agreed to, that the idea of matter or material substance or, as it is now being
cast, extension (which is the essence of matter or material substance), is
something that is mediately perceived – not immediately perceived. So, it is
not like the other qualities. The idea of extension (matter) is not sensory

after all. Unlike the other ideas of primary and secondary qualities, then, the idea of extension is inferred by the mind.

3.64   So, what is this idea of matter? Well, metaphysically or conceptually speaking, it must be that which underlies or supports whatever properties a body may actually have. It is plainly and simply a *material substratum*. Let us say that we have been convinced that the primary qualities shape and size (and the others) are solely objects of perception, and so depend on the mind for their existence. So, *they* are not "supported" by any material substratum. The issue before us now is whether extension depends on or is supported by a substratum other than a mind. For if it is, then Hylas might have a case in support of his view that extension exists independently of its being immediately perceived, and so it can be said to exist independently of a mind.

3.65   In Part I, Article 16 of *PHK*, Berkeley wrote:

> But let us examine a little the received opinion. It is said extension is a mode or accident of matter, and that matter is the *substratum* that supports it. Now I desire that you would explain what is meant by matter's *supporting* extension: say you, I have no idea of matter, and therefore cannot explain it. I answer, though you have no positive idea, yet if you have any meaning at all, you must at least have a relative idea of matter; though you know not what it is, yet you must be supposed to know what relation it bears to accidents, and what is meant by its supporting them. It is evident support cannot here be taken in its usual or literal sense, as when we say that pillars *support* a building; in what sense therefore must it be taken?

In the next article, Berkeley would go on to claim that philosophers in fact have no idea that would give sense to the term "support" in this context. To say, then, that matter or the material substratum *supports* extension is to use a word that is meaningless, and so you would really be saying nothing at all. Admittedly, you do not have an idea of a propertyless thing. The idea of a substance, as Berkeley suggested in the above passage, is "relative." It is relative in the sense that this whole business of support *implies* or *presupposes* something doing the supporting. This is another way of saying that the idea is *inferred by* the mind – that substance is only mediately perceived. But if the notion of support is meaningless, you have lost the very relation that is needed to make sense of the idea of a substance. In other words, if "support" is meaningless, then "matter" or "material substance" is also rendered meaningless (since the latter were being defined in terms of "support"). The upshot of this version of the argument is that if nothing is really meant by invoking matter or material substrate, then you have lost any grounds for your claiming that extension can exist independently of a mind. For, the whole point of invoking matter or the material substrate, which was assumed to be really distinct from mind, was to show how it is that extension could be taken to exist independently of its being perceived. The claim was that extension does not depend for its existence on a mind, but instead depends for its existence on this material substrate. But, if *matter* (or *material substrate*) is a vacuous term, then you really cannot say in any meaningful way that extension depends for its existence on *it* – for, there is no "it" to which you are referring. And so, extension, if it exists, depends for its existence on a mind that perceives it.

We find a slightly different though related argument in the *First Dialogue*. 3.66 Here is the main of it:

Philonous: *Material substratum* call you it? But by which of your senses came you acquainted with that being?

Hylas: It is not itself sensible; its modes and qualities only being perceived by the senses.

Philonous: I presume then, it was by reflection and reason you obtained the idea of it.

Hylas: I do not pretend to any proper positive idea of it. However I conclude it exists, because qualities cannot be conceived to exist without a support.

Philonous: It seems then you have only a relative notion of it, or that you conceive it not otherwise than by conceiving the relation it bears to sensible qualities.

Hylas: Right.

Philonous: Be pleased therefore to let me know wherein that relation consists.

Hylas: Is it not sufficiently expressed in the term *substratum*, or *substance*?

Philonous: If so, the word *substratum* should import that it is spread under the sensible qualities or accidents.

Hylas: True.

Philonous: And consequently under extension.

Hylas: Yes.

Philonous: It is therefore something in its own nature entirely distinct from extension.

Hylas: I tell you, extension is only a mode, and matter is something that supports modes. And is it not evident the thing supported is different from the thing supporting?

Philonous:	So that something distinct from, and exclusive of extension, is supposed to be the *substratum* of extension.
Hylas:	Just so.
Philonous:	Answer me, Hylas. Can a thing be spread without extension? Or is not the idea of extension necessarily included in *spreading*?
Hylas:	It is.
Philonous:	Whatsoever therefore you suppose spread under any thing, must have in itself an extension distinct from the extension of that thing under which it is spread.
Hylas:	It must.
Philonous:	Consequently every corporeal substance being the *substratum* of extension, must have in itself another extension by which it is qualified to be a *substratum*: and so on to infinity. And I ask whether this be not absurd in itself . . .

This argument is slightly different from the one offered in *PHK*. You now know that in *PHK*, Berkeley had argued that "matter" or "material substrate" is meaningless, and so any appeal to a material substrate as that which ontologically supported extension falls apart. What is it that you claim underlies or supports extension? Nothing? Well, Berkeley would say, that is as good as having no account at all. In the argument offered in the *First Dialogue*, the one in the above exchange between Philonous and Hylas, Berkeley argues that the very idea of a material substrate is a logical or conceptual absurdity (a contradiction). Though related, this criticism is slightly different from the one that says that the idea is empty (where the terms "matter" or "material substrate" are shown to be meaningless).

3.67   Here is the gist of the above *First Dialogue* argument. To begin, we should remind ourselves that for philosophers of the period a substance was considered the ground floor level of the ontology (a theory of being). Remember that properties or modes cannot exist all by themselves. They require the existence of some thing that is "more real" – a *substance* – of which they are the properties or modes. The ontological relation here is understood in terms of dependence: a property depends for its existence on the existence of a substance in a way that a substance does not depend for its existence on the existence of the property. According to this sort of Aristotelian view, if no substances, no properties; but if no properties, there could still be substances (though admittedly what they would be *like* would now be the big question!). Recall that Descartes had said that the technical notion of a substance, that is, the philosophical notion, was that a substance was that which required no other thing for its existence. It was able to exist without the help of anything else: it did not ontologically depend on anything other than itself. Of course, Descartes had also admitted that the only thing that met this criterion strictly was God. But he allowed mind and body *substancehood* status, keeping it in mind that although they depended on God for their existence, they did not depend on one another. Each could (and did) exist independently of the other. This, recall, was based on his analysis of his ideas of mind and body that showed that mind and body were really distinct, and was in turn the basis for his metaphysical dualism. To separate talk of created mind and body from talk of God, Descartes called the former "finite" substances. Ontologically, then, although finite substances depend on no other finite substance for their existence, they nevertheless do depend on God, the infinite substance. God was the only "thing" thought to be truly ontologically independent. The point is that whatever it is that we will eventually count as a substance in our ontology, the level of substance is the ground floor of the ontology. There is nothing more real than a substance. If any properties in the world exist, then there exists at least one substance that is the bearer of those properties.

According to Hylas, in the above argument taken from the *First Dialogue,*   3.68
the metaphysical notion of a substance, not surprisingly, depicts a substance as that which supports or underlies that which is supported. That which is supported is presumably some property or mode. Hylas claims that extension is a property or mode, and that matter or a material substrate supports and underlies it. This is slightly different from Descartes, recall, who had held that extension was not really a *mode* of some independent thing, but that extension and what we are taking to be a corporeal substance were one and the same thing. This was the import of Descartes's calling extension an *attribute.* In Descartes's terms, *extension* and *material substance* were only conceptually or rationally distinct: they were simply different ways of conceiving one and the same thing. By contrast, Hylas seems to hold the slightly different view that extension is a *property* or *mode* and that matter or the material *substrate* is the thing that has this property. On this view, which aligns more closely with an Aristotelian one (and a Lockean one for that matter), it may be possible for the substrate to exist independently of its being extended. After all, this substance is more real than any of its properties, including extension.

Philonous's analysis of the notion of "supporting" or "underlying" depicts   3.69
the thing doing the supporting or underlying as something that is *spread out.* In ordinary-speak, when we say, for example, that the foundation of a building *supports* the building, we have in mind the foundation as something that is spread out, sitting directly underneath the frame of the

building. When Atlas is said to support the world, we have in mind the world resting on Atlas' shoulders, where Atlas is located directly underneath the world, his shoulders supporting the world insofar as they are spread out underneath it. If matter or a material substrate is that which supports the property extension, then when we think of this we have in mind something that is spread out, lying just underneath the property. But the property in question is extension. This is where the problem begins to emerge. Let us pause and get clearer about the problem. To do this we will need to remind ourselves of Aristotelian metaphysics.

3.70   According to the Aristotelian picture, our language reveals important details about reality. For example, and this should be familiar, since we considered it in Chapter 1, when we say that "*This ball is blue*," "this ball" is the subject of the sentence and "is blue" is the predicate. Now, the "is" in "is blue" is not the "is" of identity. We are not saying that this ball is *identical* with blueness. We are not saying: *this ball = blue*. For, if that was how we were taking "is" (as expressing identity), then since we also say "*This shirt is blue*," the shirt would be identical to blue too, in which case this ball would be the shirt. And no one thinks that that is what they are saying when they say "*This ball is blue*" and "*This shirt is blue*." Rather, this "is" is the "is" of predication. We are saying that this ball now possesses the property of blue; it is now in a state of *being* blue. The same for the shirt: we are saying that the shirt possesses the property of blue. Ontologically speaking, in some cases, like the ball and shirt cases, the predicate is picking out the property and the subject is picking out the substance, the thing that has the property. So, "this ball" is picking out a substance and "blue" is picking out the property that this substance has.

3.71   But what if the property in question is extension? Well, presumably we tell a similar metaphysical story to the one told in the ball case. In saying that "*x is extended*," "*x*" is the subject and "is extended" is the predicate. In terms of the ontology, "*x*" is picking out a substance and "extension" is picking out the property that this substance has. So, when we say "*x is extended*" it would be, ontologically speaking, no different from our saying "*x is blue*." Here is where the trouble lurks. In thinking "*x is blue*," we might think that *x*, the substance, supports or underlies the blueness. *x* is spread out underneath the blue; it is that over which the blue is spread. What accounts for *x*'s being blue is that it has the property *blue*. Remove this property and *x* is no longer blue. But we cannot really think the same for extension. If what accounts for *x*'s being extended is its having the property extension, we cannot think that *x*, the substance, supports or underlies extension – that is, we cannot think that *x* is spread out underneath extension; we cannot think that x is that over which extension is spread. For, if x is that over which extension is spread, then in being "spread out" x is already extended, and is so even prior to or independently of its having the property extension! Of course, we might say, as Philonous suggests we might, that this "deeper" or "underlying" extension is not the same as the property initially picked out by the predicate "is extended." The former exists at a deeper or more fundamental level of the ontology. But this "deeper" extension is a kind of extendedness, right? If so, it is a kind of property, even though it is presumably found at a deeper level than the extendedness of interest at the beginning of our inquiry. Let us keep track of these different levels of extendedness by numbering them. So, let the extension with which we began be referred to as $extension_1$. And so, we now say "x is $extended_1$." Since x is "spread out" underneath its properties, it is that over which $extension_1$ is spread, we noted that x must possess some "deeper" level of extension. Call this $extension_2$, where $extension_2 \neq extension_1$. Now, if this deeper kind of extension, $extension_2$, is a property, then x, in being the substrate, must be taken as underlying it. But wait! That would mean that x has an even deeper kind of extension over which this deeper extension is spread! Call this even deeper level of extension $extension_3$, where $extension_3 \neq extension_2$. And if this yet deeper extension is also a property, then x must possess some even deeper extension over which this other is spread, and so on *ad infinitum*.

Why is this a problem? Well, the whole point of invoking x, the sub- 3.72
stance, was to identify the ground floor. Remember, a substance is the ground floor of the ontology; nothing is more fundamental. The buck stops there (to use another metaphor). But if things are as Hylas sees it, then there is *no* ground floor – there are simply deeper and ever deeper levels of the ontology! If that is the case, then what does Hylas even *mean* by "substance"? What would be the point of invoking it? Hylas' notion of a substrate, at least in our consideration as to whether extension is a property that can exist independently of a mind, is the contradictory or impossible metaphysical picture of a ground floor-ontology that has no ground floor; it is the contradictory metaphysical picture of a bottomless bottom.

This might at least show that extension is not a property of an extended 3.73
substrate. Of course, if you are Hylas (or Descartes or Locke), you will allow for only two kinds of possible substrate: a material and a mental (immaterial) substrate. Since the above argument rules out extension's depending for its existence on an extended (material) substrate, the only alternative is that it depends for its existence on an immaterial one – a mind.

An alternative and more direct (and even simpler) rendering of Philonous' 3.74
argument is this:

1. If extension *can* exist independently of a mind, there is no bottom to the ontology.
2. But if the world is *real*, there must be a bottom of the ontology.
3. The world is real.
4. So, there must be a bottom to the ontology. [from 2 and 3]
5. Therefore, extension cannot exist independently of a mind. [from 1 and 4]

3.75 If the primary qualities of body (extension, bulk, shape, size, motion, etc.) depend for their existence not on some material substrate but instead on their being perceived, just like the sensible qualities, then Philonous (i.e. Berkeley) has made his case. Everything sensed, imagined, and reasoned – *everything!* – depends on a mind. In other words, the world as you know it depends for its existence on its being perceived.

3.4 The Problem of the External World Answered: The Omni-perceiver

3.76 Return to the case of the tables and chairs in the classroom. If Berkeley was right and the *existence* of the tables and chairs is identical with *their being perceived*, then what should you say once you leave the room and neither you nor anyone else perceives them? Well, presumably you must say that if no longer perceived, the tables and chairs no longer exist. *That* does not sound like it aligns with commonsense! Remember that the tentative agreement between Philonous and Hylas was that the better view was the one that best supported and aligned with commonsense. Berkeley's view (represented by Philonous), at least without any further qualification, definitely fails to align with commonsense. Given Berkeley's view thus far, this looks to be the best you could do: You put people on a rotating watch, where you stand watch for an hour and perceive the tables and chairs, your friend stands watch for the next hour, and so on, so that *some* mind is perceiving the tables and chairs. But even though you could do this, the world is presumably so big and complex that you could not drum up enough perceivers (assuming that there are any others) to perceive everything. What about the concrete foundation hidden under the floor tiles? The dark corner of the broom closet? The underside of each table and chair? What about all past events and people? We cannot perceive the past! Even if you could get everyone on board with your plan, the world would be unfathomably *gappy;*

for, the bits that go unperceived would not exist – and, there would be a lot of bits. What if everyone closed their eyes or plugged their ears all at once? Would the world vanish? Well, no person of commonsense would think so. The world, they would say, exists whether or not anyone sees it, touches it, hears it, tastes it, or smells it. That is an important demand of commonsense.

There is another related problem: when you asked your friend to take   3.77 over the watch and to perceive the tables and chairs, in what sense can she be taken to be perceiving the *same* tables and chairs that you perceived? Are not her ideas distinct from yours? If they are, and the tables and chairs are solely collections of ideas, if she is taken to perceive the same tables and chairs, we look to be committed to saying that a single collection of ideas is there for all minds to perceive. But does not each mind perceive its own ideas? If we choose the view that there is one single collection, then another problem arises: how does this single collection persist as a single collection during the periods when it is not perceived? Let us say that you are the only mind to perceive this collection on Monday and then again on Tuesday. In what sense can the collection you perceive on Tuesday be taken to be the same collection you perceived on Monday? Did not the collection cease to exist in the interim between your perceiving it on Monday and Tuesday? If so, would not the Tuesday tables and chairs be different from the Monday tables and chairs?

Berkeley saw a way to get his view to align with commonsense. Let us be   3.78 clear about what commonsense tells us. Commonsense says that the tables and chairs, that is, *real* tables and chairs, exist independently of anyone's perceiving them. Commonsense says that although what you and others imagine may differ (you might imagine wooden chairs, for example, but someone else may imagine steel ones), the tables and chairs that you *sense*, if they are *real* tables and chairs, are the same tables and chairs that others sense. So, commonsense looks to make two demands on us about real objects, which constitutes the commonsense notion of the *objective world*:

1. **Real objects can exist independently of their being perceived by any one perceiver.**
2. **Real objects can be perceived by multiple perceivers.**

An objective world is one that exists independently of the subjective   3.79 instances of a perceiving mind. So, the tables and chairs are real – they are inhabitants of the objective world – if they meet the two criteria just noted: they would exist independently of their being perceived by you or by anyone else; and they would be perceivable by any perceiver. Something would be subjective if it failed to meet either criterion. So, for example, something that existed only when perceived by your mind would fail to meet the first criterion, and so would be taken to be subjective. The heat of the fire that you feel is subjective. No one other than you can feel that. They can have their own sensation of heat, but they cannot ever have yours. Once you no longer feel the heat, the heat, the quality felt, no longer exists. Objects that meet the first criterion meet the commonsense view that they continue to exist even during those intervals when you are not perceiving them. Objects that meet the second criterion meet the commonsense view that the objects that you perceive are the very same objects that others perceive. Berkeley's view, at least as developed thus far, seems unable to clearly secure either commonsense belief.

3.80   Descartes, recall, had secured both by way of his metaphysical dualism. He secured the first criterion by way of his showing that mind and body are really distinct: mind can exist independently of body, and vice versa. He secured the second by way of his adopting a version of the Scholastic distinction between formal and objective reality. Formal reality, recall, is the kind of reality a thing possesses in virtue of its being an existent thing. So a *real* thing possesses formal reality. We might say that a real thing is a *formal* being. So, if the tables and chairs are real, they possess some level of formal reality. But here is where things can get tricky. Objective reality is the kind of reality a thing possesses in virtue of its representing something. "Objective" in the phrase "objective reality" is importantly different from "objective" in the phrase "objective world," used a moment ago. The formal sun, Descartes said, is the sun as it exists in the heavens. The objective sun is the sun as represented in the mind. The formal sun is mind-independent, whereas the objective sun is importantly mind-dependent. No minds, no objective suns, but there could still be a formal Sun. So, Descartes's contrasting "formal" and "objective" is different from our newest (and more contemporary) distinction "objective" versus "subjective." Just to be clear, let us mark them: "objective$_1$" as Descartes used it versus "objective$_2$," this last one being the one contrasted to *subjective*. The formal sun exists in the objective$_2$ world. However, Descartes's objective$_1$ sun, since it fails to meet the two criteria just introduced, is not part of the objective$_2$ world. Rather, Descartes's objective$_1$ sun is *subjective*. If you and your friend both see the sun, using Descartes's terms, we count two objective$_1$ suns – the one presented in your mind, the other in your friend's – but we count only one formal sun, the sun existing in the heavens. Using our newest terms, the sun that is taken to meet the above two criteria is an inhabitant of the objective$_2$ world. Each mind, when perceiving the sun, has its own objective$_1$

(i.e. subjective) sun, but each mind perceives the *same* sun, the formal sun, insofar as each objective$_1$ sun represents one and the same formal sun. The formal sun is the *real* sun. It is taken to meet the two above criteria. So, it can exist independently of anyone's perceiving it; and it can be perceived by multiple perceivers. On Descartes's view, the formal sun is a material object. It is a body. Its nature is extension. It is, to use our new term, an inhabitant of the objective$_2$ world. The same goes for those tables and chairs. But Berkeley has rejected the very idea of a material substratum. On his view, there are no material things existing independently of minds. So, how can Berkeley square his view with commonsense, now having rejected the notion of matter as meeting the above two criteria?

To secure these two criteria, Berkeley introduced in the *Dialogues* the 3.81 notion of the *Omni-perceiver*. Although we will have to make this clearer as we go, one way to initially think of the Omni-perceiver is as a mind that perceives all things at all times. It should come as no surprise that Berkeley took the Omni-perceiver to be God. So, it is God who perceives the concrete hiding under the floor tiles, the dark corners of broom closets, and the undersides of tables and chairs, when no finite mind perceives them. It is God who not only guarantees that the world has no gaps, but guarantees the continued existence of the world when no finite mind perceives it. It is the appeal to God that also secures a sense in which you and others perceive the same tables and chairs. Let us now make this clearer before bringing this chapter to a close.

Recall that earlier Berkeley had noted that he had no problem accepting 3.82 the commonsense term *thing*, when talking about ordinary objects like apples, so long as we were clear that philosophically speaking things were ultimately to be understood as being nothing more or less than collections of ideas. Since a thing's existence is identical with its being perceived, Berkeley wrote in *PHK*, Part I, Article 35:

> I do not argue against the existence of any one thing that we can apprehend, either by sense or reflection. That the things I see with my eyes and touch with my hands do exist, really exist, I make not the least question. The only thing whose existence we deny, is that which philosophers call matter or corporeal substance.

In the very next article of *PHK*, Article 36, he would claim:

> There are spiritual substances, minds, or human souls, which will or excite ideas in themselves at pleasure: but these are faint, weak, and unsteady in respect of others they perceive by sense, which being impressed upon them according to certain rules or laws of nature, speak themselves the effects of a

mind more powerful and wise than human spirits. These latter are said to have more reality in them than the former: by which is meant that they are more affecting, orderly, and distinct, and that they are not fictions of the mind perceiving them. And in this sense, the sun that I see by day is the real sun, and that which I imagine by night is the idea of the former. In the sense here given of reality, it is evident that every vegetable, star, mineral, and in general each part of the mundane system, is as much a real being by our principles as by any other.

This aligns with what he had said three articles earlier:

The ideas imprinted on the sense by the Author of Nature are called *real things*: and those excited in the imagination being less regular, vivid and constant, are more properly termed *ideas*, or *images of things*, which they copy and represent. (*PHK*, Part I, Article 33)

3.83   There is much to unpack here. Let us begin with Berkeley's claim that the Author of Nature, which is God, is said to be responsible for "imprinting" certain ideas on finite human minds. These ideas are contrasted to the ones "produced" by the human mind, brought to mind by way of one's *willing* them. The ideas imprinted by God are more lively, more vivid, more distinct, and more regular and orderly than those produced by the human imagination. When you *see* the sun, for instance, Berkeley's view is that God imprints this collection of ideas on your mind. One thing to stress here is that when this sort of thing occurs, you are not in control of what you see. You might think that you can turn your head, say, and no longer see the sun, but when you turn your head back, the sun is there and there is nothing you can do to alter that. In *PHK*, Part I, Article 29, he wrote:

But whatever power I may have over my own thoughts, I find the ideas actually perceived by sense have not a like dependence on my will. When in broad daylight I open my eyes, it is not in my power to choose whether I shall see or not, or to determine what particular objects shall present themselves to my view ... there is therefore some other will or spirit that produces them.

To align with commonsense, Berkeley called those ideas (or those collections) imprinted on the human mind by God *real things*. Contrast this to what happens when you simply imagine or recollect having seen the sun. This idea (or collection) is produced by you, and is under your control – you are said to have *willed* the idea. Notice that when inspected, the imagined sun is not as lively, vivid, distinct, or regular as the seen sun. You can alter it at will. You can make the imagined sun purple, for example, or move on to other things and no longer imagine it. To again align with common-sense, Berkeley wanted to call things like the imagined sun *ideas* or *images of things*. Even so, notice that *both* the seen sun and the imagined sun are collections of ideas, maybe even the same collection. The difference between being a *real thing* and an *image of a real thing* is drawn in terms of the dif-ferences in the liveliness, vivacity, distinctness, and regularity and orderli-ness of objects that are seen, but more importantly, real things are ideas that come to you even *against* your will, while those that are the product of the imagination are completely under your control. Real things are collections of ideas made present to your mind by God; images of things are collections of ideas made present to your mind by your own mind.

Recall that Descartes had said that what had led him to believe that there existed objects "outside" his mind was the fact that they presented them-selves to his mind whether he wanted them presented or not. In the Third Meditation, in talking about his sensory ideas, he said: 3.84

> But in addition I know by experience that these ideas do not depend on my will, and hence that they do not depend simply on me. Frequently I notice them even when I do not want to: now, for example, I feel the heat whether I want to or not, and this is why I think that this sensation or idea of heat comes to me from something other than myself, namely the heat of the fire by which I am sitting. (AT VII 38; CSM II 26)

Whereas Descartes will go on to argue that the origin of the occasion for his sensory ideas are bodies existing independently of his mind, Berkeley, as we know, will reject this. The very idea of matter or material substance on Berkeley's view, understood as something that can exist independently of the mind, is either empty or internally contradictory. Even so, Berkeley saw the need, in aligning his view with commonsense, to provide some account of why it is that some of our ideas really do come to us without our willing them or without our consent. Instead of bodies existing independently of your mind, however, Berkeley claims that it is God who is the origin of the occasion of your sensory ideas. But what is more, and this is important to keep in mind, those very ideas, when they arise in your mind by way of God's willing them, are what Berkeley refers to as *real things*. The sun that you see, the ordinary sun, *is* the real sun. That aligns perfectly with commonsense.

Real things have a regularity or orderliness to them. That regularity has its origin, Berkeley said, in something other than your own mind. *You* are not regulating or ordering the objects that you sense. In the passages just   3.85

quoted from *PHK*, Berkeley had claimed that the mind or spirit doing the regulating and ordering is God, the "Author of Nature." Berkeley wrote:

> The ideas of sense are more strong, lively, and distinct than those of the imagination; they have likewise a steadiness, order, and coherence, and are not excited at random, as those which are the effects of human wills often are, but in a regular train or series, the admirable connection whereof sufficiently testifies the wisdom and benevolence of its Author. Now the set of rules or established methods, wherein the mind we depend on excites in us the ideas of sense, are called the *laws of nature*: and these we learn by experience, which teaches us that such and such ideas are attended with such and such other ideas, in the ordinary course of things. (*PHK*, Part I, Article 30)

In *PHK*, Part I, Article 48, Berkeley would go on to elaborate on the possible objection to his view that if real things are simply collections of ideas, then the entire world ceases to exist when *you* no longer perceive it:

> For although we hold indeed the object of sense to be nothing else but ideas which cannot exist unperceived; yet we may not hence conclude they have no existence except only while they are perceived by us, since there may be some other spirit that perceives them, though we do not. Whenever bodies are said to have no existence without the mind, I would not be understood to mean this or that particular mind, but all minds whatsoever. It does not therefore follow from the foregoing principles, that bodies are annihilated and created every moment, or exist not at all during the intervals between our perception of them. (*PHK*, Part I, Article 48)

When neither you or any other finite mind perceives the tables and chairs in the classroom, it would not follow, Berkeley claimed, that they cease to exist. For, there is another mind that perceives them when finite minds do not – namely, the mind of God. This is the Omni-perceiver.

3.86   Supposing this to be Berkeley's view, there are some conceptual troubles lurking. For example, since God does not sense anything, how is it that God can be said to *perceive* the tables and chairs? Berkeley does not ever really address this issue. But he may not for the simple reason that, according to his theological view, it is not possible to understand how God does anything. After all, it is God we are talking about. Berkeley did mention the notion of an *archetype*, which, together with what he said about the laws of nature, suggests that for God an apple, for example, is an archetype or pattern that God employs when imprinting those ideas on a finite mind, ideas that constitute the object called an *apple*. Since this archetype is used in all cases of imprinting, then there is a sense in which you see the same object as others see. But more importantly, this may be a sense in which God "perceives" an apple. The archetype is not some idea that God perceives, but is rather a pattern that God employs when imprinting ideas on finite minds.

The objective world, then, the world that can (and does) exist indepen-   3.87
dently of your mind (and, more generally, of any finite human mind), is this regular, orderly, series of ideas imprinted by God on the human mind. The *laws of nature* are the patterns of regularity and orderliness we detect in our sensory experience. It is in the form of a law of nature that the human mind is able to get a glimpse of the eternal *will* of God.

Let us close this chapter by making a few comparisons. Descartes had   3.88
held that although all finite things ultimately depend on God for their being and existence, the two kinds of finite substances could (and do) exist independently of one another: *mind* and *body*. Mind and body are really distinct, which means that their natures can be conceived completely independently of one another. Using Descartes's terminology, we can *exclude* the nature of mind from our idea of body and vice versa. Our sensory ideas of bodies are occasioned by actual, mind-independent, bodies. Recall that Descartes's main reason for thinking this is that were something other than bodies directly responsible for occasioning our sensory ideas, God would be a deceiver. For, in gearing us so that we are compelled to believe that bodies are "outside" the mind based upon our sensing them, God would be a deceiver were it really the case that bodies were not "outside" the mind but that instead some other thing – you, some other finite mind, or God – was the origin of those sensory ideas. By contrast, Berkeley rejected the claim that mind and body are really distinct. We cannot exclude the nature of mind from our idea of body, and vice versa. Rather, the best we can do is to *abstract* body from mind. But what is worse, said Berkeley, the very idea of a body, understood as a material substance, is either empty or contradictory. Either way, such an idea is useless to philosophy. As a replacement for body (matter or material substance), Berkeley argued that God is actually the origin of our sensory ideas. Of course, we might wonder how Berkeley will avoid Descartes's claim that the sort of view advocated for by Berkeley led to the unacceptable view that God is a deceiver.

Even so, and this is the thing to stress, both philosophers, although   3.89
they disagree about the nature of the *immediate* origin of our sensory ideas, agree that the metaphysics requires that *something* play the role of origin. Something must account for why it is that the world that we see, touch, hear, smell, and taste is regulated, ordered, and comes to us even against our will. That *something* is the basis for the notion of the "external" world of commonsense – the objective$_2$ world. For Descartes, that

something was body or material substance; for Berkeley, that something was the Omni-perceiver. You might think that Descartes's story better aligns with commonsense, but keep in mind that if Berkeley is right, Descartes's story is either empty or contradictory. So, perhaps we might want to admit simply that Descartes's story is more familiar to us than Berkeley's. But its being more familiar does not make it *better* align with commonsense. The story told to you as a kid about the moon's being made of cheese, or the story that there's a Santa, is familiar too, but, as you now no doubt know, those stories are simply false: the point is that *familiar ≠ true*. You might argue that Berkeley's story seems made up, fabricated, taken from the books of theologians. But, if Berkeley is right, Descartes's story, and the story of anyone who advocates for matter or material substance, is made up, fabricated, taken from the books of dogmatic metaphysicians. Where Berkeley may have a leg up is that his story is not empty or contradictory. For, even Descartes would hold that ultimately God is the origin of the real world, the "external" world, or in our new technical language: the objective$_2$ world.

3.90   But if Berkeley is right, is not God a deceiver? This really is the philosophical rub between the two views. Recall that Descartes had argued that were God, and not body, the origin of his idea of body, then God would be a deceiver. Recall, his argument went something like this: Your idea of body represents to you a thing whose principal attribute (i.e. essential property) is *extension* in length, breadth, and depth. Now, there are only four possible "causes" of this idea, or items whose formal reality could be the origin of this idea's objective reality: (i) the formal reality of your mind, (ii) the formal reality of God's mind, (iii) the formal reality of some finite mind other than your own, or (iv) the formal reality of an extended thing (i.e. body). Now, the trouble with claiming that a *mind* is the origin of the idea of *body* is that the idea must then be understood as falsely representing its "cause." How so? The idea of body represents to you something that is *essentially* extended. A mind is *not* essentially extended (in fact it is not extended at all!), but is instead essentially a thing that *thinks*. So, if the idea truly represented its object, the idea should represent to you a thing that is essentially a thing that thinks – not a thing that is essentially extended (which essentially does *not* think). And so, if a mind were the "cause" of *this* idea, of the idea of *body*, the idea would falsely represent its object (that which "caused" the idea). And, since it is God who ordains that you have the idea of body in such circumstances, God would be a deceiver if the idea, which represents its object as being essentially extended, was something that in fact was not essentially extended. As Descartes would put it:

So, I do see how God could be understood to be anything but a deceiver if the ideas [of bodies] were transmitted from a source other than corporeal things. It follows that corporeal things exist. (Sixth Meditation, AT VII 80; CSM II 55)

It would seem, then, that had Descartes lived long enough to read Berkeley's works, Descartes could have replied that Berkeley is in trouble. For, Berkeley seemed to be claiming that all of our ideas, including the ones representing bodies to us, such as our ideas of apples, are *false* representations of their causes or origins. God is their origin, and yet the vast bulk of our ideas represent to us things that are *not* God – that is, they represent to us things that appear to be colored, hot, smelly, extended, shaped, and so on. Descartes might argue, had he had lived long enough to see the movie *The Matrix*, that Berkeley's God is a deceiver. For, just like the computer in *The Matrix* that produces in the minds of those hooked up to the computer a world that seems material but is not, Berkeley's God produces in you and in all other finite minds a world that seems material but is not. Is there a way for Berkeley to answer this sort of charge? We will entertain a possible answer in the last section of this chapter, to which we now turn.

3.5 Possible Common Ground

Descartes's and Berkeley's metaphysical views look hopelessly at odds with   3.91 one another: Descartes was a dualist, Berkeley was a monist. And although we have yet to consider it in any detail, here is another point of possible disagreement, their epistemological views: Descartes was a rationalist, whereas Berkeley was an empiricist. We will take up this possible epistemological disagreement later in Chapter 5, the chapter on Kant. So, for the moment let us ignore this difference and stick to the metaphysical issue now before us: whether Descartes would be right in thinking that Berkeley's God is a deceiver. What will be suggested in this final subsection is that there may be a way for Descartes and Berkeley to find common ground, so that Berkeley's view does not necessarily fall prey to the charge that God is a deceiver.

3.5.1 Ontological Dependence

On Descartes's view, a primary idea is importantly related to two things: it   3.92 is related (i) to a mind, of which the idea is a mode, and (ii) to some object, whose formal reality is the origin of the idea's objective reality. (i) depicts the basic mode/substance dependence relationship: a mode depends for its existence on the existence of a substance in a way that a substance does not depend for its existence on the existence of any mode. Ideas are modes, and so they depend for their existence on a substance, which for Descartes was a mind, a thing whose principal (that is, essential) attribute was *to think*. (ii) is a bit more complex. It depicts the relationship that holds between an idea's content and the object that this idea represents. For example, the idea of the sun represents the sun and not some other object precisely because the objective reality of the idea has its origin in the formal reality of the sun. In Chapter 1, we referred to the principle that expresses this relationship as a *principle of representation* (PR). We said:

(PR) Primary idea A represents object B only if the objective reality of idea A has its origin in the formal reality of object B.

Even though we have focused on this as a principle of representation, it is for all that a piece of Descartes's ontology. The relationship between the objective reality of an idea and its origin, the formal reality of some object, is an ontological one. In fact, it is as much an ontological dependence relationship as is the relationship between mode and substance.

3.93   We noted in Chapter 1 that Descartes took the idea that represented body (or ideas that represented bodies) to be subject to this principle of representation. He argued in the Sixth Meditation that the objective reality associated with the idea of body must have its origin in the formal reality of body (or bodies). Since formal reality is the kind of reality a thing possesses insofar as it exists, then identifying body (or bodies) as the thing having formal reality (which is taken to be the origin of the idea's objective reality), Descartes was claiming is that body *exists* (or that bodies *exist*).

3.94   But also recall from our discussion in Chapter 1 that both finite mind and body, on Descartes's view, are only considered to be substances insofar as they can exist independently of one another. But neither are substances in the heavy-duty strict sense. God is the only true substance in the heavy-duty strict sense. Both mind and body depend for their existence on the existence of God in a way that God does not depend for God's existence on the existence of mind or body. In fact, it was this sort of view that led Spinoza (1632–1677) to claim that finite minds and bodies are simply modes of God. Now, if we focused on ontological dependence, and ignore the more contemporary notions of *representation*, even Descartes will have to agree that the ultimate origin of our ideas is God. How so? For starters, our ideas are either of God, of finite mind, or of finite body – right? The idea of God, as the Third

Meditation proof for God's existence demonstrated, has its origin in God. So, there's one idea that has its origin directly in God. That's easy. But what about the ideas of finite mind and body? Well, the objective reality of the idea of mind has its origin in the formal reality of a finite mind, and the objective reality of the idea of body has its origin in the formal reality of body (corporeal substance), where the formal reality of both finite mind and body has its origin in the formal reality of God, the infinite substance. So, if we were to trace out the "causal" origin of our ideas, whether understood in terms of their being modes or in terms of their content, we would discover that *ultimately* they originate in God – for all finite things, including ideas, are ultimately ontologically dependent on God. In this very special sense, then, Descartes might be able to agree with Berkeley that God is the ultimate origin or source of our ideas, a sense that might allow Berkeley to avoid the charge that his view looks to entail that God is a deceiver.

But even Descartes admitted that our sensory ideas fail to resemble the 3.95 objects they reportedly represent. For example, the sensory idea of the ice cube presents the ice cube as being cold. But Descartes argued that *cold*, the quality, was nowhere to be found "outside" the mind. As Locke would also later argue, the ice cube, understood as a body, was essentially extended, and in being finite, had some shape or other, had some size or other, and so on. Descartes seems to have thought something like this too. As he put it, the motions of the particles constituting the body that we are calling an "ice cube" affect the motions of the particles constituting one's hand, which in turn, through various nerves, affect the motions of the particles constituting the brain, especially those constituting the fine vapor-like medium referred to as "animal spirits." The motions of this fine matter, via divine institution, occasion certain ideas in the mind – in this case the sensory idea of cold. As Descartes admits, this could suggest to someone that since God had ordained it so that *this* idea (which represents the motions of certain particles of matter but utterly fails to resemble this origin) is the one that comes before the mind, then God is responsible for the false image. This idea is "materially false," Descartes says in the Third Meditation, since it represents the ice cube as having a property (the cold) that it in fact does not have. Descartes is able to avoid this conclusion by arguing that sensory ideas, like the sensory idea of cold, although useful for helping human beings (which are a union of mind and body) to get along safely in the world, do not appear to be meant for revealing the *truth* of things. Feeling heat, for instance, looks to be a better (more efficient) way to get someone to remove his or her hand from the fire than just equipping human beings with purely intellectual ideas. By the time you calculated that the fire would injure your hand if you do not remove it, it might be too late. Feeling pain, at least according to Descartes, looks like an efficient way to gear the human being so that reaction to potential injury is sped up. The point here is that Descartes says that God is not a deceiver simply because God set up human beings to have ideas that do not correlate perfectly with the way the world is. God provided us with the faculty of reason, which is perfectly reliable for acquiring the truth.

3.96   We might charitably lend some version of the above line of reasoning to Berkeley. For example, we might argue that Berkeley does not look to be committed to the view that says that our sensory ideas are the revealers of truth. As they were for Descartes, they may be better understood as a means of making human *action* possible. That is, from a theological point of view, they are simply instrumental and are not the ultimate givers of *truth*. This possible reading of Berkeley, however, requires a serious discussion about the possibility of our having knowledge. And, both Descartes and Berkeley agree that knowledge is possible. So, they have that in common. Where they seem to disagree is *what* exactly makes knowledge possible. Let us now turn to Hume before getting to Kant. We will see that Hume will adopt much of what Berkeley has laid out, but where he differs seems in part to provide to Kant a way to show that there is a sense in which empiricism and rationalism, and monism and dualism, are philosophically compatible. After our look at Kant, we will explore the work of Shepherd, who interestingly shows similarities with all of the philosophers studied here.

Readings

Primary Berkeley Readings

Berkeley, George. (1710) *A Treatise Concerning the Principles of Human Knowledge.* https://www.earlymoderntexts.com/assets/pdfs/berkeley1710.pdf.
Berkeley, George. (1713) *Three Dialogues Between Hylas and Philonous.* https://www.earlymoderntexts.com/assets/pdfs/berkeley1713.pdf.

Secondary Reading

Downing, Lisa. (2013) George Berkeley, *The Stanford Encyclopedia of Philosophy*, Edward N. Zalta (ed.). https://plato.stanford.edu/entries/berkeley/.

4

DAVID HUME

David Hume was born 7 May 1711, in Edinburgh, Scotland. At around 4.1
12 years old, he entered school at the University of Edinburgh. About his
school years, he would later write that he had developed a keen interest in
law. He did not graduate. Without a profession or wife and children to keep
him anchored, Hume traveled, spending a good deal of time in France,
where he had established relationships with several Jesuits connected to the
College of La Flèche, Descartes's alma mater. In 1739, he published *A
Treatise of Human Nature*, which set out to explain the possibility of moral
action by way of an empiricist epistemology. Hume would later claim that
the *Treatise* was a project that he had envisioned even before leaving college. In the early 1740s, Hume sought the academic position of Chair of
Pneumatics and Moral Philosophy at the University of Edinburgh, but was
denied the position. He would later rework the main themes of the *Treatise*,
to make them more palatable for readers, dividing this effort into writing
two books: *An Enquiry Concerning Human Understanding* (1748) and *An
Enquiry Concerning the Principles of Morals* (1751). Enduring several failed
attempts at establishing a career, he eventually landed the position of secretary to the British Embassy, stationed in Paris. He would leave Paris around
1766, accompanying none other than Jean-Jacques Rousseau. This interesting relationship would end bitterly. After settling down nearer home, Hume
was appointed Under Secretary of State for the Northern Department, and
would return to Edinburgh around 1770. His health seemed to be on a
steady decline, and on 25 August 1776, Hume died at home in Edinburgh.
He was 65 years old.

This Is Modern Philosophy: An Introduction, First Edition. Kurt Smith.
© 2023 John Wiley & Sons, Inc. Published 2023 by John Wiley & Sons, Inc.

4.1 Hume on Impressions and Ideas

4.2 Hume's philosophical view was grounded in dividing perceptions into two basic categories: *impressions* and *ideas*. His account of the possibility of our having knowledge required an appeal to both. He would say that the contents of all *ideas* must ultimately be traced to impressions. No ideas (i.e. no ideational contents) were innate. About impressions and ideas he wrote:

> The difference betwixt these consists in the degrees of force and liveliness with which they strike upon the mind, and make their way into our thought or consciousness. Those perceptions, which enter with most force and violence, we may name *impressions*; and under this name I comprehend all our sensations, passions and emotions, as they make their first appearance in the soul. By *ideas* I mean the faint images of these in thinking and reasoning; such as, for instance, are all the perceptions excited by the present discourse, excepting only, those which arise from the sight and touch, and excepting the immediate pleasure or uneasiness it may occasion. (*Treatise*, Book I, Part I, p. 1)

The force or vivacity of an idea, its "liveliness," in some circumstances (such as fever or madness) could approach that associated with our impressions. But, in normal "waking" experience, the difference in force and vivacity associated with impressions was almost always greater than that associated with ideas (Ibid.).

4.3 "The first circumstance, that strikes my eye," Hume would go on to write, "is the great resemblance betwixt our impressions and ideas in every other particular, except their degree of force and vivacity" (*Treatise*, Book I, Part I, Section I, p. 2). If the force and vivacity of an idea ever matched that of an impression, it would be easy to explain how one might mistake the idea for an impression.

4.4 Ideas are what the mind employs when it reasons. Using a familiar philosophical vocabulary of the period, we might say that "impressions" referred in part to our occurring *sensory* experience – vivacious, lively, forceful impressions, striking the mind without its consent – whereas our *intellectual* experience was constituted entirely of ideas, when we reason, when we imagine, when we remember, or, more generally, when we *think*. If our ideas, the items employed when thinking, constituted (in part) what we might call *rationality*, impressions might be taken as *pre*-rational perceptions. We do not think with impressions; we think only with ideas. Even so, without impressions, there would be no ideas.

4.5 Ideas, at least the simplest ones, Hume argued, are such that "all our simple ideas in their first appearance are deriv'd from simple impressions, which are correspondent to them, and which they exactly represent" (Ibid.). Hume would go on to claim that not only do simple ideas correspond and represent the impressions from which they are derived, but also that simple ideas *resemble* their corresponding impressions; so much so, that no distinction on this front between a simple impression and its corresponding simple idea could be intelligibly made. The salient cognizable difference between them was with respect to their relative force and vivacity.

The connection between simple ideas and simple impressions is ever- present before the mind. There is not a single moment of consciousness in which the two (and their connection to one another) are not present. Not so, however, when it comes to complex ideas, ideas whose contents are organized collections of simples. When imagining a fictional city, such as the New Jerusalem, for instance, Hume noted that this was clearly a complex idea that had not been derived directly from any complex impression of the city, since this city did not yet exist (*Treatise*, Book I, Part I, Section I, p. 3). But, he had seen Paris. When he imagined Paris, Hume went on to note, in contrast to the New Jerusalem, this idea, the idea of Paris, *was* derived from a complex impression (his sensory experience of Paris). Even so, this complex idea would not exhibit all of the details of the city, of the streets and houses, and would fall short of the original impression. Thus, for complex ideas, if they are derived from complex impressions, they may not perfectly correspond to or perfectly resemble the latter. 4.6

A simple idea, on the other hand, corresponded in *all* respects (except force and vivacity) to the original simple impression from which it was derived. Hume wrote: 4.7

> Thus we find, that all simple ideas and impressions resemble each other; and as the complex are formed from them, we may affirm in general, that these two species of perception are exactly correspondent. (*Treatise*, Book I, Part I, Section I, p. 4)

Like the complex impression and idea of Paris, the impressions and ideas of other ordinary objects such as tables, chairs, apples, and so on, were "collections" of perceptions. They were complex ideas. Such a collection, upon mental inspection, would reveal a variety of simple perceptions – colors, sounds, smells, and so on. "The complex are the contrary to these [i.e., the simples], and may be distinguished into parts." He would write: "Tho' a particular colour, taste, and smell are qualities all united together in this apple, 'tis easy to perceive they are not the same, but are at least distinguishable from each other" (*Treatise*, Book I, Part I, Section I, p. 2). As for the simples, "Simple perceptions or impressions and ideas are such as admit of no distinction nor separation" (Ibid.). His view seemed to be, then, that if we were to inspect a simple idea of a particular shade of red, say, we would find its content to be utterly uniform with no distinguishable internal differences. By contrast, if we were to inspect the complex idea of an apple, we would find its content to be a collection of widely diverse simples – various shades of colors, smells, taste, feels, and so on. This might remind us a bit of how Berkeley had described his complex idea of an apple, in the *Principles of Human Knowledge*.

4.8   Hume would go on to greatly emphasize the *resemblance* relation that held between simple impressions and simple ideas. He wrote:

> . . . every simple idea has a simple impression, which resembles it; and every simple impression a correspondent idea. That idea of red, which we form in the dark, and that impression, which strikes our eyes in the sun-shine, differ only in degree, not in nature. (*Treatise*, Book I, Part I, Section I, p. 3)

Let us say that we see a red flag. In Hume's terms, we can count this a complex impression. Focus on a uniform region of color we see – on some specific shade of *red* – that inhabits a specific area of the flag. For sake of explanation, let this count as a simple impression. Now, let us say that we return to a dark room and go the extra step of closing our eyes while standing in this dark room. We can recall or remember (here, we would be employing the faculty of memory) what we just saw, namely that red flag. The *red* that we imagine, which is done by bringing the simple idea of this color before the mind, is essentially no different from the *red* we saw – there is no difference in the *nature* of red exhibited in the idea and in the earlier impression. The only difference is that the impression of red was more lively and forceful than our idea, the latter the item the mind was employing when imagining. Of course, this account assumes that our memory of the seen color is trustworthy. More on *trust* shortly.

4.9   Not only was there a difference between impressions and ideas with respect to their relative force and vivacity, but Hume explained that there must also be a difference between ideas themselves on this front. For instance, he discussed how it was that, strictly speaking, one's *memory* was different from one's *imagination* in part by an appeal to the differing degrees of force and vivacity of ideas. He wrote:

> 'Tis evident at first sight, that the ideas of the memory are much more lively and strong than those of the imagination, and that the former faculty paints its

objects in more distinct colours, than any which are employ'd by the latter. When we remember any past event, the idea of it flows in upon the mind in a forcible manner; whereas in the imagination the perception is faint and languid, and cannot without difficulty be preserv'd by the mind steddy [sic] and uniform for any considerable time. (*Treatise*, Book I, Part I, Section III, p. 9)

When one remembers some event, one takes the remembered event to have been an event that one had *actually* experienced. It is not taken as something simply hoped for or conjured up by way of a daydream. Hume accounted for this fact by attributing to the ideas employed by the faculty of memory a greater force and vivacity than, say, the ideas employed by the faculty of the imagination. Although not perfectly clear, Hume's view seemed to be that the faculty of memory, the faculty itself, contributed to increasing the force and vivacity of an idea. In the above passage, Hume suggests that the faculty of memory had some hand in its ideas having greater force and vivacity, by "painting its objects" in more distinct or vibrant colors, where the force and vivacity would run closer to that found in impressions. Even so, it does not seem to be Hume's view that the faculty of memory, for instance, works in a domain of ideas distinct from that in which the imagination works. Both faculties appear to operate over the same domain. That a faculty could enhance an idea's force and vivacity might explain how it was that such ideas would compel the mind to hold that the events *remembered* are more "true" or more "real" than those simply *imagined*. The more force and vivacity associated with or imparted to an idea, the more *influence* it could have on a mind when it thinks. Any *trust* or confidence one would have in their memory would amount to the force and vivacity of the ideas brought before the mind.

When Hume cast simple ideas as having been *derived from* their corre- 4.10 sponding simple impressions, the justification, as already suggested, seemed to have been based on their respective *order*, when each made its first appearance in the mind. Hume would write:

. . . every simple impression is attended with a correspondent idea, and every simple idea with a correspondent impression. From this constant conjunction of resembling perceptions I immediately conclude, that there is a great connexion betwixt our correspondent impressions and ideas, and that the existence of the one has a considerable influence upon that of the other. Such a constant conjunction, in such an infinite number of instances, can never arise from chance; but clearly proves a dependence of the impressions on the ideas, or of the ideas on the impressions. That I may know on which side this dependence lies, I consider the order of their *first appearance*; and find by constant experience, that the simple impressions always take the precedence of their corresponding ideas, but never appear in the contrary order. To give a child an idea of scarlet or orange, of sweet or bitter, I present the objects, or in other words, convey to him these impressions; but proceed not so absurdly, as to endeavor to produce the impressions by exciting the ideas. Our ideas upon their appearance produce not their correspondent impressions, nor do we perceive any colour, or feel any sensation merely upon thinking of them. On the other hand we find, that any impressions either of the mind or body is constantly followed by an idea, which resembles it, and is only different in the degrees of force and liveliness. The constant conjunction of our resembling perceptions, is a convincing proof, that the one are the causes of the other; and this priority of the impressions is an equal proof, that our impressions are the causes of our ideas, not our ideas of our impressions. (*Treatise*, Book I, Part I, Section I, pp. 4–5)

This passage is important, since it foreshadows everything to follow in our discussion dealing with Hume's notions of cause and effect and his account of the common belief in the existence of an external world, of a world that exists independent of the mind. Let us start with Hume's account of the idea of cause and effect.

4.2 The Idea of Cause and Effect

4.11   Early in the *Treatise*, Hume challenged the reader to identify an impression from which the idea of *cause* was derived. The challenge was rhetorical, for he in fact did not expect anyone to point out such an impression. According to him, there was no such impression. Instead, he argued, all we will find when inspecting this idea is that it is a rather complex idea forged in the imagination, based on our experience, past and present. Specifically, the complex idea would be found to greatly emphasize the constant conjunction of specific impressions and ideas.

4.12   For example, let us say that someone holds an ice cube in his or her hand. Immediately, they feel a coldness in their palm. If this happened only once in this person's life, where the force and vivacity of the impressions were not noticeably greater than usual, the experience might be forgotten. But, let us say that this is something that happens more than once – more than 1000 times. The memory of each episode – the idea of holding the ice cube followed immediately by the idea of cold (each originating from their respective impression) – would find its way to the imagination, which would begin to forge the separate episodes or instances of experience into a pattern of cognition; in this case, the pattern of the perception of holding an ice cube-like object followed by a perception of an intense cold-like feeling. The greater the number of repeated episodes, the more force and vivacity is imparted to this developing complex idea (as part of the imagination's forging process). The level of force and vivacity of this complex idea can grow to be greater than any of the original episodic paired ideas taken separately, where a new experience (a new impression) of holding an ice cube-like object will trigger the forceful complex idea of the imagination-forged pattern, bringing it before the mind, which will result in the *expectation* of having an intense cold-like feeling. This expectation would be nothing short of the expression of what Hume would call *custom* or *habit*.

Hume's account of *belief* was similar to the above account about cause and effect: a belief is an idea (or a complex of ideas) that has a great force and vivacity associated with it, certainly greater than that associated with a typical simple or complex idea. For a belief, the idea's force and vivacity comes about as described above, by way of the imagination's accumulating similar episodes and then forging a complex idea that represents some pattern of perception. Like an impression, a belief, or a very lively and forceful idea (or idea complex), will command the mind's attention. As Hume would put it: "An opinion, therefore, or belief may be most accurately defin'd, A LIVELY IDEA RELATED TO OR ASSOCIATED WITH A PRESENT IMPRESSION" (*Treatise*, Book I, Part III, Section VII, p. 95). The more the belief fit in with the rest of one's lived experience, that is, the better it aligned with one's natural, everyday life, the more "entire" would be its ability to compel. "Belief," Hume would write, "being a lively conception, can never be entire, where it is not founded on something natural and easy" (*Treatise*, Book I, Part IV, Section I, p. 186). 4.13

Hume provided a working definition of a *cause*: 4.14

> We may define a CAUSE to be "An object precedent and contiguous to another, and where all the objects resembling the former are plac'd in like relations of precedency and contiguity to those objects, that resemble the latter." (*Treatise*, Book I, Part III, Section XIV, p. 170)

Here, instead of referring to the relation between an impression and an idea, or to the relation between an idea and an idea, or, more generally, to the relation between two perceptions, Hume specifically referred to "objects," where one *object* was said to precede and to be contiguous with (i.e. "next to" in terms of space or time) another, the former taken to be the cause of the latter. We will take a closer look at *object*-talk in a moment. For now, let us keep focused on the idea of cause and effect.

4.15   There is more to the relation of cause and effect than resemblance, precedence, and contiguity. There is the element of *constant conjunction*. The two objects appear to the mind *always* conjoined, the one following the other in terms of priority. Hume would argue that previous philosophers had wrongly attributed this constancy to the objects themselves, where that constancy had ultimately been declared a form of *necessity*: causes necessarily produce their effects, and effects necessarily follow from their causes. Hume took this to be wrong in that the *necessity* was not something revealed through our impressions and ideas as some metaphysical attribute of the relation between objects. Instead, the *necessity*, if one insisted on calling it that, had its origin in cognition itself. The objects of perception did not reveal anything we might identify as *necessity* holding between *them*, and no single impression was the source of the idea of necessity. Instead, necessity emerged from an activity of the mind. *Necessity* was akin to the previously mentioned expression of psychological expectation. Hume wrote:

> For after we have observ'd the resemblance in a sufficient number of instances, we immediately feel a determination of the mind to pass from one object to its usual attendant, and to conceive it in a stronger light upon account of that relation. This determination is the only effect of the resemblance; and therefore must be the same with power or efficacy, whose idea is deriv'd from the resemblance. The several instances of resembling conjunctions leads us into the notion of power and necessity. These instances are in themselves totally distinct from each other, and have no union but in the mind, which observes them, and collects their ideas. Necessity, then, is the effect of this observation, and is nothing but an internal impression of the mind, or a determination to carry our thoughts from one object to another . . .. Upon the whole, necessity is something, that exists in the mind, not in objects . . .. (*Treatise*, Book I, Part III, Section XIV, p. 165)

The mistake of previous philosophers, Hume argued, was that they had failed to see that the necessity they attributed to causation was something that their own minds had imparted to the objects perceived. Hume characterized the act as an act of *transfer*: the mind transfers the expectation of a pattern the mind "feels" to the *objects* perceived. He wrote:

> This is the case, when we transfer the determination of the thought to external objects, and suppose any real intelligible connexion betwixt them; that being a quality, which can only belong to the mind that considers them. (*Treatise*, Book I, Part III, Section XIV, p. 168)

Hume rested on two definitions of causation, which on his view ultimately amounted to making the same claim:

Cause: Definition 1
. . . [A]*n object precedent and contiguous to another, and where all the objects resembling the former are plac'd in a like relation of priority and contiguity to those objects that resemble the latter.* (*Treatise*, Book I, Part III, Section VIX, p. 172)

Cause: Definition 2
. . . *An object precedent and contiguous to another, and so united with it in the imagination, that the idea of the one determines the mind to form the idea of the other, and the impression of the one to form a more lively idea of the other . . ..* (Ibid.)

So, what is the relevance of Hume's notion of causation to our study? The answer is that Hume understood the notion to be related to his explanation of how we come to believe that there is an "external" world, a world that exists independent of the mind.

Early in the *Treatise*, Hume had claimed:

We readily suppose an object may continue individually the same, tho' several times absent from and present to the senses; and ascribe to it an identity, not withstanding the interruption of the perception, whenever we conclude, that if we had kept our eye or hand constantly upon it, it wou'd have convey'd an invariable and uninterrupted perception. But this conclusion beyond the impressions or our senses can be founded only on the connexion of cause and effect . . .. (*Treatise*, Book I, Part III, Section II, p. 74)

He would make a similar claim later in the *Treatise*:

For as all our reasonings concerning existence are deriv'd from causation, and as all our reasonings concerning causation are dervi'd from the experience'd conjunction of objects, not from any reasoning of reflexion, the same experience must give us a notion of these objects . . .. (*Treatise*, Book I, Part III, Section XV, p. 172)

Hume developed several concepts that played important roles in his account of the belief that a material world exists independent of the mind. They in turn would find their way into Shepherd's account. So, they are worth considering, if only briefly, before turning to our study of Shepherd (in Chapter 6). The procession of concepts to be discussed in what follows will be introduced in this order: *Object, Existence, Unity, Identity, Constancy, Coherence, Continued Existence,* and *Distinct Existence.*

4.3 Object and Existence

4.16 Hume used the word "object" when referring to whatever the mind was aware of at a given moment. Thus, if one perceives the color *red*, the "object" is the red. If, one perceives an apple, the "object" is the apple. Strictly speaking, objects are *perceptions*. As Hume would put it:

> We may observe, that 'tis universally allow'd by philosophers, and is besides pretty obvious of itself, that nothing is ever really present with the mind but its perceptions or impressions and ideas, and that external objects become known to us only by those perceptions they occasion. (*Treatise*, Book I, Part II, Section VI, p. 67)

As is suggested here, if one considered what philosophers "universally" allow, one would be indirectly aware of the apple, in this case an "external object," by way of being directly aware of the perceptions that this apple occasioned. The phrase "external object," however, would be problematic according to Hume's assessment, since it would presumably denote a perception (an "object") that was not perceived, the latter expressed by the word "external." The phrase amounted to expressing a contradiction. For, it amounted to saying that a perception, the existence of which depends on a mind, nevertheless existed independently of the mind. More on that shortly.

4.17   Hume's account of objecthood, for lack of a better name, is more subtle than it first appears. To be sure, we can say that one perceives an apple, where the apple is a collection of perceptions. If that sounds familiar, it is because we learned something similar when studying Berkeley. According to Hume's assessment, philosophers and the vulgar (common persons) would hold that they are aware of more than simply some collection of perceptions. The apple, they would say, is a thing, an object, that exists and possesses various properties or characteristics – for example, the apple is red, the apple is cool, the apple is smooth, the apple is sweet, and so on. Commonsense has no "theory" about the matter. It simply holds that the apple is an object which is red, smooth, sweet, etc. The apple they perceive is nothing other than the "real" apple. There is no substantive difference between the two. Philosophy, however, goes a bit farther, which, according to Hume, would lead it into making certain questionable claims. For instance, philosophy would not only agree that the apple possesses certain properties or characteristics, it would also claim that the apple was a thing that was the totality of properties *and* an underlying substrate, the latter being that in which the properties adhered. Such a substance can and does exist independently of its being perceived. It is what philosophers ultimately think they are referring to when speaking about "external" objects.

Hume would argue that this philosophical notion of *substance*, the abovementioned underlying substrate, is problematic. For starters, the notion would tell us that a substance, in being the underlying substrate, would itself lack characteristics. The properties that adhere in it are the characteristics. Colors, shapes, tastes, and the like, are properties or charac-teristics (or as Descartes would call them "modes") which presumably adhere in a substance. Ontologically speaking, properties or modes depend for their existence on the existence of the underlying substance. But such properties were not essential to the underlying substrate. It could presum-ably exist on its own, propertyless, though in such cases minds would not be able to perceive (or even conceive) it – for, minds perceive (or conceive) only the apple's properties. As Locke would puzzlingly note, contrary to a property, a substance was *a something I know not what*. Descartes, as we know, identified extension as the principal attribute (property) of body. Minus this attribute, he argued, this substance would be unintelligible. 4.18

According to Hume's analysis of this sort of view: 4.19

> The idea of a substance as well as that of a mode, is nothing but a collection of simple ideas, that are united by the imagination, and have a particular name assigned them, by which we are able to recall, either to ourselves or others, that collection. (*Treatise*, Book I, Part I, Section VI, p. 16)

As suggested in this passage, Hume would explain that even the philoso-pher's idea of a substance was initially derived from the workings of the imagination. It was not an idea derived from any impression. This initial idea of the philosophers, forged in the imagination, was nothing other than that held by the vulgar, said Hume, though unlike their philosophical coun-terparts, they were not compelled to go the extra step and claim that the apple was a substance, a something they know not what. For the vulgar, the apple was simply the ordinary thing they see, the thing they hold, the thing they eat, it is a thing they desire (if hungry). There is no talk of substrates and modes; there is no talk of ontological dependence relations. In the above quoted passage, Hume in fact seemed to be rejecting the philosophical claim that underneath the properties was a substance, a something we know not what. For him, at best, philosophers would be better off if they realized that all they could really denote by "substance" was a collection of perceptions, a collection of items perceived by the mind, which have been united by the imagination into a single, recognizable *thing*, which we call an "apple."

4.20   In several places throughout the *Treatise*, Hume confirmed this view, which, by his own admission, was consistent with at least one claim made by philosophers, and would in fact be necessary, he said, in any attempt to explain the view of the vulgar, namely, the view that "our perceptions are our only objects" (*Treatise*, Book I, Part IV, Section II, p. 213). Here, it is worth noting that Hume would speak of objects and perceptions as one and the same entities, where both were further classified as either ideas or impressions. Whether seeing *an apple*, having the *impression of an apple*, or having the *idea of an apple*, Hume was talking about one and the same sort of *object* – the apple *perceived*. Each instance could be recast as a mind's engagement with its *perceptions*. All objects, the *only* objects, of which the mind was aware were understood by Hume to be perceptions. Whether one eats the apple, sees the apple, thinks about the apple, remembers the apple, and so on, one's mind, generally speaking, perceives one and the same sort of item – a *perception*, which, with respect to the example now under discussion, we call "apple." The salient difference between the aforementioned items would be the force and vivacity associated with each; the difference would not be in terms of what is *presented*, for each collection of simples (sometimes a collection of simple impressions, sometimes a collection of simple ideas) would be that which we refer to by the name "apple" (see *Treatise*, Book I, Part IV, Section II, p. 202).

4.21   Hume understood there to be no distinction between a *perception*, a *perception of a thing*, and *existence*. This may remind you of what Berkeley had said in the *Principles of Human Knowledge*. In the *Treatise*, Hume would write:

> The idea of existence, then, is the very same with the idea of what we conceive to be existent. To reflect on any thing simply, and to reflect on it as existent, are nothing different from each other. That idea, when conjoin'd with the idea of any object, makes no addition to it. Whatever we conceive, we conceive to be existent. (*Treatise*, Book I, Part II, Section VI, pp. 66–67)

4.22   On this view, the *perception* of an apple and the *existence* of that apple were one and the same. Even so, Hume also recognized a notion of existence that was lurking in philosophy, something he had referred to as *external existence*, mentioned earlier, which, on his view, others had wrongly attributed to objects, to things existing independent of the mind.

4.23   The addition of "external" here (for both "external *existence*" and "external *object*"), Hume argued, appeared to indicate that the thing that purportedly existed did so *independent* of the mind and its perceptions. Thus, strictly speaking, an external object would be one that not only was not perceived by a mind, but *could not* be perceived by the mind. This would include our even thinking about such a thing. For, in not being a perception, and assuming that the only objects of which a mind is aware are its perceptions, such an object could not ever be something perceived (or thought) by a mind. One could not even entertain or consider the existence of such an object, for in doing so, one would be entertaining or considering a *perception*. An example of this line of reasoning was given in Part II, Section VI:

> Now since nothing is ever present to the mind but perceptions, and since all ideas are deriv'd from something antecedently present to the mind; it follows, that 'tis impossible for us so much as to conceive or form an idea of any thing specifically different from ideas and impressions. (*Treatise*, Book I, Part II, Section VI, p. 67)

That which preceded an idea, as we know, was an impression. Talk of impressions would be as far as we could go with any talk of objects. There could be no meaningful object-talk beyond (prior to) talk of impressions. As noted earlier, this view might remind you a little of Berkeley's, which, recall, had forwarded the now-famous claim: *to be is to be perceived*.

4.4 Unity and Identity

Perceiving an apple is coextensive with our having a complex perception 4.24
(or collection of perceptions), where the name "apple" denoted this complex perception. This perception presents a single, unified object – an apple. This unity (of the collection of perceptions) is forged in the imagination, where the imagination in turn "recommends" to the mind that what it perceives is a single object. This is how we arrive at the idea of a *unity*. But, this is not enough to account for the idea of *identity*. Hume wrote:

> . . . As to the principle of individuation; we may observe, that the view of any one object is not sufficient to convey the idea of identity. For in that proposition, *an object is the same with itself*, if the idea express'd by the word, *object*, were no way distinguish'd from that meant by *itself*; we really shou'd mean nothing, nor wou'd the proposition contain a predicate and a subject, which however are imply'd in this affirmation. One single object conveys the idea of unity, not that of identity. (*Treatise*, Book I, Part IV, Section II, p. 200)

That said, the idea of identity is also not made by simply considering *multi-* 4.25
ple instances (or perceptions) of objects. Hume continued:

. . . a multiplicity of objects can never convey this idea, however resembling they may be suppos'd. The mind always pronounces the one not to be the other, and considers them as forming two, three, or any determinate number of objects, whose existences are entirely distinct and independent . . . . Since then both number and unity are incompatible with the relation of identity, it must lie in something that is neither of them. (Ibid.)

4.26 Hume suggested that to resolve the matter, we should consider the idea of time or duration. He wrote:

I have already observ'd, that time, in a strict sense, implies succession, and that when we apply its idea to any unchangeable object, 'tis only by a fiction of the imagination, by which the unchangeable object is suppos'd to participate of the changes of the co-existent objects, and in particular of that of our perceptions. This fiction of the imagination almost universally takes place; and 'tis by means of it, that a single object, plac'd before us, and survey'd for any time without our discovering in it any interruption or variation, is able to give us the notion of identity. For when we consider any two points of this time, we may place them in different lights: We may either survey them at the very same instant; in which case they give us the idea of number, both by themselves and by the object; which must be multiply'd, in order to be conceiv'd at once, as existent in these two different points of time: Or on the other hand, we may trace the succession of time by a like succession of ideas, and conceiving first one moment, along with the object then existent, imagine afterwards a change in the time without any variation or interruption in the object; in which case it gives us the idea of unity. By this means we make a difference, betwixt the idea meant by the word, *object*, and that meant by *itself*, with going the length of number, and at the same time without restraining ourselves to a strict and absolute unity . . . . Thus the principle of individuation is nothing but the *invariableness* and *uninterrupted-ness* of any object, thro' a suppos'd variation of time, by which the mind can trace it in the different periods of its existence, without any break of the view, and without being oblig'd to form the idea of multiplicity or number. (Ibid.)

4.27   Think back to our chapter on Descartes. There, recall, in the Second Meditation, Descartes had analyzed his experience of a piece of wax. When he put it on the hearth of his fireplace, the wax had a particular shape, a particular color, fragrance, and so on. But after some time had passed, he noted that all those particular qualities were no longer perceived. Instead, a strikingly differ-ent set of qualities were now perceived. He asked why it was that he was com-pelled to think that this was in fact *one and the same* body. Reason would appear to dictate that the object he had placed on the hearth was *not* the same object he had later perceived, after having returned his attention to the hearth.

Now, in light of Hume's analysis given in the above passages, when 4.28
Descartes, say, was perceiving the wax at t_1, it was perceived as a thing, as a
unified *object*, not simply as a collection of qualities. Using Hume's terminology, Descartes had perceived the wax as a *unity*. So far, so good. We
should note that whereas Descartes had attributed this insight to reason,
Hume, as he does in the above passages, deferred to the imagination. But,
leaving that aside, and returning to the case at hand, at a later time, call it t_3,
Descartes had turned his attention to an object on the hearth, and, as before,
perceived the object as a *unity*. He compared his perceptions, had at t_1 and
t_3 (clearly the perception at t_1 is now the *memory* of the perception at t_1),
and noted that they presented very different objects (in terms of their having very different qualities or properties). In light of Hume's assessment,
Descartes, in considering his perceptions side-by-side, so to speak, at a single moment of cognition, was no longer engaging the idea of unity, but was
instead now engaging the idea of *number* – here, there were *two* things
being considered: the object at t_1 and the object at t_3. Neither the idea of
unity nor the idea of number is coextensive with the idea of identity.

Descartes's question was: on what grounds was he justified in thinking that 4.29
these were *not* two distinct objects, but instead was *one and the same* object?
In Hume's terms, Descartes was engaged in a philosophical search for the idea
of *identity*. Hume's account, given in the passages quoted above, gives us some
clue as to how that search would proceed. The gist of the account required
that we first perceive a unity, which required that this object not suffer any
variation and would be perceived uninterrupted. With respect to the latter, a
"fiction" arises, said Hume, a recommendation from the imagination, that the
object (the perception), a unity, has remained *the same with itself* over the
period of time perceived, where the *only* change was time. Of course,
Descartes might reply by noting that the body (the wax) remained itself insofar as it was extended. But, Hume might respond in return that although that
may account for the object or objects in question remaining *bodies*, it would
not account for the claim that it was the *same* body over time.

4.5 Constancy, Coherence, Continued Existence, and Distinct Existence

According to Hume: 4.30

> . . . philosophy informs us, that every thing, which appears to the mind, is
> nothing but a perception, and is interrupted, and dependent on the mind;

whereas the vulgar confound perceptions and objects, and attribute a distinct continu'd existence to the very things they feel or see. This sentiment, then, as it is entirely unreasonable, must proceed from some other faculty than the understanding. (*Treatise*, Book I, Part IV, Section II, p. 193)

Reason determines from experience that perceptions are ever-changing. Just walk around a table, and the table's shape changes, the colors that constitute its surface change, and so on. Even so, no one believes that from moment to moment they are perceiving a multitude of similar though distinct objects. This is so, said Hume, because the mind itself takes the table to be a single, unified thing, taking this object to be the same table over the span of time perceived. This is something "recommended" by the imagination, where the idea of the table as a persistent, unified *object* is forged. The imagination synthesizes the "moments" of perception into a single thing – the table.

4.31   But here's the rub: as one walks around the table, looks at it, one's eyes blink. The perception (of the table) at t_1 and the perception (of the table) at t_3 are interrupted by the perception (of black) at t_2. Of course, interruptions can be greater in duration than these short intervals. One leaves the room for an hour and returns. Even so, this interruption and that of the tiny interruptions (when blinking) are basically the same – interruptions of perceptions (of the table). Reason counts such interruptions to be instances of annihilation. That is, the perception at t_1, once gone, is no longer. For, a perception *exists* only *when* perceived. It has been replaced with another, distinct, impression at t_2; which, in turn is replaced with another at t_3. What rational grounds does one have for thinking that the perception at t_1 and the perception at t_3 are identical? Identity, recall, looked to require that there was no variation and no interruption. The span of time, from t_1 to t_3, not only includes variation, but they are also interrupted (by the perception at t_2). Are not the perceptions at t_1 and t_3 distinct then, and not identical? According to Hume, philosophers (and reason) should answer that they *cannot* be identical! The perception at t_1 is nowhere to be found at t_3.

4.32   But, the imagination recommends the opposite, namely that the objects perceived at t_1 and at t_3 *are* identical – it is one and the same table that one perceives over that span of time. About this, Hume wrote:

We shall afterwards see many instances of this tendency of relation to make us ascribe an *identity* to *different* objects; but shall here confine ourselves to the present subject. We find by experience, that there is such a *constancy* in almost all the impressions of the senses, that their interruption produces no alteration on them, and hinders them not from returning the same in appearance and in situation as at their first existence. I survey the furniture of my chamber; I shut my eyes, and afterwards open them; and find the new perceptions to resemble perfectly those, which formerly struck my senses. This resemblance is observ'd in a thousand instances, and naturally connects together our ideas of these interrupted perceptions by the strongest relation, and conveys the mind with an easy transition from one to another. An easy transition or passage of the imagination, along the ideas of these different and interrupted perceptions, is almost the same disposition of mind with that in which we consider one constant and uninterrupted perception. (*Treatise*, Book I, Part IV, Section II, p. 204)

Both the idea of *unity* and the idea of *identity* are products of the imagination, where despite the apparent continual change of perceptions (shapes, colors, etc.), the imagination nevertheless "recommends" that these are alterations of one and the same thing – so long as there is no variation or interruption. One might think that the changes of shapes and colors might count as variation (as happened in the case of Descartes's wax), especially in the case of continually perceiving something over some duration of time, even if no interruption is detected. But, why not think that at the very moment we perceive even the subtlest change of color, or slight change of shape, that what we perceive is a *new* object, and no longer the object perceived moments prior?

We might think, then, that even the most minute changes would violate the criteria for unity and identity. But, as Hume suggested in the above passage and elsewhere, the *resemblance* between a perceived color at one moment, say, and the perceived color at the next, is so powerful a relation that it helps the mind (via the imagination) "slide along the succession" (Ibid.), where the change goes undetected (or it is ignored). As just noted, these "micro" changes are in principle no different (for the imagination) from the "micro" interruptions. As he said in the above passage, what the imagination does with respect to creating the fiction of a single object that persists as one and the same over some duration of time, is similar to what the imagination does with respect to creating the fiction of a single object that exists unperceived during any interruptions. 4.33

Hume would go on to argue that is precisely what the imagination suggests to the mind, contrary to the fact that perceptions *are* interrupted. 4.34

An interrupted appearance to the senses implies not necessarily an interruption in the existence. The supposition of the continu'd existence of sensible objects or perceptions involves no contradiction. (*Treatise*, Book I, Part IV, Section II, pp. 207–208)

This "suggestion" by the imagination runs counter to reason, and to the logical criteria for identity. Even so, the imagination might be better understood here as in fact trying to resolve the contradiction between the fact of interruption of perception and the tendency to hold that, despite the interruption, we perceive the same objects over time. Despite the interruptions, our tendency is to think that the table we see upon returning to the room is the same table we saw when in the room earlier. About this, Hume wrote:

> We may easily indulge our inclination to that supposition. When the exact resemblance of our perceptions make us ascribe to them an identity, we may remove the seeming interruption by feigning a continu'd being, which may fill those intervals, and preserve a perfect and entire identity to our perceptions. (Ibid.)

The "feigning" of a continued being, of an object that exists even when not perceived, would appear to resolve the contradiction, the latter related to the contradiction expressed by the phrase "external existence."

4.35   In addition to *constancy*, a concept rooted in *resemblance*, Hume would consider another concept – *coherence*. He would write:

> After a little examination, we shall find, that all those objects, to which we attribute a continu'd existence, have a peculiar *constancy*, which distinguishes them from the impressions, whose existence depends upon our perception. Those mountains, and houses, and trees, which lie at present under my eye, have always appear'd to me in the same order: and when I lose sight of them by shutting my eyes or turning my head, I soon after find them return upon me without the least alteration ... [Even so] ... Bodies often change their position and qualities, and after a little absence or interruption may become hardly knowable. But here 'tis observable, that even in these changes they preserve a *coherence*, and have a regular dependence on each other; which is the foundation of a kind of reasoning from causation, and produces the opinion [belief] of their continu'd existence. When I return to my chamber after an hour's absence, I find not my fire in the same situation, in which I left it: But then I am accustom'd in other instances to see a like alteration produc'd in a like time, whether I am present or absent, near or remote. This coherence, therefore, in their changes is one of the characteristics of external objects, as well as their constancy ... [in this way] continu'd existence of body depends on the COHERENCE and CONSTANCY of certain impressions .... (*Treatise*, Book I, Part IV, Section II, p. 194–195)

In other places, Hume would claim that this natural "hypothesis," that there are bodies that exist not only between the interruptions of our perceptions, but even if not perceived at all, looked to serve as the best explanation for the constancy and coherence we observe (see *Treatise*, Book I, Part IV, Section II, p. 212).

The claim of reason and the strong recommendation of the imagination 4.36 stand in internal conflict. Hume's clearest account of the resolution of this conflict is provided in Section II, with which, as we shall see, Shepherd takes issue. He wrote:

> In order to set ourselves at ease in this particular, we contrive a new hypothesis, which seems to comprehend both these principles of reason and imagination. This hypothesis is the philosophical one of the double existence of perceptions and objects; which pleases our reason, in allowing, that our dependent perceptions are interrupted and different; and at the same time is agreeable to the imagination, in attributing a continu'd existence to something else, which we call *objects*. This philosophical system, therefore, is the monstrous offspring of two principles, which are contrary to each other, which are both at once embrac'd by the mind, and which are unable mutually to destroy each other. The imagination tells us, that our resembling perceptions have a continu'd existence and uninterrupted existence, and are not annihilated by their absence. Reflection tells us, that even our resembling perceptions are interrupted in their existence, and different from each other. The contradiction betwixt these opinions we elude by a new fiction, which is conformable to the hypothesis both of reflection and fancy, by ascribing these contrary qualities to different existences; the *interruption* to perceptions, and the *continuance* to objects. (*Treatise*, Book I, Part IV, Section II, p. 215)

Thus, for Hume, *continued existence* is an hypothesis, so to speak, that the mind forwards as a way to resolve the conflict between what reason claims and what the imagination recommends. Once the idea of continued existence is in play, Hume noted that the idea of distinct existence was not far off. The latter, the idea of distinct existence, was derived from continued existence, where the emphasis is on an object's *independence* of the mind (*Treatise*, Book I, Part IV, Section II, p. 188). Such an object is taken to be able to exist independently of the operations of the mind.

The philosophy of "double existence" is the view that our perceptions, 4.37 which are a kind of object, are ultimately the effects of another kind of object, presumably a material object, that is the cause of our perceptions. When having sensory experience, the two kinds of object exist simultaneously. Even so, material objects are taken to exist whether perceived or not. That they are taken to be *material* is presumably part of the move to divorce them from being *mental*. That way, as even Descartes would contend, conceptual ground has been prepared for the claim that such objects can exist independently of the mind. The double-existence "hypothesis" apparently serves a greater purpose: it eases the mind with respect to the looming contradiction that arises between reason and the imagination.

4.38   At the opening of Section II, Hume wrote about the human being:

> Nature has not left this to his choice, and has doubtless esteem'd it an affair of too great importance to be trusted to our uncertain reasonings and speculations. We may well ask, *What causes induce us to believe in the existence of body?* But 'tis in vain to ask, *Whether there be body or not?* That is a point, which we must take for granted in all our reasoning. (*Treatise*, Book I, Part IV, Section II, p. 187)

So, how does this "hypothesis" become a belief? Hume argued, as seen in the above passage, that this hypothesis was so strong in its ability to put the mind at ease, that it forces itself on the mind, despite the fact that reason can call it into question (but only while doing activities like philosophy). Nature, he said, would always in time eventually bring the mind back to this "belief" whether it liked it or not. Hume's view is this: that human beings believe there exists a world external to their experience is not a mistake, but is in fact a feature of human nature.

Readings

Primary Hume Readings

Hume, David. (1739) *Treatise of Human Nature*, Analytical Index by L.A. Selby-Bigge, revised text and notes by P.H. Nidditch, Oxford: Oxford University Press, 1978. https://oll-resources.s3.us-east-2.amazonaws.com/oll3/store/titles/342/0213_Bk.pdf.

Secondary Reading

Morris, William Edward & Brown, Charlette R. (2019) David Hume, in *Stanford Encyclopedia of Philosophy*. https://plato.stanford.edu/entries/hume/.

5

IMMANUEL KANT

Immanuel Kant was born on 22 April 1724, in Königsberg (East Prussia). He 5.1
attended the University of Königsberg, where he studied philosophy. He was
exposed to the philosophical work of Christian Wolff (1679–1750), who was
a widely known scholar of the philosophical work of Gottfried Leibniz (1646–
1716). According to biographers, Kant was greatly influenced by Martin
Knutzen (1713–1751), who exposed Kant to the works of Wolff, the (British)
philosopher John Locke (1632–1704), and the (British) natural philosopher,
Isaac Newton (1642–1727). Unlike many philosophers of this period, Kant
was a professional academic. He taught philosophy at the University in
Königsberg (the Albertina) for 40 years, retiring in 1796. He was 72 years old.
He published the first of his most famous works, the *Critique of Pure Reason*,
when he was 57. He died 12 February 1804. He was 79.

5.1 Kant's Critical Period

Kant's *Critique of Pure Reason* (hereafter *CPR*) is an important book in the 5.2
history of Western philosophy. The principal question that it asks is: Can
human beings have knowledge that is not derived solely or completely
from sensory experience? The answer to this question, Kant said, "will
therefore decide as to the possibility or impossibility of metaphysics in
general" (*CPR*, "Preface to First Edition," A xii, p. 9). Traditionally understood, as we learned in Chapter 1, metaphysical knowledge was thought to
provide the knower with something that was necessarily true (it could not
be false), and just as importantly, its truth was knowable independently of

This Is Modern Philosophy: An Introduction, First Edition. Kurt Smith.
© 2023 John Wiley & Sons, Inc. Published 2023 by John Wiley & Sons, Inc.

the particulars of sensory experience. It was understood to be knowledge of the conditions that underwrite the very possibility of the everyday and familiar world. So, as Kant would make clearer in a relatively short book he wrote in response to critics of *CPR*, the *Prolegomena to Any Future Metaphysics* (1783), and in the Second Edition of *CPR* that soon followed, the central question of *CPR* is:

Is metaphysics possible?

As we will see, Kant's answer to this was: Yes.

5.3　　There is a lot going on in *CPR*, too much to work through in a single chapter. Our plan therefore will be to use our focus on the Problem of the External World to help us narrow things down, where we will only consider a relatively small number of arguments found in *CPR* that will help us to see how Kant addressed the philosophical problem of the external world. Now, some scholars take Kant to have forwarded solely an epistemological view in *CPR*, while others take him to have forwarded both an epistemological and a metaphysical view. In this chapter, we will explore *CPR* in light of this second view, the view that takes Kant to be doing both epistemology and metaphysics. But there is a caveat: Kant did not take himself to be offering a complete, systematically worked out metaphysics, but instead took himself to be laying down the groundwork for others who were willing to provide a complete metaphysical system. Kant characterized his own view as something he calls *Critical Idealism*, which he contrasted to what he called Descartes's *Empirical Idealism* and to what he called Berkeley's *Mystical Idealism* (*Prolegomena*, p. 45). So, in addition to understanding Kant's answer to the question concerning the possibility of metaphysics, in this chapter, we will also get clearer about the kind of idealism for which Kant advocated, since, as we will see, it will speak directly to the Problem of the External World.

5.4　　*CPR* was first published in 1781, this first edition now known as the "A-edition." The revised edition appeared in 1787. This is the "B-edition." Norman Kemp-Smith's translation, the one that we will be using, is primarily a translation of the B-edition, which nevertheless includes bits of the A-edition. References to the text, then, will employ the "A" and "B" numbers. These are found in the book's margins. So, for example, if reference is made to text on page 68 of Kemp-Smith's translation, we will also make reference to the corresponding "A" or "B" number: in this case, it would be "B38." This can help you find the relevant text if you find yourself looking at a different translation. In all, Kant wrote three *Critiques* that form a kind of trilogy: *CPR* (B-edition, 1787), the *Critique of Practical Reason* (1788), and the *Critique of Judgment* (1790). Perhaps not surprisingly, given Kant's emphasis on the notion of a *critique*, scholars have come to refer to this period of his philosophical work as his "critical period."

5.2 Knowledge: Preliminaries

In the seventeenth and eighteenth centuries, the concept of *knowledge* was 5.5
applied when speaking about a "system" of thought, or what in the period
was referred to as a *science* (Latin: *scientia*). Specifically, a science was taken
to be a systematic body of hierarchically interrelated true propositions. So,
a science or a body of knowledge was not simply some arbitrary collection
of true propositions. We discussed this in some detail in this book's
Introduction and in Chapter 1. Euclidean geometry is a good example of a
science in this sense. Understood as a science, geometry is a body of knowledge. The true propositions and their relations express a hierarchy, where
some propositions are more fundamental in the system than others – more
fundamental in the sense that the latter are propositions which are based on
(or are justified by) the former. Axioms are examples of basic propositions
in Euclidean geometry. Newtonian physics was also thought by Kant to be
another good example of a science. As in Euclidean geometry, in Newtonian
physics, the true propositions and their relations expressed a hierarchy,
where some propositions were taken to be more fundamental in the system
than others in the sense that the latter were based on (or were justified by)
the former. The laws of motion are examples of basic propositions in
Newtonian physics. Kant accepted both mathematics and physics as examples of *actual* systematic bodies of knowledge – as *actual* sciences. So, he is
not asking whether knowledge understood as science is *possible*, since he
recognized there to already be *actual* bodies of knowledge.

In addition to both mathematics and physics, Kant would count *logic* 5.6
among the sciences. In fact, he took logic to be a salient example of an
actual (and complete) science, a science that he took to be importantly fundamental to both mathematics and physics, in the sense that these latter
sciences presupposed logic (*CPR*, "Preface to Second Edition," Bix, p. 18).
"The sphere of logic," Kant wrote, "is quite precisely delimited; its sole concern is to give an exhaustive exposition and a strict proof of the formal rules
of all thought . . ." (*CPR*, "Preface to Second Edition," Bviii, p. 18). The formal rules of thought in part describe how the mind successfully produces a
line of reasoning, a line of reasoning that guarantees that if one begins with
true statements, one will end with a true statement. In fact, the rules of discursive reasoning (the sort of reasoning that "moves" from one statement to

another) guarantee something more: if one begins with true statements, one *cannot* end with a false statement. We engage discursive reasoning when thinking within the framework of a science like mathematics or physics. Logic in effect would be the intellectual tool by which we navigate a science, or a system of hierarchically interrelated statements. As a formal system itself, logic is understood to be the system of formal rules that "govern" or "determine" thought in its salient operations – namely, in *cognizing* and *thinking*.

5.7   Recall from Chapter 1 that Descartes was greatly interested in establishing the ground of reason. In *Rules for the Direction of the Mind*, Descartes had identified *deduction* as the unique "movement" that a mind undertakes when moving from one thought or proposition to another. This looks to be akin to Kant's notion of discursive reasoning. As we also know from Chapter 1, in his *Meditations*, Descartes grounded the guarantee of reason, or deduction, in God's nature. Kant suggested that he agreed with this, but said that the limitations that he set for himself would not allow him to establish this in *CPR* (*CPR*, "Preface to Second Edition," Bxxx, p. 29). To establish the ultimate ground of the guarantee of discursive reasoning, he must assess the use of reason in practical terms (as it is in fact employed) – the ground of the guarantee can be shown only when considering what is *necessary* for the "practical employment of my reason" (Ibid.). Specifically, this would be *reason* understood as it emerges within the context of human action. Kant would go on to argue for this ultimate ground in the second *Critique*, the *Critique of Practical Reason*.

5.8   It is important to note that for Kant, the formal rules of thought extended beyond discursive reasoning, or as Descartes would have put it, beyond deduction (or as Berkeley might have put it, beyond mediate perception). For, engaging in discursive reasoning is but one element or component that goes into what it is to possess knowledge. Kant wrote that the formal rules also *determine* the possible objects of knowledge. They account for how it is that the mind is able to represent to itself such objects. This seems to also involve what Kant referred to as "the pure forms of sensibility," which are not born from the understanding, but are the principles of *a priori* knowledge specific to sensibility (*CPR*, B35-36, pp. 66-67). Some of this seems to be akin in some ways to what Descartes had referred to in the *Rules for the Direction of the Mind* as *intuition*, and some of this even seems to be akin to what Berkeley had referred to in the *First Dialogue* as *immediate perception*. As this chapter progresses, we will be taking a very close look at what Kant said about the forms of sensible intuition.

5.9   Here are some things to emphasize before moving forward: in granting logic, mathematics, and physics the status of being actual bodies of knowledge (the status of being genuine sciences), Kant is banking on the widely accepted philosophical view that whatever is actual is possible. So, insofar as there is at least one actual body of knowledge, it follows trivially that knowledge is possible. As he unambiguously would argue in *CPR*:

> Since these sciences actually exist, it is quite proper to ask *how* they are possible; for that they must be possible is proved by the fact that they exist. (*CPR*, "Introduction," B20–21, p. 56)

As Kant made clear in this passage, having established the claim that knowledge is possible, the challenge in *CPR* would be to figure out *how* knowledge is possible, which in part will require us to identify the underlying conditions that account for this possibility. To put this in terms used in earlier chapters, Kant planned to ferret out the underlying *necessary conditions* that make knowledge possible.

5.3 Transcendental Philosophy

In the "Introduction" of *CPR*, Kant wrote: 5.10

> I entitle *transcendental* all knowledge which is occupied not so much with objects as with the mode of our knowledge of objects in so far as this mode of knowledge is to be possible *a priori*. A system of such concepts might be entitled transcendental philosophy. (*CPR*, B25, p. 59)

Constructing such a *system*, he would go on to say, would be "too large an undertaking" given his focus in *CPR* (Ibid.). And even then, he would say in the next paragraph, transcendental philosophy, at least given the limitations set out in *CPR*, could express at best only "the idea of a science" (*CPR*, B27, p. 60). The good news, he suggested, is that his investigation in *CPR* should be able to ferret out the necessary conditions that make *sensibility* and *understanding* possible, where sensibility and understanding are in Kant's view the two sources of knowledge. Knowing these underlying conditions would be an important part in our knowing the *mode* of our knowledge of objects – where "mode," recall, meant something like a *way*; so a mode of knowing was a *way* something is known, or the *way* in which knowledge of an object was produced. But more importantly, knowledge of *the mode of knowledge of objects,* of the *way* an object is known, where the way something is known is prior to the result, the object known, would be knowledge of something that is *a priori*, since it is knowledge of what makes possible *the knowledge of objects*. It is a search for that which underwrites the very possibility of the knowledge of objects – and, to be clear, it is not a search for that which *might* underwrite this possibility, so Kant was not offering a speculative hypothesis, but instead was a search for that which *must* underwrite this possibility.

5.11   Kant introduced several analogies to help make clearer how we can better understand what it was that a transcendental investigation was after, and what it would mean for something to count as *a priori* in the sense that it is something knowable independently of actual sensory experience. The first analogy is from business (*CPR*, "Preface to Second Edition," Bx. p. 18). Think of the profit-making aim of a business. Let us say that the business is a manufacturer of shoes. To find the profit, we take the gross income and then consider the cost of making the shoes, which will include the initial cost of materials and labor. We take that number and subtract it from the gross income number, and arrive at the net income, which is our profit. Although the gross income seemed to be simply income from sales, it really was not *all* income from sales since a portion of it was really the initial cost of production, our initial contribution (our initial investment) in the whole process, working its way back to us through sales. Likewise, we might think of knowledge (in the sense of a science) like gross income. But just as with the shoe manufacturer analogy, some of this gross income is actually not income at all but is capital initially contributed by the manufacturer – some aspect or some part of knowledge of objects is not generated by *objects*, but by the *mind* itself (analogue to the manufacturer's initial investment of capital). The mind is investing something that makes knowledge possible. In the same way that we can isolate the cost of production, we can isolate what the mind contributes to our knowledge of objects. Knowledge of what the mind contributes, insofar as this contribution is prior to the production (of the knowledge of objects), would count as *a priori* knowledge. As Kant would put it: ". . . we can know *a priori* of things only what we ourselves put into them" (*CPR*, "Preface to Second Edition," Bxviii, p. 23), and a few pages later: "Nothing in *a priori* knowledge can be ascribed to objects save what the thinking subject derives from itself . . ." (*CPR*, Bxxii, p. 25).

5.12   The second analogy, which typically gets more press in the secondary literature, comes from astronomy (*CPR*, "Preface to Second Edition," Bxvi, p. 22). The Polish astronomer Copernicus had challenged the Ptolemaic model of the solar system. Ptolemy had argued that the earth was the center of the solar system, and had successfully calculated the orbits of the planets and sun accordingly. It was a very complicated mathematical model. Copernicus offered a sleeker model, where he allowed the sun to be at the center of the solar system. His model was mathematically much simpler than Ptolemy's. Instead of "explaining the movements of the heavenly bodies on the supposition that they all revolved around the spectator, he [i.e. Copernicus] tried whether he might not have better success if he made the spectator to revolve and the stars to remain at rest" (Ibid.). The point is that by shifting from earth as center to sun as center, where now the earth moved, astronomical science was advanced. Kant noted that philosophers had up until his day "assumed that all our knowledge must conform to objects" (Ibid.). But this assumption, he said, always led to failure. He asked, what would happen if instead we held "that objects must conform to our knowledge?" (Ibid.). If objects must conform to *us*, to our *minds*, then there must be something that our mind is doing when engaged in making objects conform. This would be a sense in which the mind is *determining* objects of knowledge. This is akin to the initial contribution the company made in the manufacturing of those shoes. "This new point of view," said Kant, "enables us to understand how there can be knowledge *a priori*" (*CPR*, Bxix, p. 23). If we can know what it is that the mind is doing when determining the objects of knowledge, which would account for how it is that our minds make them conform to us, we would have *a priori* knowledge. For, that which is determining an object of knowledge is *prior* to the object's being given in the product, that is, it is prior to the mind's representation of the object. Kant's focus was not on how an object imposes itself on the mind, then, but instead was on how the mind does whatever it does that accounts for its making the object *conform* to the mind, when the mind represents to itself an object. The focus, in other words, is on how the mind imposes certain conditions on objects that account for the possibility of their being objects of knowledge.

Kant wrote that there was an important and startling implication in all this: 5.13

> For we are brought to the conclusion that we can never transcend the limits of possible experience, though that is precisely what this science is concerned, above all else, to achieve. This situation yields, however, just the very experiment by which, indirectly, we are enabled to prove the truth of this first estimate of our *a priori* knowledge of reason, namely, that such knowledge has to do only with appearances, and must leave the thing in itself as indeed real *per se*, but as not known by us. (*CPR*, "Preface to Second Edition," Bxix–xx, p. 24)

So, *a priori* knowledge will *not* be about objects as they exist independently of human cognition. Instead, it will be knowledge about the conditions that underlie the very possibility of representing and knowing objects, where these conditions are contributions that the *mind* makes in its representing and knowing objects – in its *cognizing* objects. So, such knowledge is not knowledge of objects as they exist independently of human cognition, but is instead knowledge of the conditions that make possible the objects as they *appear* in experience.

5.14   As noted above, Kant begged off from seeking the *ultimate* ground of knowledge, since that looked to require us to go beyond what the narrow introspection into reason could reveal. And, as he suggested in the passage quoted in the previous paragraph, our *a priori* knowledge cannot ever be about anything "outside" (or independent of) the domain of the possibility of human cognition – where the ultimate ground would be "outside" or completely independent of the possibility of human cognition. Even so, Kant thought that reason could reveal its *immediate* ground, where this immediate ground (which is distinct from its *ultimate* ground) would be those formal rules that determine all of its operations. Reason can reveal whatever it is that the *mind* must be doing when it contributes to our having knowledge of objects. The challenge would be to show that the mind can reveal such a thing.

5.15   In the "Preface to the First Edition" of *CPR*, Kant wrote:

> Pure reason is, indeed, so perfect a unity that if its principle were insufficient for the solution of even a single one of all the questions to which it itself gives birth we should have no alternative but to reject the principle, since we should then no longer be able to place implicit reliance upon it in dealing with any of the other questions . . .. (*CPR*, Axiii, p. 10)

This should remind you a little of Descartes. Recall that in the *Meditations*, he had said something very similar. After having secured his first principle (*If I am thinking, I exist*) in the Second Meditation, Descartes examined it in the Third Meditation, trying to ferret out what it was about this first principle that guaranteed his now knowing something, or his now being certain of something. This first principle was something, he said, that he clearly and distinctly perceived. He wrote:

> Do I not therefore also know what is required for my being certain about anything? In this first item of knowledge there is simply a clear and distinct perception of what I am asserting; this would not be enough to make me certain of the truth of the matter if it could ever turn out that something which I perceived with such clarity and distinctness was false. So I now seem to be able to lay it down as a general rule that whatever I perceive very clearly and distinctly is true. (AT VII 35; CSM II 24)

This is pretty straightforward. Let us grant Descartes the following: *If you clearly and distinctly perceive something, then what you perceive is true.* This would make your perceiving the truth a necessary condition for your clearly and distinctly perceiving something; but it would also make your clearly and distinctly perceiving something a sufficient condition for your perceiving the truth. The logic here shows that if it were true that you clearly and distinctly perceived something, and yet false that you perceived the truth, then the conditional – *If you clearly and distinctly perceive something, then what you perceive is true* – would be false. Since Descartes had claimed that this conditional *could not* be false, at least it could not if *being certain* is possible, then in every case in which it is true that you clearly and distinctly perceive something, it is also true that you perceive the truth. The point was that if the immediate ground of reason was insufficient to guarantee your perceiving the truth, then you must abandon reason and place no confidence in what it tells you. And this seemed to be exactly Kant's point in the previously quoted passage from *CPR*.

Soon after that point was made, Kant wrote:

> As to *certainty*, I have prescribed to myself the maxim, that in this kind of investigation it is in no wise permissible to hold *opinions*. Everything, therefore, which bears any manner of resemblance to an hypothesis is to be treated as contraband . . .. (*CPR*, Axv, p. 11)

This, too, should remind you of Descartes. Recall that in the *Meditations*, Descartes had claimed about his search for the ground of certainty: "Anything which admits of the slightest doubt I will set aside just as if I had found it to be wholly false . . ." (AT VII 18; CSM II 12). The only claims that could be maintained, then, were those that could not be false – or, perhaps more accurately, those that *we* could not conceive to be false. Descartes's first principle, as we know from Chapter 1, met this very criterion. Likewise, Kant would suggest that within the context of a transcendental investigation, only propositions that are *a priori* (or whose truth is knowable *a priori*) could be held.

Given the ever-increasing emphasis on the concept of *a priori* in our discussion, this is a good place to make this and other importantly related concepts clearer before moving forward. 5.16

5.4 Two Distinctions and the Category of Synthetic *a priori* Propositions

Kant developed an important category of proposition in which he located 5.17 the salient propositions of metaphysics. He called this category "synthetic *a priori*." The category is constructed from two distinctions: a distinction between *analytic* and *synthetic* judgments, and a distinction between *a priori* and *a posteriori* propositions (or *a priori* and *a posteriori* truths). The import of the synthetic *a priori* category is as part of a response to a view laid out by David Hume (1711–1776), in *An Enquiry Concerning Human Understanding* (1748). As in Hume's earlier book, *A Treatise of Human Nature* (1739), Hume had argued that the propositions of metaphysics were meaningless. This was so since the more important terms used by the metaphysicians were such that the contents of the ideas to which the words were "annexed" were empty – Hume's view assumed that the meanings of words were the contents of ideas. He divided all propositions into two basic categories: *Relations of Ideas* and *Matters of Fact*. What he took himself to have shown was that metaphysical propositions, at least the more important ones, fell into neither category. What Kant would show in *CPR* was that Hume made a mistake in formulating his two categories, and that once cleared up, the category of synthetic *a priori* emerged, a category that secured a meaningful place for metaphysical propositions. We will want to take a close look at this, since it will have some bearing on Kant's answer to the Problem of the External World. Let us begin by taking a brief look at Hume's view, and then turn to an examination of Kant's response to it.

5.4.1 Hume's Two Categories of Proposition

5.18 In Section 4, Part I of *An Enquiry Concerning Human Understanding* (1748), Hume introduced two categories of proposition: *Relations of Ideas* and *Matters of Fact*. He wrote:

> Of the first kind are the sciences of geometry, algebra, and arithmetic; and in short, every affirmation which is either intuitively or demonstratively certain. *That the square of the hypotenuse is equal to the square of the two sides*, is a proposition which expresses a relation between these figures. *That three times five is equal to the half of thirty*, expresses a relation between these numbers. Propositions of this kind are discoverable by the mere operation of thought, without dependence on what is anywhere existent in the universe . . ..
>
> Matters of Fact, which are the second objects of human reason, are not ascertained in the same manner; nor is our evidence of their truth, however great, of a like nature with the foregoing. The contrary of every matter of fact is still possible; because it can never imply a contradiction, and is conceived by the mind with the same facility and distinctness, as if ever so conformable to reality. *That the sun will not rise tomorrow* is no less intelligible a proposition, and implies no more contradiction than the affirmation, *that it will rise*. We should in vain, therefore, attempt to demonstrate its falsehood. (*Enquiry* 28)

The criteria of the two categories are:

Relations of Ideas

1. Their truth can be demonstrated by reason (or logic) alone.
2. Their truth can be known independently of any reference to how the world is.
3. Their negation implies a contradiction.

Matters of Fact

1. Their truth cannot be demonstrated by reason (or logic) alone.
2. Their truth cannot be known independently of any reference to how the world is.
3. Their negation does not imply a contradiction.

Examples that Hume gave of *Relations of Ideas* were the Pythagorean theorem, taken from Euclidean geometry, and the equation $3 \times 5 = \frac{30}{2}$, taken from arithmetic. Consider the latter. Begin with the ideas of the numbers 2, 3, 5, and 30, and the ideas of the relations *multiplication, division,* and *equality*. The equation is simply one way to express how these numbers are related to one another. Or, as Hume would put it, the equation expresses how the *ideas* of these numbers are related to one another. On Hume's view, the truth of this proposition (the equation) can be demonstrated by reason (logic) alone; it can be known independently of how the world is; and, to show its necessity, we note that its negation implies a contradiction. For instance, to claim that it is not the case that $3 \times 5 = \frac{30}{2}$, or alternatively that $3 \times 5 \neq \frac{30}{2}$, is to imply that $15 \neq 15$, which is a contradiction.

Examples of *Matters of Facts* are the propositions "The Sun will rise tomor- 5.19 row" and its negation "It's not the case that the Sun will rise tomorrow" (or, alternatively, "The Sun will not rise tomorrow"). On Hume's view, the truth of "The Sun will rise tomorrow" cannot be demonstrated by reason (or logic) alone; it cannot be known independently of the way the world is; and, its negation does not imply a contradiction. You may believe that "The Sun will rise tomorrow" is true based on past experience and the unlikelihood of some catastrophe, but that is far from securing the truth of this belief by way of a logical demonstration. In order to know whether it is true or not, you'll simply have to wait and see how the world shakes out. In other words, knowledge of its truth ultimately depends on sensory experience. What is more, its negation does not imply a contradiction. That is, "The Sun will not rise tomorrow" is just as intelligible as "The Sun will rise tomorrow." That is very different from the negation of the earlier equation. For "$15 \neq 15$" is a contradiction; it is *unintelligible*. You cannot conceive something as not being identical to itself. Do not mistake the *unlikelihood* of "The Sun won't rise tomorrow" for its being a *contradiction*. Remember that a contradiction can *never* be true (it is always false!). It is possible (even though improbable) that "The Sun won't rise tomorrow" is true. So, "The Sun won't rise tomorrow" is not a contradiction. To be sure, it is the negation of "The Sun will rise tomorrow," so both cannot be true at the same time. That is a logical point. But, taken by itself, despite your thinking that it is improbable, it is nevertheless *possible* that "The Sun will not rise tomorrow" is true. This is very different from a *Relations of Ideas* proposition.

5.20   Hume associated the use of deductive reasoning primarily with the category of *Relations of Ideas*, and the use of inductive reasoning primarily with the category of *Matters of Fact*. You can see that the reasoning in support of the claim that "The Sun will rise tomorrow" is inductive. Your belief that it is *probable* or *likely* that "The Sun will rise tomorrow" is true, is based upon the evidence you have gathered over the years, where the knowability of the evidence (expressed by the premises) is dependent on sensory experience. Your belief that it is improbable or unlikely that "The Sun won't rise tomorrow" is true, is based on the same body of evidence. To know which is in fact true, however, you will have to wait until tomorrow to see. The point is that the knowability of the truth of such claims, whether by inductive reasoning or by direct observation, is dependent upon sensory experience and on the way the world is. Logic by itself can get you only so far with *Matters of Facts*.

5.21   Hume held that empirical science operates almost exclusively within the domain of *Matters of Fact*. This will include our coming to formulate what today we call the *laws of nature*. On Hume's view, a law of nature is a general proposition that expresses a pattern of correlation that we observe among our perceptions. Ideally, a law of nature will be the conclusion of a cogent inductive argument. The truth of a law of nature is not absolute, but at best is highly probable or likely. Since we take it to be highly probable, it takes on a law-like status. So, it might be better to say that a law of nature is a law-*like* proposition. It is certainly not a law in the sense that the tax or zoning ordinances are laws. Be that as it may, since its probable truth is only knowable from inductive reasoning, which ultimately relies on sensory experience, it falls within the domain of *Matters of Fact*.

5.22   The reason for bringing all of this up is to show why it is that Hume would classify propositions such as a *law of nature* (which, as just noted, is simply a law-like proposition drawn from sensory experience) in the category of *Matters of Fact*. By contrast, as we already know, he classified propositions from mathematics in the category of *Relations of Ideas*. What about propositions from metaphysics? Into which category might they be classified? Well, for Hume, propositions from metaphysics were meaningless, and so, strictly speaking, are not propositions at all. They are found *nowhere* in Hume's category scheme. They are neither to be found among *Relations of Ideas* nor *Matters of Fact*. Of course, if philosophers defined some term they wished to use in a metaphysical investigation, then that is okay, and the definition would be an example of a *Relations of Ideas* proposition. But this would be no different from defining "God," or "Pegasus," or "Unicorn." Such propositions are simply true *by definition*, and so really would not carry any great "metaphysical" weight. You simply cannot make God or Pegasus or unicorns *real* by simply conjuring up definitions of them. At least, that is Hume's point. And remember that metaphysics is in part supposed to *explain* what it is for something to be *real*. So, as just noted, metaphysical terms that simply arose as the result of definition would carry no heavy weight, and terms annexed to ideas whose contents are empty would be meaningless. Such propositions would not guarantee that they pick out anything real, since their truth does not rely on how the world is. So, if a metaphysical proposition were either true by definition, or meaningless (and so not a proposition), Hume's view suggested that metaphysics would be lame indeed.

5.4.2 Kant's Response to Hume's View

The category of synthetic *a priori* propositions is constructed from two distinctions. Let us look at each and then construct the category from them.   5.23

5.4.2.1 A Priori/A Posteriori

This distinction would be used when talking about propositions and knowledge – specifically when talking about how one can come to know the *truth* of propositions. For instance, some propositions are said to be *a priori* true, while others are said to be *a posteriori* true. In casting this specifically in terms of knowledge, *a priori* propositions can be known – i.e. their *truth* can be known – independently of all sensory experience, whereas *a posteriori* propositions can be known – i.e. their *truth* can be known – only by way of (or only by an appeal to) sensory experience. What is more, *a priori* propositions are *necessarily* true – i.e. they *must* be true and *cannot* be false. We cannot even conceive of their being   5.24

false. Kant made it a point to say that their truth must be knowable independently of experience since their necessity "cannot be derived from experience" (*CPR*, "Introduction," Section V, B14–15). The proposition "The square of the hypotenuse of a (Euclidean) right triangle equals the sum of the squares of the other two sides" is, for Kant, an example of an *a priori* proposition. It will be made clear shortly how it is that Kant held that we can know that this claim is true independently of any particular sensory experience, and what is more, we will want to get clear on how Kant took its truth to be necessary. For the moment suffice it to say that what makes *a priori* propositions unique, if any such propositions there be, is that their truth would be knowable independently of the particulars of sensory experience.

5.25   By contrast, *a posteriori* propositions are only *contingently* true – i.e. they *could be* true, they *could be* false, depending on how the world is. This is related to the fact that we can conceive of situations in which they are true, and equally we can conceive of situations in which they are false. The proposition "Michelle is at her yoga studio" is an example of an *a posteriori* proposition. We can know whether this is true only by way of (or only by an appeal to) sensory experience, and its truth is contingent. If it is the case that Michelle is at her yoga studio, the proposition is true; if it is not the case that she is at her yoga studio, the proposition is false.

5.26   Here is the second distinction:

5.4.2.2 Analytic/Synthetic

5.27   Kant drew a distinction between analytic and synthetic judgments. "Analytic judgments," he wrote, "are . . . those in which the connection of the predicate with the subject is thought through identity" (*CPR*, Introduction, Section IV). The predicate does not really "add" anything to the subject. Rather, it simply expresses what we take the subject *essentially* to be. His example of an analytic judgment was "All bodies are extended." What it is *to be* a body is that it be extended. When you conceive of a body, you conceive of an extended something. By contrast, synthetic judgments are propositions whose predicates "add to the concept of the subject a predicate which has not been in any wise thought in it" (Ibid.). In this same passage, he said that predicates in synthetic judgments *amplify* the subject, telling us something more about the subject than what an examination of the subject concept would reveal when examined in isolation from other concepts. His example of a synthetic judgment was "All bodies are heavy."

Let us get crystal clear about this. Here is the distinction in Kant's own 5.28 words:

> If I say, for instance, "All bodies are extended," this is an analytic judgment. For I do not require to go beyond the concept of which I connect with "body" in order to find extension as bound up with it . . .. But when I say, "All bodies are heavy," the predicate is something quite different from anything that I think in the mere concept of body in general; and the addition of such a predicate therefore yields a synthetic judgment. (*CPR*, Introduction, B11)

As just noted, when you conceive of a body, you think of a thing that is extended. If you were not thinking of an extended thing, you were not thinking of a body. Or, as stated earlier, what it is *to be* a body is to be extended (and vice versa). This much of Kant's view sounded like Descartes's. So, "A body is extended" is analytic. The predicate "extended" does not really *add* anything new to the subject "body." Instead, the predicate "extended" simply expresses what we think when thinking about a body. In Kant's terms, the concept "extendedness" *is contained in* the concept "body." To use a now familiar term, our thinking about body *presupposes* our thinking about extendedness.

But what about the statement "This body is heavy"? When thinking 5.29 about a body must we think that it is heavy? We know that when thinking about a body that we must think of it as being extended, but *must* we think of it as being heavy? In Kant's terms, we can ask: Is the predicate "heavy" contained in the subject-concept "body"? Here is another way of asking this: Can we conceive of a body that was *not* heavy? Well, the answer to this should be clear: Yes, we can. Bodies in deep space are not *heavy*. Imagine that you were born aboard a ship traveling in deep space. It would never occur to you that bodies were heavy, right? (Keep in mind that a body's mass is not the same as its weight or heaviness – in deep space, a body will not be heavy but it will still have mass.) Let us say that as part of your ship's plan to return to earth, you were scheduled to first land on the moon. Let us say that when on the moon, you noticed that you felt a little weird. You went outside the space craft and noticed, for example, that it was difficult to move your feet, that the wrench you were using was . . . what? . . . well, it was "heavy." Your ship leaves the moon and all is back to normal. Now you land on earth, and again your body feels weird. Moving your feet is noticeably much more difficult than when on the moon – and that wrench, well you cannot even budge it. Clearly, you have learned something *new* about the subject "body," something that was not included in its concept (when considered in isolation from other concepts). The predicate "heavy" in this case *amplifies* or tells you something more about the subject "body" than what is included in the isolated concept.

5.30   Let us now put the two sets of distinctions together:

5.4.2.3 Synthetic *A Priori* Propositions

5.31   Kant developed a category of proposition in which the salient or more important propositions of metaphysics are to be found. As noted earlier, he called this category "synthetic *a priori.*" The category is constructed from the two distinctions just discussed: the distinction between *analytic* and *synthetic* judgments, and the distinction between *a priori* and *a posteriori* propositions (or *a priori* and *a posteriori* truths). If we combined the items from both distinctions, we would get the following four categories:

1.   Analytic *a priori*
2.   Analytic *a posteriori*
3.   Synthetic *a priori*
4.   Synthetic *a posteriori*

Coming up with examples for all of the categories has proven difficult for scholars (give it a try and you will see). Even so, it should be easy to understand that propositions like "Michelle is at her yoga studio" are classifiable in the category of synthetic *a posteriori*. The proposition about Michelle is synthetic since the predicate-concept "being at her yoga studio" is not contained in the subject-concept "Michelle." (When conceiving of Michelle, you need not think that she is at her yoga studio, right?) This predicate, "being at her yoga studio," amplifies the subject by telling us more about Michelle. And, it is *a posteriori* since we must rely on (or must appeal to) the particulars of sensory experience when determining its truth.

5.32   And, it should also be easy to understand that propositions like "A thing is identical to itself" (e.g. "A = A") are classifiable in the category of analytic *a priori*. Such a proposition is analytic since the concept of A "contains" A (whenever you conceive A you conceive *A*, right?), and it is *a priori* since we need not rely on (or need not appeal to) the particulars of *sensory* experience when determining its truth. You know that the thing that you are thinking about is the thing you are thinking about, and you could know this independently of the particulars of sensory experience.

5.33   But let us now focus on the prize: the category of synthetic *a priori*. This is the category that *CPR* (and the *Prolegomena*) aimed at establishing. For a proposition to count as synthetic *a priori*, it would have to be one in which the predicate-concept was not included in the subject-concept, but instead amplified the subject by telling us something more about the subject than the subject concept tells us when considered by itself. Further, the truth of the proposition would have to be knowable independently of the particulars of sensory experience.

5.4.3 Synthetic A Priori Propositions, Mathematics, and the Laws of Nature

Many philosophers before Kant had held that the propositions of mathematics 5.34 were simply *analytic*. No doubt Hume's category of *Relations of Ideas* expresses at the very least the notion of analyticity. Where we might find some disagreement among these earlier philosophers is with whether they would take such propositions to be *a priori* or *a posteriori*. Since Hume, for instance, believed that all knowledge is *ultimately* derived from sensory experience (from impressions), it is not clear how he could allow those propositions that fall into his category of *Relations of Ideas* to be taken to be *a priori*. To be sure, their truth does not rely on the way the world is, and can be demonstrated by way of the principle of contradiction (i.e. by way of logic alone), but since no ideas are innate, then even the ideas of numbers and triangles must be ultimately derived from the particulars of sensory experience (with some help perhaps from the imagination). So, analytic, yes; but *a priori*, no. Kant disagreed with Hume on both fronts: Kant said that the propositions of mathematics are not only *synthetic*, but are in addition to that *a priori*. They are synthetic *a priori*.

Suppose that someone defines for you the "+" operation (the operation of 5.35 addition). Kant suggested that knowing this, you could know that 7 added to 5, for example, would equal some definite number. And, you could know that *analytically*. That is, "the sum of $7 + 5$ is some definite number" is an analytic proposition. But that 7 plus 5 equals the specific number *12* and no other number is not analytic; that is, the proposition "$7 + 5 = 12$" is not analytic. He wrote:

> We might, indeed, at first suppose that the proposition $7 + 5 = 12$ is a merely analytic proposition, and follows by the principle of contradiction from the concept of a sum of 7 and 5. But if we look more closely we find that the concept of the sum of 7 and 5 contains nothing save the union of the two numbers into one, and in this no thought is being taken as to what that single number may be which combines both. The concept of 12 is by no means already thought in merely thinking this union of 7 and 5; and I may analyze my concept of such a possible number as long as I please, still I shall never find the 12 in it. (*CPR*, B15, pp. 52-53)

To see that 7 added to 5 equals 12, and not some other number, Kant said that we must "go outside these concepts, and call in the aid of the intuition" (Ibid.). By this, he meant that we must imagine or sense counting our fingers, or consider marks perhaps drawn on a piece of paper, or some other scenario that involves the realm of sensibility. His point is strengthened if we consider less familiar numbers. Think of 4376 added to 3988. Can you tell their sum simply by conceiving these two numbers? Kant's answer was – No. Rather, you will need to perform some procedure, whether seen, spoken, heard, felt, or imagined, which will involve fingers, or marks on a page, or some such, where you would arrive at their sum being equal to 8364 and no other number. The proposition "4376 + 3988 = 8364" is *synthetic*. Knowing that the sum equals 8364 amplifies the concept of the union of these two numbers (where the union of these numbers, "4376 + 3988," is the subject). This is equally true for the more familiar proposition "7 + 5 = 12". It is synthetic. Knowing that their sum equals 12 amplifies the concept of the union of 7 and 5. So, how mathematical propositions can be understood to be synthetic should be clear. But Kant still owes us an account of how they can be understood to be *a priori*. We will get to that shortly.

5.36   As in *CPR*, in the Second Part of the *Prolegomena*, Kant would explain how the laws of nature are also synthetic *a priori*, arguing that this was the account of the very possibility of pure natural science. He introduced two laws of nature: the law of the conservation of the quantity of matter in the universe and the law of the conservation of the quantity of motion in the universe. Here is how he explained their being *synthetic*. Consider the first law, for instance, which states: "in all changes of the material world the quantity of matter remains unchanged" (*CPR*, "Introduction," B17, p. 54). He noted that "in the concept of matter I do not think its permanence, but only its presence in the space which it occupies" (*CPR*, "Introduction," B18, p. 54). The predicate-concept expressing *permanence* is not contained in the subject-concept expressing *matter* or *extendedness*. Instead, this predicate-concept amplifies our concept of matter. The view seems to be that we acquire knowledge of this "permanence" by way of intuition or sensory experience, in the same way that the synthetic judgments of mathematics required the appeal to intuition or sensory experience. So, for Kant, the laws of nature are *synthetic*.

5.37   Now, as with the synthetic propositions of mathematics, Kant still owes us an account of how it is that such propositions are *a priori*. Let us now look at this. The challenge is: Kant's account of the abovementioned synthetic propositions of mathematics and physics *requires* us to appeal to intuition or to the sensible. But an *a priori* proposition's truth is supposedly knowable *independently* of sensory experience or intuition. It is just not clear, then, *how* the truth of a synthetic proposition can be known independently of intuition or sensory experience. Kant is fully aware of this challenge.

In the *Prolegomena*, he wrote: 5.38

> For now the question runs: *How is it possible to intuit something* a priori? An
> intuition is a representation of the sort which would depend immediately on
> the presence of an object. It therefore seems impossible *originally* to intuit *a*
> *priori*, since then the intuition would have to occur without an object being
> present, either previously or now, to which it could refer, and so it could not
> be an intuition. (*Prolegomena*, "First Part," §8, p. 33)

To understand how such a proposition can be synthetic and at the same
time be *a priori*, we will need to carefully examine Kant's account of intuition. Let us turn to doing that.

So, as we now turn to looking carefully at Kant's account of intuition,   5.39
here is a summary of where we are at this point: Hume put the propositions
of mathematics in the category of *Relations of Ideas*, and put the law-like
propositions of physics, which express the *laws of nature*, in the entirely different category of *Matters of Fact*. So, mathematical propositions and natural law-like propositions are in completely different categories. What is
more, according to Hume, there was no place for the propositions of metaphysics. By contrast, Kant put *both* the propositions of mathematics *and* the
propositions expressing the laws of nature in the *same* category, the category of synthetic *a priori*. And, it is in this very same category that Kant
would locate the salient propositions of metaphysics. That is a pretty big
difference. What Kant took himself to have shown, then, was that contrary
to Hume's claim, metaphysics was at least *possible*, since there was a category of proposition that would allow for the meaningfulness of metaphysical claims (of the non-lame sort!). Let us now turn to Kant on intuition and
get clearer on how synthetic propositions, which require an appeal to intuition, are nevertheless *a priori*, or knowable independently of intuition.

5.4.4 Intuition, the Manifold of Intuition, and the Forms of Intuition

5.4.4.1 Intuition

At the opening of the "Transcendental Doctrine of Elements" of *CPR*, Kant   5.40
would give us the nuts and bolts of what he meant by *intuition*. The passage
is worth quoting in full. Let us do that and then spend some time unpacking
it. Kant wrote:

> In whatever manner and by whatever means a mode of knowledge may relate
> to objects, *intuition* is that through which it is in immediate relation to them,

and to which all thought as a means is directed. But intuition takes place only in so far as the object is given to us. This again is only possible, to man at least, in so far as the mind is affected in a certain way. The capacity (receptivity) for receiving representations through the mode in which we are affected by objects, is entitled *sensibility*. Objects are *given* to us by means of sensibility, and it alone yields us *intuitions*; they are *thought* through the understanding, and from the understanding arise *concepts*. But all thought must, directly or indirectly, by way of certain characters, relate ultimately to intuitions, and therefore, with us, to sensibility, because in no other way can an object be given to us.

5.41   The effect of an object upon the faculty of representation, so far as we are affected by it, is *sensation*. That intuition which is in relation to the object through sensation, is entitled *empirical*. The undetermined object of an empirical intuition is entitled *appearance*.

5.42   That in the appearance which corresponds to sensation I term its *matter*; but that which so determines the manifold of appearance that it allows of being ordered in certain relations, I term the *form* of appearance. That in which alone the sensations can be posited and ordered in a certain form, cannot itself be sensation; and therefore, while the matter of all appearance is given to us *a posteriori* only, its form must lie ready for the sensations *a priori* in the mind, and so must allow of being considered apart from all sensation. (*CPR*, B33–34, pp. 65–66)

5.43 As we know from earlier sections, Kant took the sources of knowledge to be two: *sensibility* and *understanding*. These are capacities or faculties that the mind possesses inherently. Sensibility is the capacity the mind has to be affected by objects, where the result of this affectation is a *representation* of the object. The effect of this object on the mind *via* sensibility is *sensation*. His view is that when you see a red apple, for example, the *red*, the quality of which you are immediately aware, is a sensation. When you bite into the apple and it tastes sweet, the *sweet* is a sensation. When the representation of the object is by way of sensation, it is an *empirical* intuition.

5.4.4.2 The Manifold of Intuition

5.44 Kant's view suggested that the object *itself* is not before the mind, but instead presumably an *appearance* of the object is. The passage quoted at the opening of the previous section also suggested that an object, a "real" object, was *completely* determined. But an *appearance* (the object appearing before the mind) is not completely determined, which suggests that it is not in some sense "real." Consider your experience of the apple. You see one side of it, as you hold it in your hand, but you do not see the other side, the side that you take to be facing away from you. Okay, turn it around and see the other side. You see it. But now you do not see the side seen just a moment ago. There is always something about the apple that you *do not* see at what we might say is during any *single go* of intuition. The apple you *see* is always incomplete – that is, there is always something missing. This would include, say, the "inside" of the apple. You take there to be an inside, even though all you see is its outside. Even if you cut the apple in half, and now see its "inside," do you see its inside? Or, are you still seeing an outside, an outer surface, and the inside still escapes you?

    You might say that in turning the apple around in your hands, you eventually 5.45
see all of it. But that takes time, right? You do not see the whole thing at a single go. Your experience of the apple, in spanning some duration of time, can be thought to be like an old film that is basically a bunch of single frames put together. The single frames here would be the analogues to single intuitions – each intuition a single go of experience. Kant says that our single intuitions are synthesized together. Their synthesis is what he calls a *manifold*. Your experience *is* the manifold. There would be no experience if all you had was just a single intuition – *blip* and done! You actually do not ever have a single-go-experience. That is, you do not have experience one frame at a time. Your experience is fluid. The manifold is seamless. The manifold is what is given; not the single "instances" of experience. Unlike the film, however, you could never actually slow things down enough to have a single – one off – experience. That intuitions are synthesized is not something *itself* seen or experienced. It *is* the experience; where *what* you experience are things like apples and such. That we understand experience to be a synthesis of intuition is something known by way of reason, by an analysis of what makes experience possible; which sounds like Descartes when he reasoned in the Second Meditation, in his analysis of his experience of a piece of wax, that the nature of a body is not found in the particulars of sensory experience, but is instead something brought to light by reason. The synthesis of intuitions *must* be the case, Kant argued, for without it experience, as we humans have it, would be *im*possible.

5.4.4.3 The Forms of Intuition: Space and Time

So, your experience of the apple is a manifold of intuition. What makes the 5.46
synthesis or ordering of intuitions possible is *time*. It is what accounts for the very possibility of a manifold. And so, time underwrites the very possibility of your experience of the apple – or, as just mentioned, it is what Kant referred to as one of the *forms* of intuition. The other form of intuition is *space*. The apple appears as a spatial object, right? It is given to you as though it were at some distance from you, the perceiving *subject* – or, at some "distance" from what Descartes, Berkeley, and Kant would take to be the "I" of experience. Intuition, or sensory experience, is essentially *spatial*. Even at a single go,

where our analysis ignores the synthesis of multiple intuitions, if an "object" were given, it would nevertheless be represented "in" space. Think of that apple. What becomes of such an object if you "take away" space? No space, no apple! Same with time of course: No time, no apple! But, to be clearer, if no space and time, no *experiences* (or *appearances*) of apples. Now, what is interesting about Kant's view is that he is not talking about what above we clumsily called the *apple-in-itself*. He is talking about the apple *as it appears*. You might think that he must be talking about the apple-in-itself, the apple that exists independently of human cognition, since space and time surely exist independently of experience, and are features that constitute material reality. Okay, but by "apple-in-itself," what apple do you have in mind exactly? You reply: the "physical" one that you are thinking about; the one that you *imagine* to be "existing" there all by itself, all material-like, the apple that exists without anyone's perceiving (sensing, imagining, thinking, etc.) it. But, remember what Berkeley showed. Such an apple is a contradiction! Recall an exchange between Hylas and Philonous from *The First Dialogue*:

Hylas:	. . . What is more easy than to conceive a tree or house existing by itself, independent of, and unperceived by, any mind whatsoever? I do at this present time conceive them existing after that manner.
Philonous:	What are you saying, Hylas – can you see a thing which is at the same time unseen?
Hylas:	No, that would be a contradiction.
Philonous:	Is it not as great a contradiction to talk of *conceiving* a thing which is unconceived?
Hylas:	It is.
Philonous:	The tree or house, therefore, which you think of is conceived by you.
Hylas:	How should it be otherwise?
Philonous:	And what is conceived is surely in the mind.
Hylas:	Without question, that which is conceived is in the mind.
Philonous:	How then did you come to say you conceived a house or tree existing independent and out of all minds whatsoever?

Clearly, then, if we are going to make sense of the view that things like apples can and do exist independently of our seeing them, or even independently of our thinking about them, we have got some work to do.

5.47   Okay, so we want to see whether we can figure out a way to say, without contradiction, that there is a difference between the apple that appears (in experience) and the apple *itself*. The apple that appears surely falls into the category of what Kant referred to as *phenomena*, right? It is a *phenomenal* apple. It is the apple of experience. It is the apple that appears. It is the apple that we can never experience at a single go. By contrast, it would seem that the apple itself would fall into the category of what Kant referred to as *noumena*. It is the *apple-in-itself.* It is the *noumenal* apple. It is the apple that exists independently of human cognition. It is the apple that is all there at a single go. But not so fast! Although it is true that Kant employed the distinction between *phenomena* and *noumena*, or the distinction between *appearance* and *thing-in-itself*, he also gave reasons for holding that, strictly speaking, we cannot know anything about things-in-themselves. This is so, since a thing-in-itself is presumably not subject to the conditions of human cognition – specifically, it would not be subject to the conditions of space and time, the forms of intuition. And, we know what happens if we "take away" space and time – the very intelligibility of the thing is lost. So, strictly speaking, there is no easy way to talk about or to refer to any noumenal *apples*. At best, this so-called noumenal apple, or the "apple-in-itself," which is simply formed in the imagination, is no different from any apple that *appears*. So, as noted a moment ago, we still have some work to do. Now, there is a way to sort some of this out. We can do that if we get a bit clearer on the import of space and time being taken as forms of intuition, as opposed to being taken as features of objects that exist independently of human cognition. This will be Kant's "Copernican" move. Once we do that, we will be in a position to see how Kant was able to understand those synthetic propositions taken from mathematics and physics to be *a priori*. And, finally, after getting that straight, we will be in a position to bring this chapter to a close by seeing how Kant dealt with the Problem of the "External" World – the world that commonsense says exists independently of your mind.

5.4.4.4 Space and Time: Some Details

In the First Part of *CPR*, in the "Transcendental Aesthetic," Kant argued that space and time are the *forms* of intuition. They underwrite the very possibility of intuition. The arguments about space parallel the arguments about time. So, if you understand the import of his arguments about space, you would have a good idea about his view of time. To keep this concise, then, we will just look at one of his arguments about space.   5.48

Introducing his view on space and time, Kant wrote: 5.49

> By means of outer sense, a property of our mind, we represent to ourselves objects as outside us, and all without exception in space. In space their shape, magnitude, and relation to one another are determined or determinable. Inner sense, by means of which the mind intuits itself or its inner state, yields

indeed no intuition of the soul itself as an object; but there is nevertheless a determinate form [namely, time] in which alone the intuition of inner states is possible. And everything which belongs to inner determinations is therefore represented in relations of time. Time cannot be outwardly intuited, any more than space can be intuited as something in us. (*CPR* A23/B37)

Space and time not only are what make possible a cognitive *distinction* between sensory qualities (like colors, sounds, smells, and so on), but make an *ordering* of them possible.

5.50   Recall something from a passage quoted earlier:

That in the appearance which corresponds to sensation I term its *matter*; but that which so determines the manifold of appearance that it allows of being ordered in certain relations, I term the *form* of appearance. That in which alone the sensations can be posited and ordered in a certain form, cannot itself be sensation; and therefore, while the matter of all appearance is given to us *a posteriori* only, its form must lie ready for the sensations *a priori* in the mind, and so must allow of being considered apart from all sensation. (CPR, B33–34, pp. 65–66)

Here, the sensible qualities are what Kant referred to in this passage as the *matter* of intuition. They are the *material* of intuition. These are the *particulars* of sensory experience. But that which accounts for the possibility of the "positing" of these particulars (and their being distinct) and their being ordered or related, Kant referred to as *form*. Such an item would be a form of intuition. Since space and time are what underwrite the possibility of positing and ordering, Kant called them the *forms* of intuition. But there is more. Although the particulars of sensation (particular colors, sounds, and what not) are given *a posteriori* (where knowledge of what *red* is, for instance, requires the immediate experience of this quality), the forms of intuition are *prior* to these particulars in that they lie at the ready, functioning as the underlying framework in which the particulars appear. Without this underlying "framework," there are no particulars and no order (at least, such would be inconceivable). In other words, the forms of intuition, space and time, are *a priori*. They are prior in the sense that they must be in place in order for the particulars of intuition to be *given*. They are necessary conditions for the very possibility of experience.

5.51   As noted above, Kant had arguments that are intended to demonstrate their priority. Here is one that dealt with space:

Space is a necessary *a priori* representation, which underlies all outer intuitions. We can never represent to ourselves the absence of space, though we can quite well think it as empty of objects. It must therefore be regarded as the condition of the possibility of appearance, and not as a determination dependent upon them. It is an *a priori* representation which necessarily underlies outer appearances. (*CPR*, A24/B39)

This should remind you a bit of Descartes and his notion of presupposition. Remember that for Descartes "*A* presupposes *B*" meant something like "In every case in which we conceive *A*, we conceive *B*, though not in every case vice versa." *Shape* presupposes *extension*, we learned, since in every case in which we conceive *shape*, we conceive *extension* – though not vice versa. This was in turn related to *intelligibility*. "Shape," Descartes wrote, "is unintelligible except in an extended thing . . ." (*Principles*, Part I, Art. 53: AT VIIIA 25; CSM I 210). That is, *extension* is what underlies the intelligibility of *shape*; *extension* is a necessary condition for the possibility of *shape*. This seems to be Kant's view, too. An "outer object," that is, an object given in sensory experience, *presupposes* space. Likewise, space is what underwrites the very intelligibility of an object of "outer" sense; space is a necessary condition for the very possibility of an object of intuition (sensory experience). In this sense, space is *a priori*.

Okay, we are now in a position to understand how Kant took the synthetic 5.52 propositions of mathematics and physics (the laws of nature) to be *a priori*. Geometry, for instance, is *about* space – about all of the various possible relations that it affords. Arithmetic has its origins in time; it is about all of the various possible relations that it affords. Since the propositions of mathematics (geometry and arithmetic) are about the *forms* of intuition, and the forms of intuition are *a priori*, then such propositions are *a priori* (are *a priori* true). Their truth can be known independently of any *given* intuition. So, on Monday you draw up the Pythagorean theorem on the chalkboard and demonstrate that it is true. You do the same on Tuesday. In fact, on every occasion when you draw it on the chalkboard, or draw it on a piece of paper, or even think it, the theorem is true. But you do not say that it is *necessarily* true based off of some Humean inductive line of reasoning. That is, you do not inductively argue that the theorem was true on Monday, on Tuesday, on Wednesday, and so on, and then concluded that it is highly likely that it will be true tomorrow. Its being *necessarily* true has nothing to do with any of the particulars of sensory experience, it has nothing to do with any specific experience. Instead, it is *always* true, and will *always be* true, since what the theorem is about is about that which underlies *all* possible experience – that which underlies the very possibility of experience, namely the form of intuition called *space*. You simply could not have an experience in which geometry failed to be true, since you cannot have an experience in which space was absent. The same sort of reasoning works for the laws of nature. They are ultimately about space and time (and the possible relations they afford; though they may also include the concept of causation), not about the particulars of experience.

5.53   So, we now have an idea of what Kant meant when claiming that the propositions of mathematics and physics (specifically the laws of nature) are synthetic *a priori*.

5.5 The External World

5.54 Kant introduced two senses of "external to the mind." The first is what we will call an *empirical* sense, the other a *transcendental* sense. An object is "external to the mind" in the empirical sense in that it is taken to exist independently of the subjective particulars of sensory experience. So, the apple that is said to be *empirically* external to the mind is taken to exist independently of the particular instance of *red* that you sense when seeing the apple. This sense of "external" aligns with commonsense. By contrast, the transcendental sense of "external to the mind" is quite different and will require some discussion to better understand it. We will see that an "object" that is said to be *transcendentally* external to the mind is not subject to the conditions of space and time; it is not subject to the forms of intuition. Since this is so, such an "object" would be inconceivable (which is why *object* is put in quotes here).

5.55   Kant built these important senses of "external to the mind" out of two versions of his distinction between *ideality* and *reality*. There is an *empirical* version of the distinction between *ideality* and *reality*, which we will call the *empirical ideality–reality distinction*, and there is a *transcendental* version, which we will call the *transcendental ideality–reality distinction*.

5.56   About these distinctions, Henry Allison explained:

> Taken in its empirical sense, "ideality" characterizes the private data of an individual mind. This includes ideas in the Cartesian-Lockean sense or, more generally, any mental content in the ordinary sense of "mental". "Reality", construed in the empirical sense, refers to the intersubjectively accessible, spatiotemporally ordered realm of objects of human experience. At the empirical level, then, the ideality-reality distinction is essentially between the subjective and the objective aspects of human experience. When Kant claims that he is an empirical realist and denies that he is an empirical idealist, he is really affirming that our experience is not limited to the private domain of our own representations, but includes an encounter with "empirically real" spatiotemporal objects.[1]

---

[1] Allison 1983, pp. 6–7.

Here, we get the distinction between what we might take to be the purely subjective sensory "data" that only your mind has access to, versus what you take to be a spatiotemporal world of objects that exist independently of the particulars of your own mind. That you are even able to conceive anything like "your own," private sensory data presupposes the conception of something that is not "your own." Something that depends for its existence on a particular mind is said to be *empirically ideal*. By contrast, something that does not depend for its existence on a particular mind is said to be *empirically real*. The empirical sense of "external to the mind" is derived from this. As just noted, empirical ideality and empirical reality look to be internally related, so that the one requires the other. An object that is said to be empirically real is said to be (empirically) external to the mind. This should remind you of earlier discussions of what we called concept-pairs, our examples being inside-outside, up-down, concave-convex, cause-effect, and so on.

In *Remarks on Colour*, Ludwig Wittgenstein very briefly mentions what 5.57 it might mean to say that two things are "internally related" versus being "externally related":

> A language-game: Report whether a certain body is lighter or darker than another. –But now there's a related one: State the relationship between the lightness of certain shades of colour. (Compare with this: Determining the relationship between the lengths of two sticks – and the relationship between two numbers.) –The form of the propositions in both language-games is the same: "X is lighter than Y". But in the first it is an external relation and the proposition is temporal, in the second it is an internal relation and the proposition is timeless. (Paragraph 1).

Consider the stick and number example. Let us say that you take two sticks and compare them – call them "stick A" and "stick B." You note that stick A is longer than stick B (or, conversely, that stick B is shorter than stick A). Compare this to what you understand about the numbers 2 and 3: the number 3 is greater than the number 2 (or, conversely, the number 2 is less than the number 3). Both employ the grammatical form "x is greater than y" (or, "y is less than x"). Just to be clear, for the sticks, you say, "Stick A is greater (in length) than stick B." Wittgenstein's point is that although you employ the same grammatical form in both the stick and number cases, something very different is being expressed in each case. In the stick-case, the relationship between the sticks is utterly contingent, and is only true for the duration of time in which one is longer than the other. It is easy to imagine that stick B is longer than stick A. This would be akin to Hume's noting that it is as intelligible to imagine that sun's not rising as it is to imagine that it rises. As a way of emphasizing the contingency, Wittgenstein says that this relation is temporal. The number-case is importantly different. That 3 is greater than 2 is not contingent, and time is irrelevant. Unlike the stick-case, you cannot imagine that 2 is greater than 3. Wittgenstein says that this relation is timeless (eternal). There is more. You could easily understand what stick A is (it is a stick), that it has some length, and so on, independently of your ever considering anything at all about stick B. That is, you can consider all sorts of things about stick A and not even be aware that there is a stick B. But the number case is different. You could not be said to understand the number 3, what it is, and yet not know that it is greater than 2. What it is *to be* 3 is that it is greater than 2 (and less than 4). The relation between the sticks, in terms of their respective lengths, is external – it is an *external* relation. Here, we might think of "external" as meaning something like "accidental." The relation between the numbers, in terms of their very "being," is internal – it is an *internal* relation. Here, we might think of "internal" as meaning something like "essential" (though Wittgenstein himself might caution against taking it this way). Applied to Kant, we are saying that the concepts of "empirical ideality" and "empirical reality" are *internally* related – they are like the number-case.

5.58   G.E. Moore also looked carefully at this distinction, in his famous essay, "Proof of an External World" (1939).[2] Moore's analysis employed two phrases introduced by Kant, namely, the phrases "to be presented in space" and "to be met with in space."[3] Let us look at them. Suppose that you look at the sun a bit too long and now notice what we might call its *after-image*. This after-image of the sun is presented *as though it were* a spatial object, located at some distance from you, the perceiving subject (the "I" of experience). Even when you close your eyes, the after-image appears to be "out there." It is circular shaped, whitish-yellow, and "exists" so long as you perceive it. Note that once the after-image fades, it is no longer taken to exist. Moore says that such an "object" meets the criterion for being *presented in space*.

5.59   Contrast this with what we believe about the sun. Although the sun is also presented in space (that is, it is when you look at it), it is also taken by you and others to be an object that can (and does) exist independently of your perceiving it. Moreover, it is taken to be an object that other perceivers, in addition to you, can (and do) perceive. Such an object is to be *met with in space*.[4] This is

---

[2] Moore 1959, pp. 127–150. The paper was originally published in *Proceedings of the British Academy*, Vol. XXV, 1939.

[3] Moore 1959, pp. 130–131. Moore suggests that Kant may have taken these phrases to be coextensive, but Moore's analysis shows that they can be taken as denoting two distinct classes of object.

[4] Kant actually lands on *"things which are to be found in space,"* (Kant, p. 348 (A373)); Moore does not mislead by using "met with" (see, e.g., Kant, p. 348 (A372)).

importantly *unlike* the after-image, which, when perceived by you, is some-thing that only you can perceive, and when no longer perceived by you is taken to no longer exist. The after-image, when perceived, is presented in space, but because it cannot be perceived by multiple perceivers (only you can perceive your after-image), and it is not taken to exist when no longer per-ceived, the after-image is *not* to be met with in space. By contrast, since we take the sun to be perceivable by multiple perceivers and can exist independently of anyone's perceiving it, the sun *is* to be met with in space. When not seen, of course, we might say that the sun is not presented in space. The point is that it is possible for something to be presented in space but not to be met with in space (the after-image), and it is possible for something to not be presented in space but to be met with in space (the sun when no one is looking at it).

Moore wrote: 5.60

> My body, the bodies of other men, the bodies of animals, plants of all sorts, stones, mountains, the sun, the moon, stars, and planets, houses and other buildings, manufactured articles of all sorts – chairs, tables, pieces of paper, etc., are all of the "things which are to be met with in space". In short, all things of the sort that philosophers have been used to call "physical objects", "material things", or "bodies" obviously come under this head.[5]

Things that are solely presented in space (so they are not to be met with in space) depend importantly on the mind. The after-image is our salient example. Moore says that such things are said to be "internal to" a mind. By contrast, he argued, things that are to be met with in space are, in an equally important sense, independent of the mind. The sun is our salient example. Such things are said to be "external to" a mind.[6] Moore's "internal to a mind" is coextensive with what Allison says is "empirically ideal," and Moore's "external to a mind" is coextensive with what Allison says is "empirically real." Empirically real objects are, as Moore notes in the above-quoted pas-sage, typically taken (by commonsense) to be *physical* or *material* objects (i.e. *bodies*), which in being such, exist independently of the mind. (Casting something as physical or material may turn out to be a short-cut to express-ing that it meets the conceptual criteria for being met with in space.)

Now, what accounts for our even being able to draw the distinction 5.61 between the *empirically ideal* and the *empirically real*? What accounts for our being able to conceive of an objective, mind-independent world? Answering this question is tricky business – remember that Berkeley had claimed that you contradict yourself if you claim to conceive of a world that

---

[5] Moore 1959, p. 130.
[6] Moore 1959, pp. 129–130.

stands independently of your conceiving it! Moore's list of empirically real objects in the above passage suggests that the empirically external world, that is, the world that is taken to exist independently of the mind, is perfectly intelligible – it is the commonsense world of tables, chairs, pieces of paper, and so on. But, as Berkeley had argued, if all we have immediate access to are our ideas (specifically, the particulars of them), which in this context are items categorized as empirically *ideal*, a world independent of our ideas would be unintelligible.

5.62   Berkeley appeared to be denying the possibility of empirical reality (an intelligible world of bodies in motion that exists independent of the mind). But, as we noted in Chapter 2, in introducing the *Omni-perceiver*, Berkeley looked to have actually accounted for the category of empirical reality in the end. For, Berkeley now had available to him a sense in which objects could exist independently of any *finite* mind. That certainly aligned his view with commonsense. But Kant saw a problem for Berkeley. We find it lurking in what Kant said about those who cling too tightly to certain forms of idealism. He wrote:

> It is, in fact, this transcendental realist who afterwards plays the part of empirical idealist. After wrongly supposing that objects of the senses, if they are to be external, must have an existence by themselves, and independently of the senses, he finds that, judged from this point of view, all our sensuous representations are inadequate to establish their reality. (*CPR*, A369, p. 346)

A few paragraphs later, he would make a related point:

> Transcendental realism . . . inevitably falls into difficulties, and finds itself obliged to give way to empirical idealism, in that it regards the objects of outer sense as something distinct from the senses themselves, treating mere appearances as self-subsisting beings, existing outside us. (CPR, A371, p. 347)

To better understand Kant's concern, we need to take a closer look at the transcendental version of the *ideality–reality* distinction, which, it is important to note, is different from the empirical ideality–reality distinction just introduced. Concerning the *transcendental ideality–reality distinction*, Allison explained:

> At the transcendental level, which is the level of philosophical reflection upon experience (transcendental reflection), "ideality" is used to characterize the universal, necessary, and, therefore, a priori conditions of human knowledge. . .Kant affirms the transcendental ideality of space and time on

the grounds that they function as a priori conditions of human sensibility. . .Things in space and time (empirical objects) are ideal in the same sense because they cannot be experienced or described independently of these sensible conditions. Correlatively, something is real in the transcendental sense if and only if it can be characterized and referred to independently of any appeal to these same sensible conditions. In the transcendental sense, then, mind independence or being external to the mind (*ausser uns*) means independence of sensibility and its conditions. A transcendentally real object is thus, by definition, a nonsensible object or noumenon.[7]

The answer to the earlier question about what accounts for our being able to draw a distinction between the *empirically ideal* and the *empirically real* is found in Kant's notion of the *transcendentally ideal*. Kant showed that the very conceivability of an empirically real world (an intersubjective, mind-independent world) is actually underwritten by certain conditions – among them space and time. When considering what underlies our even being able to conceive of an empirically real world, in contrast to the domain of empirical ideality, we are now engaged in what Kant calls *philosophical reflection*. We are examining the *concepts* we use. *Transcendentally ideal* objects are those very same objects found in the category of *empirical reality*, such as the sun, but *now* considered in terms of the conditions of their conceivability. In considering what underwrites the very possibility of our conceiving objects that exist independently of the particulars of one's own mind (of things that are to be met with in space), then, these objects are now classified in the category of the *transcendentally ideal*. For, we are no longer talking about the objects *per se* (that is, we are no longer talking about the sun in the heavens), but are talking about what the *mind* contributes in its conceiving (or perceiving) such an object. Whatever is not subject to these conditions, the principal conditions here being space and time, is (by default) categorized in the domain of *transcendental reality*. These are, in the strict-sense, Kant's *noumena*.

To make this clearer, consider the following table (Figure 5.1):   5.63

	Ideality	Reality
Empirical	A	B
Transcendental	C	D

Figure 5.1 Table of the Empirical and Transcendental versions of the Ideality/ Reality distinction.

---

[7] Allison 1983, p. 7.

A-type objects are *empirically ideal*. Like the after-image, they are subjective mental contents that depend for their existence on an actively perceiving mind. B-type objects are *empirically real*. Like the sun, they are objects that are taken to be perceivable by multiple perceivers, and can exist independently of their being perceived by anyone. Keep in mind that this is not an empirical *hypothesis*. Rather, the very possibility of making such hypotheses already presupposes the distinction between empirical ideality and empirical reality. Think back to our earlier example of the apple. The particular *red* that you see when seeing the apple, is an A-type item, whereas the apple, the "physical" apple, the one that you believe exists independently of this particular experience you are having, is a B-type item. The B-type apple is the apple of commonsense.

5.64   Here is where things get tricky. C-type objects are all those objects that are subject to the conditions of space and time – that is, they are subject to the forms of intuition (that is, to the universal conditions that underwrite the very possibility of experience). These objects, of course, were, in light of the empirical distinction, the B-type objects of empirical reality – so, the sun in the heavens and the apple that you are holding. But now cast in light of the *transcendental* distinction, these same objects are taken to be transcendentally *ideal*. For, when you *think* about the sun in the heavens, or the apple in your hand, and consider them to be empirically real, your very thinking about the sun or apple involves the forms of intuition, space and time. Here, instead of taking the sun or the apple to be the sorts of things to which the mind conforms, Kant is saying, now in light of his remarks about Copernicus, that the sun and the apple are made to conform to the mind – it is the *mind* that is "making" the sun and the apple spatiotemporal, where this is what is underwriting your even being able to think of those "external" objects, those empirically real objects – the sun and that apple! D-type objects are *transcendentally real*, and as such they are *not* subject to the conditions of space and time. Because of this, transcendental reality (and any "object" that inhabits it) is unintelligible or inconceivable.

5.65   The category of transcendental reality is admittedly difficult to nail down. Kant realized this, and noted that any further discussion of the items that we might locate in the category will have to be done post-*CPR*. Several of those who followed in Kant's philosophical wake also found this category difficult. Georg Wilhelm Friedrich Hegel (1770–1831), Johann Gottlieb Fitche (1762–1814), and Arthur Schopenhauer (1788–1860), to name three. Here seems to be the problem: Suppose that you are shown a flat piece of sheet metal. It is smooth. Now, someone grabs a hammer and strikes the piece of metal, clearly modifying it by introducing a big dent. The person strikes again. You see the new dent. A few more strikes. Now that you understand what modifications this hammer makes to the sheet metal, you could in turn be shown a hammered piece of sheet metal and be asked whether you can imagine what this piece was like before the hammer was applied, before it was modified. Your answer should be – Yes. Through the imagination you simply backwards engineer the hammering, basically removing the dents or modifications. Right? So, you *can* understand what the object was like before any instrument was applied to it. Now, if space and time are like that hammer, and the mind modifies objects by "making" them spatiotemporal, *can* you imagine what these objects are like prior to the mind's doing its thing? Well, you would have to be able to backwards engineer the application of space and time. So, "take away" space and time. What is left of the object? Notice how this differs from the more familiar sheet metal case. Transcendentally real "objects" cannot be *made* intelligible, since the underlying conditions of intelligibility, namely space and time, are presumably no longer in play. Even so, Kant seemed pretty confident, even in *CPR*, that this category was not empty. You would have to go on to read his *Second Critique*, the *Critique of Practical Reason*, to see how Kant dealt with this category.

Now, you may believe that, in being B-type objects, the sun and the apple 5.66 not only can but *do* exist independently of the particular, subjective contents of your sensory experiences. Fine. But, as noted a moment ago, this cannot be an hypothesis, since there's no way for you to actually confirm or disconfirm that the sun and apple are there when you are not perceiving them (that's Berkeley's point!). Kant's answer to Berkeley was a logical or conceptual (a philosophical) one: the very meaningfulness of the *concept* of a subjective mental realm presupposes the *concept* of an objective extramental realm – no differently than the meaningfulness of the concept of *up* presupposes the concept of *down*, the meaningfulness of the concept of an *inside* presupposes the concept of an *outside*, the meaningfulness of the concept of *truth* presupposes the concept of *falsity*, and so on. These are the sorts of concepts we earlier referred to as concept-pairs. In any context in which it makes sense to say *up*, for example, it will also make sense to say *down*. Likewise, in any context in which it makes sense to talk of the *subjective*, it will make sense to talk of the *objective*. So, *ideality* and *reality* form a concept-pair. In terms established earlier, such concepts are *internally* related.

Allison relates these distinctions to Kant's concepts of *appearance* and 5.67 *thing-in-itself*, which, as just suggested, form a concept-pair (they are internally related). In the empirical sense, *appearance* refers to what is empirically ideal, whereas *thing-in-itself* refers to what is empirically real. Since the latter are taken to exist independently of perceptual acts of a particular mind, Kant seemed okay with referring to them as *things-in-themselves*. But, this is the less-strict sense mentioned earlier, the commonsense notion of a "physical" object. So, we could refer to the "physical" apple, the empirically real apple, as the *apple-in-itself*, but this would be to use the less-strict sense of "thing-in-itself." However, when these same objects, like the sun and the apple, are recast within the context of the transcendental distinction, Allison notes that Kant will now refer to them as *appearances* (and sometimes as *phenomena*). This is so because understood as an *appearance* the sun or apple are now understood within the context of what the *mind* does in making them appear. One of the things the mind *does*, of course, is that it subjects whatever it will represent to the conditions of space and time. When understood this way, as *appearance*, Kant takes the sun and the apple to be transcendentally *ideal*. In contrast, *thing-in-itself* now refers to what is transcendentally *real*. This is the strict-sense of the phrase, and in this sense you cannot even conceive of a thing-in-itself (since such "things" are not subject to the conditions of space and time). You might be able to argue that the category must have at least one member, but you would not be able to say anything substantive about this "object." The point is that Kant is not confused when sometimes referring to the "external" world (and the objects in it) as constituting empirical *reality*, and referring to this same world (and the objects in it), now in light of the transcendental distinction, as constituting transcendental *ideality*. Likewise, he is not confused when sometimes referring to what are taken to be empirically real objects as things-in-themselves, and yet when referring to these things now taken to be transcendentally ideal as appearances.

5.68   The above allows Kant to say, "We assert, then, the *empirical reality* of space, as regards all possible outer experience; and yet at the same time we assert its *transcendental ideality* . . ." (*CPR*, A28/B44, p. 72), where in calling it the latter, "it is nothing at all" (Ibid.). But in this context, calling it "nothing" is supposed to mean that it is not in any way related to anything "outside" the mind, that is, to *noumena* or to things-in-themselves (taken in the strict or transcendental sense). He expresses the same with respect to time.

5.69   What is important to stress is that there does not appear to be anything incoherent in Kant's view. "The transcendental idealist," Kant wrote, ". . . may be an empirical realist or, as he is called, a *dualist*" (*CPR*, A 370, p. 346). A few paragraphs later, he made the even stronger claim, "The transcendental idealist is, therefore, an empirical realist, and allows to matter, as appearance, a reality which does not permit of being inferred, but is immediately perceived" (*CPR*, A371, p. 347).

Where Berkeley went wrong, claimed Kant, was that he had wrongly 5.70
contrasted the category of *empirical ideality* with the category of *transcendental reality* (CPR, B70–71, p. 89; B274–275, p. 244). For, he thought that a
world that existed independent of one's mind was inconceivable – in the
way that transcendental reality is inconceivable. But once properly formulated, we see that the proper counterpart to *empirical ideality* in the concept-pair is *empirical reality*, not *transcendental reality*. And, given the role of the
Omni-perceiver introduced by Berkeley, it seems reasonable to think that
Berkeley could have embraced the category of empirical reality – it would
be the world of objects that exists independently of any finite mind, the
world that the Omni-perceiver "perceives." But Berkeley's kind of idealism,
which according to Kant was a form of empirical idealism (in other places,
Kant referred to it as *dogmatic idealism* and as *fanatical idealism*), is not the
right kind on which to base one's philosophical view – well, it is not the
right kind according to Kant. Kant argued that transcendental idealism is
the better philosophical view, and is the antidote to Berkeley's bad view. For,
it accounts for the very possibility of the distinction drawn between the
empirically ideal and empirically real, and prohibits the mistake of contrasting transcendental reality with empirical ideality.

As for Descartes, Kant thought that his (empirical) idealism emerged as 5.71
an artifact of his method of doubt – where one secured the existence of
one's own mind (the *cogito*), but doubted the existence of the material world
(the empirically real world). Although Descartes took himself to ultimately
prove the existence of the material world, a world that can and does exist
independently of one's mind, Kant suggested that Descartes had failed to
see that even that world, the "material" world, in the end must be understood in light of the conditions under which such a world is conceivable (or
given). Kant pointed out that Descartes's *cogito*, his first principle (*If I am
thinking, I exist*), as formulated in the Second Meditation, actually presupposed the category of empirical reality, which would have allowed him to
claim as early as the Second Meditation that a spatiotemporal world exists
(CPR, B275–276, pp. 244–245). This, too, seems to be in line with the
concept-pair notion. The meaningfulness of the concept of a *subject* of
experience requires its contrast to an *object* of experience, and vice versa.
The "I" or "me," in other words, only makes sense in contrast to a "not-I" or
a "not-me." So, according to Kant, Descartes's analysis did not go far enough.
What he should have understood was that the meaningfulness of empirical
idealism, as entertained in the First and Second Meditations, *required* a
contrasting empirical realism (and vice versa). And, to understand that
would have put Descartes at the threshold of transcendental idealism.

References

Allison, Henry. (1983) *Kant's Transcendental Idealism: An Interpretation and Defense*, New Haven, CT: Yale University Press, pp. 6–7.

Moore, George Edward. (1959) Proof of an external world, in *Philosophical Papers*, Lewis, Hywel David (ed), London: George Allen & Unwin LTD, pp. 127–150.

Readings

Primary Kant Reading

Kant, Immanuel. (1781) *Critique of Pure Reason*, translated by Norman Kemp Smith, London: MacMillan and Co. Limited, 1929. https://archive.org/details/immanuelkantscri032379mbp.

Kant, Immanuel. (1783) *Prolegomena to Any Future Metaphysics*, translated by James W. Ellington, Indianapolis, IN: Hackett Publishing Company, 2001. The online text is based on 1902 translation by Paul Carus. http://www.webexhibits.org/causesofcolor/ref/Kant.html.

Secondary Readings

Moore, George Edward (1939) Proof of an external world. https://rintintin.colorado.edu/~vancecd/phil201/Moore1.pdf.

Rohlf, Michael. (2020) Immanuel Kant in *Stanford Encyclopedia of Philosophy*. https://plato.stanford.edu/entries/kant/.

6

LADY MARY SHEPHERD

Mary Primrose was daughter of Neil Primrose, the Third Earl of Rosebery, 6.1
and Mary Vincent. She was born in December 1777 at Barnbougle Castle in
Scotland, near Edinburgh. She was one of five children, and along with her
sisters was educated at home. In 1808, she married Henry John Shepherd.
According to Shepherd's daughter, Shepherd was philosophically active
long before her marriage. One of the first books to appear under the
Shepherd name took Hume's notion of causation to task, titled *An Essay
upon the Relation of Cause and Effect, controverting the Doctrine of Mr.
Hume, concerning the Nature of Relation; with Observations upon the
Opinions of Dr. Brown and Mr. Lawrence, connected with the same subject*
(1824). A second, which will be important to our study in this chapter, was
titled *Essays on the Perception of an External Universe and other Subjects
Connected with the Doctrine of Causation* (1827), a further critique of the
idealist elements in both Hume's and Berkeley's views. She died in January
1847. She was 69 years old.

6.1 Cause and Effect, and a Proof of the External World

The concept of causation played a central role in Shepherd's philosophical 6.2
system. She proposed it in her first book, *Essay upon the Relation of Cause
and Effect* (1824; hereafter *ERCE*, p. 36). Her principle of causation presupposed two claims, namely, (i) something could not come from nothing and
(ii) something could not be the cause of itself. Thus, if something comes to
be, or begins to exist, as Shepherd would put it, some *other* thing must be
responsible for this thing's coming to be, or its beginning to exist. This

This Is Modern Philosophy: An Introduction, First Edition. Kurt Smith.
© 2023 John Wiley & Sons, Inc. Published 2023 by John Wiley & Sons, Inc.

other thing (the cause) is taken to exist independently of that which was caused.

6.3   In the Preface to a short treatise that followed, titled *Essay on the Academical or Skeptical Philosophy* (1827; hereafter *EASP*), Shepherd reveals an important role that she had intended her causal principle to play:

> It was my intention in a former publication to have introduced an appendix containing some inquiry into the nature and proof of the existence of matter, and of an external universe . . . (*EASP*, p. xi)

EASP was included along with several supporting shorter essays in a collection titled *Essays on the Perception of an External Universe* (1827; hereafter *EPEU*). This is a title that aligns almost perfectly with the theme of our study of the period, of our examination into what we are calling The Problem of the External World. We shall explore Shepherd's view as laid out in *EASP*.

6.4   According to Shepherd, the knowledge of a material world, of a world that exists independent of the mind, was to be obtained by way of a proper understanding of the relation between *cause* and *effect*. In *EASP*, still in the Preface, Shepherd continued:

> Now the question concerning the *nature* and *reality* of external existence can only receive a satisfactory answer, derived from a knowledge of *the relation of Cause and Effect*. (*EASP*, p. xii)

Her view, as we shall see, was meant to challenge the views of both Berkeley and Hume (and Thomas Reid's response to Hume's view). In this chapter, we will focus mostly on Shepherd's account of the belief that a material world exists independent of the mind. As she makes clear in the opening of *EASP*, she was not interested in offering a point-by-point criticism of Hume's view. So, we will have to do some work to ferret out how it is that her view controverts Hume's. Berkeley's view suffers a different fate. Shepherd specifically addresses what she sees to be Berkeley's failings. But even here, as Margaret Atherton has suggested, Shepherd may have either ignored or misunderstood the subtleties of Berkeley's view (Atherton 1996). So, it is not perfectly clear that Shepherd's critique does as much damage to Berkeley's view as Shepherd herself had originally estimated. For our purpose, which is primarily to understand Shepherd's view, we need not concern ourselves with the fine details of her critique of Berkeley's view. It will be enough for us if we can bring to light how her arguments against *idealism*, at least against the type of empirical idealism forwarded by Berkeley and Hume, supported her rejection of the views of both philosophers.

Shepherd's account of the *belief* in the existence of a material world, a world that exists independently of the mind, at least at one point in her writings looks to appeal to what we might call "commonsense philosophy," a philosophical approach that had in fact emerged out of the Scottish school, which looks to have later influenced the work of such philosophers as Cambridge philosopher G.E. Moore. This is worth mentioning insofar as there appear to be remnants of Shepherd's view lurking in Moore's now famous paper focused on the proof of an external world. But before we get to the commonsense reading of her work, we will begin with taking a closer look at Shepherd's view on causation and how that was understood by her to yield a proof of an external world. We will consider one of her more interesting references to mathematics that may suggest a fruitful way of understanding her view. Along the way, we will see that her view had some interesting connections to views we have already examined – specifically, the views of Descartes, Hobbes, and Kant.
6.5

6.2 Hume and The Problem of the External World

Let us start with Shepherd's own recounting of that part of Hume's view she had intended to address. In Section I of the Introductory Chapter of *EASP*, she writes:
6.6

> The question intended to be investigated in the following pages is thus stated in the "Treatise on Human Nature," "Why we attribute a continued existence to objects even when they are not present to the senses?" And, "why we suppose them to have an existence distinct from the mind; i.e. *external in their position*, and *independant* in their existence and operation?" Mr. Hume argues at great length, that it is not by means of the "*senses*, or of *reason*;" that "we are induced to believe in the existence of body;" but that we gain the notion entirely by an operation of the "*imagination*" which has "a propensity to *feign* the continued existence of all sensible objects, and as this propensity arises from some lively impressions on the memory, it bestows a vivacity on that fiction, or in other words, makes us believe the continued existence of body." It is not my intention to analyze Mr. Hume's reasoning on this subject, which I conceive to be altogether erroneous, and which it would be very tedious to examine; I prefer, therefore, answering the question as it stands, according to my own views of it, setting down what experience and reflection suggest to my mind as the operations of nature in

this matter; and I shall endeavor to point out what complication of objects, and what arrangement of them is necessary towards that result which appears to us from its familiarity and constancy of appearance, perfectly simple and easy to be understood. But, first, I shall shortly observe, that Mr. Hume's error in general is similar to that in the essay on "necessary connexion," viz. of substituting "*imagination*" and "*vivacity of thought*," as a ground of belief, instead of "*reason*." "An idea," says Mr. Hume, "acquires a vivacity by its relation to some present impression," and this at once, according to him, forms the whole ground upon which our "belief" rests, of the necessity there is, that *similar effects* should flow from *similar causes*, and *that objects should continue to exist unperceived.* It is my intention to shew here, as upon a former occasion, that as the very *act of reasoning consists in drawing out to observation the relations of things as they are included in their juxta-position to each other*; so upon this question, concerning our "knowledge of the existence of body," it is REASON, which taking notice of the *whole* of our perceptions, and of their *mutual relations*, affords those proofs "of body" which first generate, and after examination will substantiate, the belief of its existence. (*EASP*, Chapter I, Section I, pp. 1–3)

When we look over *EASP*, it becomes clear that Shepherd had structured it in line with how Hume's discussion had unfolded in *A Treatise of Human Nature*, Book I, Part IV, Sections I and II. In these sections, as we know from our earlier study (Chapter 4), Hume had reminded his reader of his account of the origins of the notion of *causation*, and then provided his account of what he saw to be the philosophically problematic *belief* in the existence of a world that exists independent of the mind, of a world that exists even when not perceived by the mind. It is worth reminding ourselves that his accounts of both, of the notion of causation and of the belief in the existence of an external world, ran along similar lines, both rooted in how he saw the influence of the *imagination* in conjunction with the influence of *custom* or *habit*.

6.3 Consciousness and Sensation

6.7 Shepherd took all "objects" of consciousness, whether purely intellectual, emotional, imaginary, or sensory, to be *sensations*. She wrote:

I know, indeed, that it is usual to apply the term *sensation* to those perceptions only which are unaccompanied with the notion *of their inhering* in *an outward object*, as the pain arising from the incision of a sharp instrument is a sensation, which is *not in the instrument*. But in reality every thought, notion, idea, feeling, and perception, which distinguishes a sentient nature from unconscious existence, may be considered generally as sensation. (*EASP*, Introductory Chapter, p. 7)

Consider the sensation of pain. Let us say that this is pain felt upon one's being stuck with a sharp pin. Unlike the sharpness, which is attributed to the pin, the pain is not taken as a property or quality of the pin, that is, it is not something that one takes to inhere in the *outward* object. This pain instead is taken to be a purely mental, fleeting entity, available only to the mind that perceives it, which represents to the perceiver of the pain some harm to the perceiver's body. Shepherd, as seen in the above passage, extends "sensation" to refer to *all* objects of consciousness. Thus, not only is the pain a sensation, but so is the pin *as seen*, the thought had when thinking about the sharpness of the pin, the mental image one might conjure when recalling having been stuck, and the fear about being stuck again.

She claims that her use of the word "perception" was for the most part 6.8 aligned with Hume's. But, there was a caveat: "However, when I occasionally use the word 'perception', I use it in the sense of '*consciousness of sensation*', a SENSATION TAKEN NOTICE OF BY THE MIND" (Ibid., p. 9), noting that this was the sense in which Locke had also used the term. She allows that not every perception is "*the perception of an exterior object*," but insists that "there can be *no perception* of such objects without that *inward act* of consciousness, which, as a consciousness, is in truth a sensation of the mind" (Ibid., pp. 6–7). So, to count as a *perception*, whether the perception of pain or the perception of the pin, the mind must be *aware of* this pain or the pin (specifically the visual sense *qualia* constituting the pin *as seen*). A perception, then, requires at least two components: a *sensation*, which is the "object" of which one is immediately aware, and the *act* of being aware. This is true even when *perceiving* a thought about the Pythagorean theorem – the immediate object would be the theorem thought, where it would have to also be the case that one was *aware of* the theorem thought. Given her view that "as a consciousness" a perception was "in truth a sensation of the mind," and given that "*all we know* must be by means of *consciousness*, or *sensations*" (Ibid.), Shepherd seems to take "perception," "consciousness," and "sensation" to be synonymous. Taking them as such may lead to confusion, however, so we will be avoiding taking them this way. To keep things as clear as possible for us, let us proceed by taking *perception* to be the *awareness of a sensation*, where at the very least *perception* includes both sensation and an act of consciousness (here, awareness of a sensation).

We shall take "sensation" to denote the immediate *object* of consciousness, whether that object be a pain, a pin, a thought about the pain or pin or the Pythagorean theorem, and, as just suggested, we will let "perception" denote the unified moment in which a perceiver is *conscious of* a *sensation*.

6.9   At several places in *EASP*, Shepherd casts sensations as expressing a "dual" aspect – what we might call, for lack of a better name, an *external* and an *internal* aspect. A sensation is *one* item, or *one* being, or *one* essence, with *two* aspects. In having a sensation, or, in being conscious of a sensation, the sensation is *given* to the mind, expressing both aspects, immediately informing the perceiver of both. She suggests that the sensation would typically occur *prior* to reason's using the external and internal aspects to draw conclusions, so that even the conclusions drawn (subsequent *thoughts*) would now count as sensations. They would be new sensations. This is suggested, for example, when she considers how one might go about making corrections with respect to what one senses. She writes:

> For under any illusion of the senses, a person would say, (as of sight, for instance,) "I thought there had been a bird in this room; until I *perceived* it was only a painting:" meaning that he made use of the *whole knowledge relating to the subject*, then in the mind, as an instrument, an inward eye, to correct the impressions at first received; and when the doctrine I propose becomes unfolded, the following is the conclusion to which I wish it may lead, viz. *That the relations of various sensations generate conclusions, which become new sensations or perceptions, and which, as so many inward objects of sense, afford an evidence of the existence of the exterior objects to which they refer, equal to the evidence there is for any existing sensation whatever, in the mere consciousness of its presence.* (*EASP*, Introductory Chapter, Section II, p. 8)

The sensation, in being present to the mind, not only provides "evidence" for something *internal*, for something with which the mind is directly and immediately acquainted, presumably arising from the sensation's *internal* aspect, but it also provides at the same time "evidence" for something *external*, which is a result of the sensation's *external* aspect. The "evidence" for the latter, for the *externality* given, is as compelling to the mind as is the "evidence" for the former, for the *internality* given. One might think that the presence of the sensation would speak only to the internal. But, she insists, the sensation's very presence will also speak to the external – in other words, the "object" is at the very least given as being *other* than the "I" that is aware of this "object," but also suggests to the perceiver that the "object" perceived has it origin in something other than the perceiver (the "not-I" or *other* has an origin in something other than the "I").

A few pages later, she again emphasizes the *giveness* of the "external"   6.10
aspect of sensation, and how that is able to prompt reason to conclude that
the objects responsible for a sensation's "beginning to exist," exist not only
during the occurring sensation, but even prior:

> For by a *general* sensation present to the mind, it *always* possesses the notion
> of the *possibility* of the existence of unperceived objects; and from the facts
> which take place; it can only explain the appearance of objects, by the sup-
> position that they actually do exist when unperceived or unfelt. For the mind
> perceives that unless they are *created purposely, ready to appear*, upon each
> irregular call of the senses, they must CONTINUE *to exist, ready to appear* to
> them upon such calls. (Ibid., pp. 13–14)

This sounds a little like what Hume had said, when talking about his experiences of mountains, trees, and the furniture in his room. We will look more
closely at this similarity shortly.

Martha Brandt Bolton has argued that Shepherd looked to have devel-   6.11
oped two versions of the *external/internal* distinction (which Bolton refers
to as "layers"): a *thin* layer and a *thick* layer. Bolton writes:

> Shepherd has a layered definition of this pair of notions. In the first instance,
> internal existence pertains to the capacity for sensations in general, that is the
> mind, or power of thought and feeling. External existence pertains to the
> exciting cause of any particular sensation (*EASP*: 40). In context of CP
> [Shepherd's *Causal Principle*], nothing that satisfies one of these definitions
> can satisfy the other. A mixture of both is necessary for the existence of a sen-
> sation. Now sensations are nothing other than appearances in consciousness,
> realizations of the general capacity for sensations, i.e. the mind. With this in
> view, Shepherd advances the thick notion of internal existence: an entity is
> thickly internal just in case one and only [one] individual can be conscious of
> it. A thing is thickly external, then, just in case it can be perceived by more
> than one human being. The thick distinction marks the difference between
> what is private and what is public . . .. The thick distinction divides the subjec-
> tive and objective components of sense perception. (Bolton 2017)

We will adopt Bolton's take on Shepherd. By chapter's end, we will see that
it dovetails nicely with some of the earlier discussion of Kant (Chapter 5),
and also suggests some similarities with things said by Descartes (Chapter 1)
and Hobbes (Chapter 2).

Bolton points out that Shepherd had declared that anything that begins   6.12
to exist must have a cause, and that this was the basis for her causal principle

(Bolton 2017, Section 2.1). This is interesting, since Hume had admitted that it was a general maxim in philosophy "that *whatever begins to exist, must have a cause of existence*" (*Treatise*, Book I, Part III, Section III, p. 78). He had also noted that philosophers had simply taken it for granted, not ever really offering anything that looked like a knockdown proof (Ibid.). But Hume was not perplexed by this, since, on his view, no proof *could* be given, at least no acceptable deductive argument, since such a proof would require one to employ the relations of *resemblance, proportions in quantity and number, degrees of any quality, and contrariety,* "none of which," he claimed, "imply'd in this proposition, *Whatever has a beginning has also a cause of existence*" (Ibid.).

6.13   Hume's argument against this general maxim was based on the fact that one could easily imagine the sudden appearance of something, where its appearance was not preceded by anything related to it. In other words, we could separate in thought the idea of some *object* and the idea of *cause*. Thus, it was not *necessary* that anything *precede* another thing; or that whatever begins to exist must have a cause. He wrote:

> . . . as the ideas of cause and effect are evidently distinct, 'twill be easy for us to conceive any object to be non-existent this moment, and existent the next, without conjoining to it the distinct idea of a cause or productive principle. The separation, therefore, of the idea of a cause from that of a beginning of existence, is plainly possible for the imagination; and consequently the actual separation of these objects is so far possible, that it implies no contradiction nor absurdity; and is therefore incapable of being refuted by any reasoning from mere ideas; without which 'tis impossible to demonstrate the necessity of a cause. (Ibid., pp. 79–80)

He went on to argue further that any arguments in support of this general maxim would presuppose the very thing they were claiming to prove (Ibid.). According to Bolton, Shepherd's view may very well succumb to Hume's criticism here, for "the texts offer no non-question begging argument for her central metaphysical doctrine. They assume the theory of causality they purport to prove" (Bolton 2017, Section 2.1). That said, perhaps Shepherd could overcome such an assessment if her view was looked at from a different point of view. The point of view on which we might focus is found in Shepherd's discussions of cause and effect being *compositional*, where there is understood to be a *union* of the items involved (agent and patient, or cause and effect); this compositional entity expressing a *synchronicity* between or among the two constituents, "cause" and "effect" being nothing "but different words for the same *Essence*" (*ERCE*, p. 57; Bolton 2017, Section 2.1). As Bolton puts it: ". . . the ideas of cause and effect are two ways of representing the same thing which are not entirely without basis in the thing" (Ibid.). Let us pause and make this clearer. To do this, we will refer back to Descartes and Hobbes.

Shepherd's *external/internal* distinction looks to hearken back to something we found in Descartes's characterization of sensation. Recall that in the Third Meditation, Descartes had raised the question about his believing that objects existed "outside" his thought. He wrote: 6.14

> But the chief question at this point concerns the ideas which I take to be derived from things existing outside me . . .. Nature has apparently taught me to think this. But in addition I know by experience that these ideas do not depend on my will, and hence that they do not depend simply on me. Frequently I notice them even when I do not want to: now, for example, I feel the heat whether I want to or not, and this is why I think that this sensation or idea comes to me from something other than myself, namely the heat of the fire by which I am sitting. And the most obvious judgment for me to make is that the thing in question transmits to me its own likeness rather than something else. (*Meditations*, AT VII 38; CSM II 26)

Here, the "external" aspect is given in experience as the "against my will" element. This is as much felt as is the *heat*. This "against my will" element presented in experience prompts the mind to make the judgment that the *heat* originates in something other than, or external to, the mind, something that resembles or is like the *heat*. Descartes was quick, however, to revise this claim, so that this initial "judgment" was not taken as anything originating in the will, but was in fact a kind of spontaneous impulse, something that he said *nature* had taught him (Ibid.).

In the Sixth Meditation, Descartes would take up the issue again, where he would recast sensations as having an *active* and a *passive* aspect. He wrote: 6.15

> Now there is in me a passive faculty of sensory perception, that is, a faculty for receiving and recognizing the ideas of sensible objects; but I could not make use of it unless there was also an active faculty, either in me or in something else, which produced or brought about these ideas. But this faculty cannot be in me, since clearly it presupposes no intellectual act on my part, and the ideas in question are produced without my cooperation and often even against my will. So the only alternative is that it [a sensation's origin] is in another substance distinct from me . . .. (*Meditations*, AT VII 79; CSM II 57)

The "against my will" element is again appealed to as indicating that the sensation has its origin in something other than the mind. This counts as "evidence" in some sense for something external (i.e. *independent* of the mind). To be sure, *reason* may subsequently conclude that from the experience there must be some object, distinct from the mind, that produces these sensations, but the "evidence" is apparently given in the experience *prior* to one's making that judgment. Shepherd's view appears to be similar.

6.16   The only active faculty of the mind for Descartes was the *will*. If the will was the origin of a sensation, then the sensation would not be experienced as coming before the mind *against* the will. In the *Passions of the Soul* (1649), Descartes would say: "For it is certain that we cannot will anything without thereby perceiving that we are willing it" (AT XI 343; CSM I 335). So, if the will had produced the sensation in question (e.g. *heat*), the mind would experience this sensation as coming before the mind as a *result* of the will. Since the mind experiences sensations as coming *against* the will (they appear before the mind without the will's consent), it follows that the mind is not that which "produces" sensations, or, to put it in Shepherd's terms, the mind is not that which is responsible for a sensation's *beginning to exist*. The external aspect of a sensation points the way to "outward" or to "other," where that which is causally responsible for a sensation's beginning to exist must be something other than the mind.

6.17   Descartes would again raise the notion of passive and active aspects belonging to one and the same thing. In this context, the "thing" he was talking about was something present before the human mind, which, cast in one light was a *thought*, and which cast in another light was *motion(s)* in the brain (body). In the *Passions*, he writes:

> In the first place, I note that whatever takes place or occurs [in the mind] is generally called by philosophers a "passion" with regard to the subject to which it happens and an "action" with regard to that which makes it happen. Thus, although an agent and patient are often quite different, an action and passion must always be a single thing which has these two names on account of the two different subjects to which it may be related. (Ibid., AT XI 328; CSM I 328)

He goes on to write: "Consequently we should recognize that what is a passion in the soul is usually an action in the body" (Ibid.). Shepherd's view on sensation seems to be akin to this: the sensation that is present before the mind can be cast in two lights – in one light, the sensation is cast as that of which the mind is directly and immediately aware, something belonging to the mind (the internal aspect); in the other light, the sensation is cast as that whose origin is not the mind (the external aspect), but is something that must be *independent of* and *other than* the mind.

*

Shepherd's notion is a bit more nuanced than Descartes's and appeals to *three* items. Margaret Atherton explains the view as follows:

> Shepherd holds the fact of the matter is that sensible objects are the product of the union of three things: 'first, the unknown, unnamed circumstances in nature, which are unperceived by the senses; secondly, the organs of sense, whose qualities mix with these; and thirdly, the living, conscious powers necessary to sensation in general' (*EASP*, pp. 71–72). The result of the joint operation of these causal factors is the apprehension of ideas. (Atherton 1996, p. 350)

Shepherd strengthens her appeal by emphasizing the fact that in normal cases of sensory perception, the objects perceived can be perceived again and again – we see a large oak tree on a walk in the park, and upon our return home we again see the large oak. We return to the park the next day, and we see the oak tree yet again. The details are found in what Shepherd says in *EASP*. Atherton continues her examination:

> Thus, our sensations exhibit what Shepherd refers to frequently as a 'readiness to reappear.' This readiness to reappear can't be due either to our sense organs or to our minds since both of these are on-going unchanging existences. Therefore, there must be something else whose continuous existence accounts for the variety and pattern among our sensations. What Shepherd says is: '*The readiness, therefore, to appear when called for* by the use of the organs of sense, mixed with the reasoning, that the organs of sense and mind being the same, a *third* set of objects is needed in order to determine those perceptions in *particular* which are neither the organs of sense nor mind *in general* . . . [and so it is that these three items form] together . . . the notion of the continual existence of objects unperceived.' (pp. *EASP*, p. 15) (Atherton 1996, p. 351)

As noted earlier, this looks familiar, for it hearkens back to what Hume had said about his experience of the mountains, houses, trees, the furniture in his home, and the fire burning in his fireplace. Hume wrote:

> After a little examination, we shall find, that all those objects, to which we attribute a continu'd existence, have a peculiar *constancy*, which distinguishes them from the impressions, whose existence depends upon our perception. Those mountains, and houses, and trees, which lie at present under my eye,

have always appear'd to me in the same order: and when I lose sight of them by shutting my eyes or turning my head, I soon after find them return upon me without the least alteration . . . [Even so] . . . Bodies often change their position and qualities, and after a little absence or interruption may become hardly knowable. But here 'tis observable, that even in these changes they preserve a *coherence*, and have a regular dependence on each other; which is the foundation of a kind of reasoning from causation, and produces the opinion [belief] of their continu'd existence. When I return to my chamber after an hour's absence, I find not my fire in the same situation, in which I left it: But then I am accustom'd in other instances to see a like alteration produc'd in a like time, whether I am present or absent, near or remote. This coherence, therefore, in their changes is one of the characteristics of external objects, as well as their constancy . . . [in this way] continu'd existence of body depends on the COHERENCE and CONSTANCY of certain impressions . . ..
(*Treatise*, Book I, Part IV, Section II, p. 194–195)

Given the similarity between their views on this front, how might Shepherd's view be understood to differ from Hume's? An important difference that stands out is that whereas Hume would beg off from claiming any knowledge of what exactly is "out there," beyond our impressions, and thus remain a skeptic, Shepherd will claim that the unperceived causes will be neither the sense organs nor solely the mind itself (i.e. none of the operations of consciousness) but will be *bodies*.

6.18   Although she does not offer an argument with explicit premises and conclusion against Hume's view on this specific issue, the argument that Descartes had offered in the Sixth Meditation would support her claim. There, recall, Descartes had set up a version of a disjunctive syllogism. Simply put the argument looked like this:

1. Either the cause of my sensations is my mind, some other finite mind, God, or body.
2. The cause of my sensations is neither my mind, nor some other finite mind, nor God.
3. Therefore, the cause of my sensations is body.

A good hunk of the Sixth Meditation had focused on establishing premise (2). As part of that focus, Descartes had ruled out God as a direct or immediate cause of our sensations. Shepherd's view is consistent with this analysis, suggesting not only an important difference between her view and Hume's, but more to the point, a difference between her view and Berkeley's. For whereas Berkeley will claim that the unperceived cause of sensation is God, Shepherd, along with Descartes and Locke, will claim that the unperceived cause is body. Although she does not say it explicitly, as just suggested perhaps she would be friendly to Descartes's arguments on this front (which in part established premise (2) above), for his own line of reasoning led him to the same view – bodies, and not God, are the direct causes of sensations. The short version of the argument in support of premise (2), recall from Chapter 1, was that if God were the cause of our sensations or of our sensory ideas of body, God would be a deceiver. God is not (*cannot* be) a deceiver. Therefore, God is not the cause of our sensations or of our sensory ideas of body. Perhaps, Shepherd could accept this argument as a way of rejecting both Berkeley's and Hume's views. Her argument, using Atherton's summation of it as our guide and Descartes's use of the Disjunctive Syllogism form, might look like this:

1. Either the cause of my sensation is an act of my consciousness, or a sensory organ, or a mind-independent unperceived thing (which we call "body").
2. The cause of my sensation is neither an act of my consciousness nor a sensory organ.
3. Therefore, the cause of my sensation is a mind-independent unperceived thing (which we call "body").

But this argument is not quite right, for, as Atherton makes clear in her 6.19 analysis, Shepherd took a sensation (or a sensible object) to be caused by *all three* items – by some mind-independent unperceived thing, the sensory organ, and the mind (one of its operations). In identifying the mind-independent unperceived thing as the cause in *this* context, Shepherd would appear to be focusing not so much on the *occurring* sensation (on the sensible object now present before the mind) but on its *beginning* to exist, on what *initiates* its occurrence. The occurring sensation, the sensible object now before the mind, is maintained by a collaboration of all three items – the mind-dependent unperceived thing, the sensory organ, and the mind (one of its operations). But what is responsible for *initiating* the activity of the sensory organ and the mind (what recruits them as collaborating causes) is the mind-independent unperceived thing. So, we might alter premises (1) and (2) above thus, which can then yield (3):

1. Either the cause of a sensation's beginning to exist is an act of consciousness, a sensory organ, or some mind-independent unperceived thing (which we call "body").
2. The cause of a sensation's beginning to exist is neither an act of consciousness nor a sensory organ.
3. Therefore, the cause of a sensation's beginning to exist is a mind-independent unperceived thing (which we call "body").

6.20   Atherton describes the gist of Shepherd's reasoning:

> The idea is that various relations among our sensations constitute a proof
> there are external existences, because, roughly speaking, the existence of the
> sensations we experience, related as they are, could not be explained unless
> bodies existed. (Atherton 1996, p. 350)

Though not perfectly clear, the basic line of reasoning in support of our
new premise (2), in our modification of Shepherd's argument above, can be
found in Shepherd's discussions of one's experience of oneself as an enduring "thing," a self, that appears to remain one and the same self over time. I
appear to be the same self that experiences *now* as that which experienced
a few seconds ago. Nothing is more obvious or certain to me than that. Her
account also requires that sensory organ systems remain relatively constant
and stable, for they serve as the material media by way of or through which
motion is transferred. Drop a pebble in a pond. The ripple effect (motion)
that moves outward to the shore does so by way of the water, the material
medium. The water remains relatively constant, as a medium, which allows
the ripple, initially caused by the pebble, to "travel" from a point where the
pebble had entered the water outward to the shore. The sensory organ is
analogue to the water. It serves as the material medium for the transfer or
the communication of motion. Motion conveyed from a body in contact
with a sensory organ will, like the ripple, "travel" through the sensory organ
(itself a body). And, like the water, the sensory organ, as medium, can do
this only if it remains relatively constant and stable.

6.21   In pre-philosophical ordinary experience, it would be easy to show that a
sensory organ remains relatively stable by way of a simple experiment: alter
the sensory organ and one will alter one's perception. Children find that if
they push on the corner of the eye that visual perception is altered. Release
the pressure and perception returns to "normal." Thus, ordinary experience
would show that a sense organ has something to do with how we experience
things; the sense organ would appear to stand between the world "outside"
and the mind's perception of that world. Of course, when doing philosophy,
this insight afforded to the one who conducts this sort of experiment done
in a moment of ordinary experience can be challenged. So, the results of the
experiment are not philosophically definitive. That said, there is something
to be said about the insights of ordinary experience. Even Descartes had
noted that there was something good to be said about what *nature* taught
him – it was just that the good was not an *epistemological* good.

6.22   Shepherd does not seem as interested in accounting for why it is that sensible *qualia* or sensations vary in the sense that there is a variety of *kinds of*

sensations such as colors, sounds, feels, tastes, and the like, as she does in accounting for the fleeting and ever-changing coming to be and ceasing to be of the individual sensations themselves. Descartes and Locke had already provided a reasonable account of the variety of different kinds of sensations: variation in the material configuration of the organs accounted for the variety. Suppose that one sits close to a fire. Let the motion of the particles constituting what we are calling "the fire" contact this human's body. The motions of the particles are transferred through one sensory organ system (e.g. the eyes) resulting in the perception of color (*yellow*); the motions of the *same* particles transferred through another sensory organ system (e.g. the skin) result in the perception of *heat*. The difference in *qualia* does not stem from any difference in the motions of the particles constituting the fire *per se*, but in the difference in the material configurations of the respective sensory organ systems (which is another good reason for thinking that sensory organs play some causal role in producing the sensations we perceive). This account takes the fire (the particles constituting it) to be responsible for *initiating* the appearance of the *yellow* and the *heat*, but not for the difference between *yellow* and *heat*. Minus this part of the account, the part that requires there to be some prior unperceived thing that initiates sensory experience, the door is opened for the sort of idealism advocated for by Berkeley and Hume. Shepherd shows more than having a little interest in keeping that door shut, and one way to do that would be to show that the best way to account for the flux of fleeting sensations in experience – for the *beginning* and *ceasing* to exist of sensations – is the account that posits that *bodies* exist independently of sensory experience, and are the causes of the flux perceived.

In identifying one's mind and one's sensory organ systems (or sensory faculties) as remaining relatively stable and constant, then, Shepherd was able to identify an unperceived mind-independent thing as the culprit responsible for the continual flux one experiences. If we do not include body as part of the account, then we are left with the sort of account offered by Hume. But there is more. Ironically, perhaps, the account that makes reference to body best explaining the sort of constancy and consistency of objects perceived (think of one's experience of that tree in the park), the account that goes further than Hume was willing to go, aligns perfectly with the account of the flux of fleeting *qualia*. Conjoining these two contrary issues, flux and constancy, may be where Shepherd takes her view to make its advance on Hume's view. 6.23

The dual role played by *body* in the accounts just mentioned is hard at work in the following analysis. When one closes one's eyes and then opens them, what would guarantee (epistemically) that the *yellow* perceived before closing the eyes is the same *yellow* perceived after opening them? Hume denies any guarantee. In fact, he argued that logically the *yellow* perceived 6.24

at t_1 and the *yellow* perceived at t_3, where t_2 is an interruption of the two (one closes one's eyes, say, and does *not* perceive *yellow* at t_2), would fail to meet the criterion of identity. On logical grounds, reason should deny that we perceive the same *quale* over time, the denial strengthened when perception was taken to have been interrupted. According to Hume, the imagination succeeds at overriding reason, giving rise to the belief that not only is *yellow* at t_1 the same *yellow* that one sees at t_3, but to the belief that whatever is responsible for producing the *quale* at t_1 and t_3 continues to exist even during the interval t_2. Hume argued that neither of these beliefs is justified via reason. Shepherd argues the contrary. The intellect, when considering ordinary experience, has *every* reason to include the claim that an unperceived mind-independent thing is a causal collaborator in producing sensations. The challenge in overcoming Berkeley and Hume would be to show that this something, in being other than one's mind, is best conceived as being *material*, as being extended in length, breadth, and depth, as having a shape, as having a size, and so on.

6.25   Appealing to discussions in *EASP*, Atherton suggests that Shepherd had in mind something like the following argument:

1. Minds are stable things and do not change.
2. Sensory organs (as media for transmission of motion) are stable and do not change.
3. We are aware of changes, of a flux of sensible items such as colors, sounds, etc.
4. The changes (or flux) that we are aware of must be caused by something.
5. Therefore, something other than the mind and sensory organ is the cause of these changes, of the flux of sensible items such as colors, sounds, etc.

Contending that the cause of a sensation is the causal collaboration of a mind-independent unperceived thing, a sensory organ, and the mind (one of its operations), Shepherd reasons that based upon the stability of mind and sensory organ, it follows by default that the flux of sensory experience (understood in terms of the *beginning* and *ceasing to exist* of instances of sense *qualia*) must have its causal origin in the mind-independent unperceived thing. Something that was not a mind, which is in part meant in our calling it "mind-independent," would have a different nature. There were several philosophically popular accounts of such a difference, the most obvious being that offered by Descartes, who had claimed in the Synopsis of his *Meditations* (AT VII 13; CSM II 9–10), for instance, that the natures of mind and body are not only different but *contrary* in some sense: minds *think*, bodies *are extended in length, breadth, and depth*. Minds are not extended, and bodies do *not* think. Although she does not explicitly make the connection to Descartes, Shepherd's account seems consistent with Descartes's, casting this unperceived mind-independent something as a *body* – as a thing that is essentially extended in three dimensions, with a definite shape and size, and so on. This, she contends, best aligns with everyday ordinary experience of the world. Very likely, however, her view is rooted in Locke's view, which was very close to Descartes's, the view that the conceptual necessity related to conceiving body as extended, as shaped, as sized, as moving or at rest. For, it would explain why this unperceived thing would require us to conceive it as having these properties.

Before moving forward, it is worth reminding ourselves that Descartes 6.26 had claimed that both finite mind and body ultimately depend ontologically on God. So, although body is directly causally responsible for producing (or occasioning) sensations in the mind, ultimately God is causally responsible for the existence of body, and for instituting the causal relationship between body and mind. So, by a kind of causal transitivity, one might argue that ultimately God (and not body) is the cause of sensations in a (finite) mind. That was, after all, the sort of view entertained by Nicolas Malebranche (1638–1715), a devoted Cartesian who followed almost immediately in Descartes's wake. But more importantly for us, it appears to be aligned with the view of Berkeley – who had claimed that the cause of our sensations is God. If we allowed the above line of reasoning to extend far enough, there might be a way of entertaining an agreement between Descartes, Locke, Berkeley, and Shepherd. For, they might agree that *ultimately* God is the cause of all perceptions. But to be clear, Descartes and Shepherd seem poised to resist this suggestion. And, of course, Hume would continue to remain the skeptical outlier, since he would almost certainly reject any of the claims made here about God.

As mentioned earlier, Shepherd's view also shares some elements with 6.27 Hobbes's, the latter discussed at some length in Chapter 2. As we know from our discussions in that chapter, Hobbes held that sensations were nothing more than *motions*. Let us remind ourselves what he had said about motion generally. For instance, he wrote: "As when one body by putting forwards another body generates motion in it, it is called the agent, and the body in which motion is so generated, is called the patient" (*De Corpore*, Part 2, Chapter IX, Section 1, p. 87). He would go on to relate the agent to the *cause* and the patient to the *effect*. He would claim that an aggregate of accidents (i.e. corporeal properties) possessed by the agent, "required for the production of the effect, is called the *efficient cause*" (Ibid., Section 4, p. 88). And, he would claim that the aggregate of accidents in the patient, required for its being affected by an agent, is called the *material cause* (Ibid.). Each by itself, the efficient and material cause, is only a "partial cause." It is only when both are together "joyned" that they constitute what Hobbes called the "entire cause" (Ibid.). In plain terms, Hobbes seems to have had in mind the view that the agent possesses the *ability* to produce motion in a patient, and that the patient possesses the *ability* to be moved by an agent.

6.28   About *cause* and *effect*, Hobbes would go on to claim that they are one and the same with what he identified as *power* and *act*, where he related *cause* to *power*, and *effect* to *act* (Ibid., Chapter XI, Section 1, p. 93). In Chapter 2, we speculated that perhaps the aggregate of accidents of the patient were what allowed the agent to *actualize* what is only a power (an ability to impart motion to the patient), which may be why Hobbes had referred to the former (the aggregate of accidents of the *patient*) as the *act*. Without the aggregate of accidents of the patient, the agent would forever remain a potential imparter of motion, say, but would never be an *actual* imparter of motion.

6.29   Return to Hobbes' claim that efficient and material causes are only partial causes. They must be *joined*, he said, where they are then understood as constituents of an *entire cause*. Likewise, power and act must be joined, where they are then understood as constituents of what Hobbes called a "plenary power," which, he would write, "is the same thing with entire cause" (Ibid.). One way to understand all of this is to think of Hobbes' *entire cause* or *plenary power* as a model of what Shepherd would later identify as *sensation*. The *entire cause*, for instance, presupposes its constituents, the *agent* and the *patient*; likewise, Shepherd's *sensation* presupposes its constituents, the *external* and *internal* aspects, which look to align with agent and patient, respectively.

6.30   Finally, it should not go unmentioned that there is the further possible similarity with respect to Hobbes's identifying the aggregate of accidents of the *patient* with the *act*. Suppose that there are two bodies, A and B. A is in motion, B at rest (relative to A). In *De Corpore* and in *Leviathan*, Hobbes had declared that a body in motion will remain in motion, unless another body causes it to rest (*De Corpore*, Part 2, Chapter XX, p. 84; *Leviathan*, Chapter 2, Section 1, p. 7). A body at rest, of course, will remain at rest, unless another body causes it to move. A is in motion; B is at rest. Let us say that A strikes B. A is the agent; B is the patient. A (its motion) is the cause of B's *beginning* to move. We might rephrase this and say (though a bit odd and wordy): A (its motion) is the cause of B's motion's *beginning to exist*. The motion that is produced, that *begins to exist*, is located in B. Apply this to Shepherd's view. Suppose that a sensation is now present before the mind. It is akin, we said, to what Hobbes had called an *entire cause*. The latter, recall, presupposes the agent and patient. Likewise, according to Shepherd, a sensation that is now present before the mind, say, presupposes an external and internal aspect, which we said is akin to the agent and patient. Now, in the case of A and B, the motion that "begins to exist" is said to be "located" in body B, the patient. Even though a sensation is akin to an entire cause, which presupposes both agent and patient, we nevertheless "locate" the sensation in the mind, the patient. We say that the first appearance of the sensation in the mind marks its "beginning to exist." This take on Shepherd aligns with Bolton's bringing to light that for Shepherd "The productive aspect of an object is called 'power', defined as a productive principle" (Bolton 2017, Section 2.1).

*

6.31   Antonia LoLordo (2019) has suggested an interesting take on what Shepherd may have had in mind in *ERCE* and in *EASP* when claiming that the sensible object (the sensation occurring before the mind) is the (causal) result of the three items operating in tandem. LoLordo's proposal is based on what Shepherd says when rejecting a common way of expressing the cause/effect relation in terms of the conditional, where "A causes B" is cast as "A followed by B," or, in its more logically rigorous form, "If A, then B". Shepherd wrote:

> To represent the relation of Cause and Effect, as A *followed by* B, is a *false* view of the matter. Cause and Effect, might be represented rather by $A \times B = C$, therefore C *is included in the* MIXTURE OF THE OBJECTS called CAUSE. (*ERCE,* p. 141)

LoLordo argues that this way of casting the cause/effect relation looks to have its origin in chemistry (LoLordo 2019, p. 4). To be sure, the equation $A \times B = C$ itself does not suggest the connection to chemistry, but LoLordo argues that Shepherd's use of the term "mixture" strongly suggests it. The idea is that the sensible object, C, comes about by way of a "mixing" of causes, here A and B. Of course, if we take the idea of the identity expressed here seriously (by the *equation*), then C is nothing more nor less than the mixing of A and B. The mixing of A and B, expressed by way of the multiplication operator, *is* C. To get this exactly right, however, we might want to propose representing the "mixing" of the *three* elements mentioned earlier as $A \times B \times D = C$, where A = mind-independent unperceived thing; B = sensory organ; D = act of consciousness; and C = sensible object (sensation).

6.32   The above is but one of several appeals to mathematics as a model of cause and effect. Deborah Boyle has noted that there are several places in her work where Shepherd makes reference to mathematics when speaking about causation and sensation.[1] Atherton, too, brings to light Shepherd's reference to "algebraic signs." The reference is made in *EASP*, where Shepherd writes:

> For all our ideas are as algebraic signs, which give evidence both of their own existence, and the quantities also signified; where proportions among themselves are known thereby, as well as their positive values. (*EASP*, p. 38)

Thus far, not much has been said by scholars about the reference to algebra specifically. Even so, we might offer the following as a possible interpretive device.

6.33   Shepherd was friend to mathematician Charles Babbage (1791–1871), who was Lucasian Professor of Mathematics at Cambridge. Some of their correspondence focused on algebra. In a 10 July 1836 letter, for example, Shepherd tells Babbage that she had been engaged in doing quite a bit of algebra.[2] Thus, her references to "algebraic symbols" were likely not just passing remarks. Emerging in this period among Babbage, George Peacock (1791–1858), and other members of the Analytical Society, was a recognition of two "fields" of algebra: *arithmetical* and *symbolical* algebra. The latter would have introduced Shepherd to algebraic notions such as *function* or *operation, solving for the unknown, domains* and *ranges*. These are clearly much more sophisticated mathematically than the previously mentioned $A \times B = C$.

6.34   The phrase "algebraic symbols," used by Shepherd, could be based on several basic ideas of symbolical algebra. Start with a *domain* of "objects." Unlike arithmetical algebra, in symbolical algebra, these need not be numbers. As Babbage himself would note in a manuscript (unpublished) titled *The Philosophy of Analysis* (c. 1821):

> Thus did letters whose signification was at first restricted to pure number gradually acquired other secondary meanings and in various situations they denoted time, space, direction, and a variety of other circumstances. (Babbage 1821)[3]

---

[1] Boyle, *The Philosophers' Magazine*. Also see her Boyle (2020).

[2] According to the scholars at Project Vox, an excellent online scholarly resource that highlights marginalized thinkers of the modern period, Shepherd's work in algebra was very likely related to her work on the notions of cause and effect. https://projectvox.org/shepherd-1777-1847/.

[3] This is quoted by David Phillips, in his paper found on the Cambridge mathematics departments website, "George Peacock and the Development of British Algebra 1800–1840":https://www.maths.cam.ac.uk/opportunities/careers-for-mathematicians/summer-research-mathematics/files/Phillips.pdf.

Now devise a function or a mathematical operation that will operate over the objects in the domain. The function or operation will include a "blank" or a *variable*, **x**, which we can "fill in" with objects taken from the domain. The function or operation, a kind of "rule," will tell us what to do to an object taken from the domain, so that when we perform the operation, the function will yield a result. This result will be a member of a new class of "object," which mathematicians call the function's *range*. The basic picture is this (Figure 6.1):

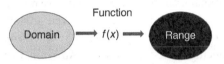

Figure 6.1 The anatomy of a function.

Suppose, for example, that the *domain* is the class of Whole Numbers 6.35 (the basic counting numbers 0, 1, 2, 3, and so on). And, let our function be $f(x) = x^2$. This *function* or *operation* tells us that whatever we "fill in" or substitute for x, the variable, we are to square it (multiply it by itself). If we do this, the function will yield a result. This result will be a member of this function's *range*. So, let us take 2 from the domain and substitute it for x:

$$f(2) = 2^2 = 4$$

This function when operating on 2, taken from the domain, yields 4, 6.36 which is a member of this function's range. We can now substitute 3, say, for the variable and get:

$$f(3) = 3^2 = 9$$

This function when operating on 3, taken from the domain, yields 9, 6.37 which is a member of this function's range. Another way to put this is that such functions or operations can take any member from the domain and relate it (the relation understood in terms of the function itself) to a member in the range.

If we know the function and what it yields, we can backwards engineer 6.38 and discover the correlated member in the domain. So, given the above function, and given the result is 9, we can easily determine that the correlated member in the domain is 3 (assuming that the domain is the class of Whole Numbers). In a more complex scenario, for instance the scenario in which we do not know anything about the domain class, we could at the very least know that if the function is well-defined, and a result is given, there will be *some* "object" that when substituted for the variable will yield this result. This idea may be what was behind Shepherd's reference to symbolic algebra when discussing causation, sensation, and the external world.

6.39   For instance, let a sensible object, or a sensation, of which a mind is aware be analogue to the particular *result*. It is what the mind is *directly* aware of when having a sensation. We could let the mind's awareness of such results (the sensations) be analogous to the *range*, where we might loosely take this to mean that sensations (the results) are to be "located" in minds (the range). But, the mind is more than a depository for sensations; it is one of the causal collaborators in producing the result. Following Atherton, then, who emphasizes Shepherd's claim that with respect to the production of a sensation "that the organs of sense and [the] mind" work so closely together that they (as causes) can be taken as constituting a unified cause, we might let the causal role played by the sensory organ and mind (together) be analogous to the function or operation. So, let us say that we are given the function and its result. We can backwards engineer. The sensory organ and the mind work together (analogous to the function) to produce the sensible object, or the sensation (analogous to the result). What the algebraic analogy suggests is that in having these two items before us (the function and its result), we can infer that there must be *something* over which this function operates. It is this *something* that when inserted for the variable in the function results in the sensation. If there were no such "object," there could be no result. That is, if this something is not there to initiate the function's work (i.e. there is nothing there over which this function can operate), there will be *no* result – so, no *something* initiating the work of the sensory function, no *sensation* of which the mind is aware. Or, put another way, if the domain is empty, so too will be the range (at least with respect to our example). In addition to the function and result, we require this something, this *third* item. Thus, as Shepherd claims, the very occurrence of a sensation before the mind cannot be simply the sensory operation itself (which involves both the sensory organ and mind), but must be something other than this – in this case, this something will be an unperceived mind-independent thing. It is *unperceived* because sensory perception is the *result* of the sensory operation, and whatever this something is, it is *prior* to both the function and its result (this is almost sounding transcendental!). And, analogous to a member of the domain, this something is "mind-independent" because, as a member of the domain, it is independent of the function or operation, the latter understood in the analogy as analogous to the collaborative operations of sensory organ and mind. In light of the algebraic analogy, then, an analysis (a backwards engineering) of sensory functions and their results will *logically* or *conceptually* point to there being some domain of object – objects that activate or initiate the sensory/mental function to do its work, resulting in perceived sensations, the latter "located" in the mind (if we take the mind to also be analogous to the *range*).

*

In our chapter on Kant, recall, we focused on two versions of his   6.40 *ideality/reality* distinction: the empirical and transcendental versions. You may have already been struck by a similarity between what above we were calling Shepherd's *internal/external* distinction, and Kant's *ideality/reality* distinction. Recall that by "ideal" Kant had something like "internal" in mind, where something was said to be *ideal* if, and only if, it depended for its being or existence on the mind (or on one of its operations). Something was *real* or "external" if, and only if, it did not depend on the mind (or on any of its operations) for its being or existence. In our analysis of Kant, we borrowed from G.E. Moore's (1873–1958) examination of Kant, in his now famous essay "Proof of an External World" (1939). There, Moore had identified two phrases used by Kant in his discussions of the *empirical* version of the ideality/reality distinction.

The first phrase was "to be presented (in space)." This phrase denoted a   6.41 thing's being *presented* in consciousness, as a spatial object, not only at some distance from the perceiving subject, but spatially related to other objects also presented in (to) consciousness. The second phrase was "to be met with (in space)." This phrase had nothing to do with presentation *per se*. Instead, what it denoted was that a thing that was *to be met with* (in space) was something that in principle could be perceived by other perceivers, and when not perceived (by any perceiver) would nevertheless remain, existing independent of perception. Both of the latter criteria are similar to the criteria Shepherd assigns to *external*.

Moore introduced a case of our staring a bit too long at the sun, where   6.42 our doing so resulted in the production of an after-image – an after-image of the sun. Now, as a matter of ordinary experience, both the sun and the after-image of the sun would be presented in space, as though they were "out there," at some distance from you, the perceiving subject. With respect to the after-image, although *presented* in space, once the after-imaged "faded" and was no longer presented in consciousness, it is typical to hold that it no longer exists. Its existence depended solely on the mind. The after-image is *presented* in space, but is never *to be met with* in space, for it is not taken to be something that can exist when not perceived, and it is not something that other perceivers can perceive – only you can perceive your after-image. By contrast, even though the sun is also *presented* in space (when perceived), unlike the after-image, we hold that the sun continues to exist even when no longer perceived, and is in fact the same object that others perceive when perceiving the sun. It is *to be met with* in space. Clearly, Moore reminds us, there is really no way to ever "prove" that the sun exists when no longer perceived, or that it is the *same* object that others perceive. This sounds akin to Bolton's analysis of Shepherd's thin and thick layers of the internal/external distinction, which, recall, produced the private and public, or subjective and objective senses, of *experience*.

6.43   The above are not criteria to be *proven*, but instead form the deeper conceptual "framework" that makes proving other things *possible*. As Ludwig Wittgenstein (1889–1951) noted, in his assessment of Moore's essays: "'Doubting the existence of the external world' does not mean for example doubting the existence of a planet, which later observations proved to exist . . ." (*On Certainty*, 20). To prove that Saturn existed would presuppose an already established "framework," where this framework sets the stage, so to speak, for engaging in an activity such as proving, and it would presuppose the existence of an "external" world. It was one thing to doubt whether a planet existed, but quite another, philosophically, to doubt the existence of the (external) world. The former may be warranted, but the latter may indicate mental illness (unless done as a philosophical exercise). Doubt would require that we understand how the matter at hand *could* be settled. The grounds for settling whether a planet existed can be clearly articulated, but what grounds are there for settling whether a world existed independent of one's mind? That the possibility of mental illness was entertained at all shows that skepticism about an "external" world, a world that exists independent of one's mind, was a very peculiar or strange kind of doubt. We found this expressed even by Descartes, in the First Meditation, when he had cast such doubt as likely being taken by others as a form of madness. Such a doubt would, in Hume's view, fly against what one "normally" experiences as one's life unfolds. Shepherd's assessment of Berkeley's view, though less so of Hume's, seemed in part motivated by a peculiarity she found in one's denying the existence of a material world, of a world that existed independent of the mind. Unlike Hume, Berkeley was not a skeptic about the existence of a material world. Berkeley does not doubt but *denies* the existence of such a world. Shepherd, like Descartes, seemed to suggest that this should be taken as an expression of madness.

6.44   Now, back to Moore: an object that was *met with* in space, on Moore's reading of Kant, was what Kant meant by "empirically real." The sun and objects like it are empirically real objects. By contrast, objects like the after-image, which were solely *presented* in space, but never *to be met with*, was what Kant meant by "empirically ideal." Objects that were empirically ideal were *internal* to the mind in the empirical sense. Objects that were empirically real were *external* to the mind in the empirical sense. This looks to run interestingly close to what Shepherd may have had in mind by her *internal/ external* distinction, as brought to light in Bolton's discussion of Shepherd's thin and thick layers of this distinction.

Kant, recall, drew the *empirical ideality/reality* distinction by way of his   6.45 engaging in a *transcendental* philosophical examination. It was by way of the category of transcendental ideality, recall, that the necessary, *a priori*, conditions of the intelligibility of empirical reality were brought to light. Transcendental idealism revealed the underlying conditions for the *intelligibility* of drawing a distinction between the empirically ideal and empirically real. The two defining criteria – that an empirically real object can exist independent of the mind and that an empirically real object can be perceived by multiple perceivers – are themselves not *empirical* claims, but, as noted just a moment ago, form part of the conceptual framework that underwrite the very notion of the *empirical*. Specifically, the empirical ideality/reality distinction is the "framework" that accounts for the very *possibility* of talking about "inside" and "outside" the mind. Moore's point is that talk about "external" objects, *empirically* external objects, is baked into the very "logic" of commonsense. On Kant's view, remember, a transcendental idealist could be a perfectly good "dualist," that is, she could accept the empirical ideality/reality distinction, where what is ideal is mental, and what is real is not mental, but is "material;" this, even though ultimately this person was an *idealist*. Not an *empirical* idealist, like, say, Berkeley, but a *transcendental* idealist, like Kant. Much more would have to be shown in order to establish any philosophical kinship between Kant and Shepherd, but it looks to be there at least on the surface (Bolton 2017, Section 2.2).

6.4 A Commonsense Reading

Let us return to Shepherd's case of the painting of the bird, in which her   6.46 hypothetical person was cast as having initially held that he had seen a bird in the other room. As we know, in this case, Shepherd describes this man as ultimately making a correction, subsequently coming to hold that what he had seen was actually a *painting of a bird* in the other room, and not a bird. There are several interesting philosophical issues lurking here, the least of which is Shepherd's noting that this man uses *the whole knowledge* he possesses of things to make the correction. There is not anything in particular, no one sensory or intellectual element that forces the correction. There is no argument. But, just as importantly, there is no *causal* story. Rather, this man relies on a *context*, a "world picture" formed by available past experience, held together by the aforementioned framework, to make the determination that he was mistaken about the bird and that what he had instead seen was a painting of a bird. This sounds a bit like Hume, when, for example, he told the story of what is involved in his *experience* of hearing a simple sound:

> I hear on a sudden a noise as of a door turning upon its hinges; and a little after see a porter, who advances towards me. This gives occasion to many new reflexions and reasonings. First, I never have observ'd, that this noise cou'd proceed from any thing but the motion of a door; and therefore conclude, that the present phænomenon is a contradiction to all past experience, unless the door, which I remember on tother side the chamber, be still in being. Again, I have always found, that a human body was possest of a quality, which I call gravity, and which hinders it form mounting in the air, as this porter must have done to arrive at my chamber, unless the stairs I remember be not annihilated by my absence. But this is not all. I receive a letter, which upon opening it I perceive by the hand-writing and subscription to have from a friend, who says he is two hundred leagues distant. 'Tis evident I can never account for this phænomenon, conformable to my experience in other instances, without spreading out in my mind the whole sea and continent between us, and supposing the effects and continu'd existence of posts and ferries, according to my memory and observation. To consider these phænomena of porter and letter in a certain light, they are contradictions to common experience, and may be regarded as objections to those maxims, which we form from concerning the connexions of causes and effects. I am accustom'd to hear such a sound, and see such an object in motion at the same time. I have not receiv'd in this particular instance both these perceptions. These observations are contrary, unless I suppose that the door still remains, and that it was open'd without my perceiving it: And this supposition, which was at first entirely arbitrary and hypothetical, acquires a force and evidence by its being the only one, upon which I can reconcile these contradictions. There is scarce a moment of my life, wherein there is not a similar instance presented to me, and I have not occasion to suppose the continu'd existence of objects, in order to connect their past and present appearances, and give them such an union with each other, as I have found by experience to be suitable to their particular natures and circumstances. Here then I am naturally led to regard the world, as something real and durable, and as preserving its existence, even when it is no longer present to my perception. (*Treatise*, Book I, Part IV, Section II, p. 196–197)

The connection between Hume and Shepherd should be clear: both appeal to an already present framework or active "world picture" in which perceptions are to be "situated," so to speak, and subsequently understood, relative to one another, the framework making possible the "situating." Perceptions do not by themselves intrinsically "tell" a mind what they are about – rather, what they are *about*, how they are to be understood, requires an active conceptual framework, which makes possible one's *making sense of* the perception, "situating" the perception, so to speak, determining its significance within the context of the framework. Identifying what has occurred as a *mistake* and explaining it as such are now possible for the man. The view that there is a world of material objects that exists independently of one's experience perhaps has its origin here. It is the sense of some underlying persistent world (the aforementioned framework) in terms of which all instances of experience are to be understood. Although we cannot make the case here, perhaps thinking of Shepherd's view this way would help her to overcome the sort of criticism that Bolton had suggested concerning circular reasoning.

The above is not only akin to what Moore would say in his now famous 6.47 essays "A Defence of Common Sense" (1925), and "A Proof of the External World," already mentioned, but is akin to what Wittgenstein would say in *On Certainty* (1969), a work inspired by Moore's essays. The latter seem to fall within the family of views that constitute what we have been calling "commonsense philosophy." Consider, for instance, several insights made by Wittgenstein, whose take on Moore we considered earlier:

94. But I did not get my picture of the world by satisfying myself of its correctness; nor do I have it because I am satisfied of its correctness. No: it is inherited background against which I distinguish between true and false.

115. If you tried to doubt everything you would not get as far as doubting anything. The game of doubting itself presupposes certainty.

141. When we first begin to believe anything, what we believe is not a single proposition, it is a whole system of propositions. (Light dawns gradually over the whole.)

144. The child learns to believe a host of things. I.e. it learns to act according to these beliefs. Bit by bit there forms a system of what is believed, and in that system some things stand unshakeably fast and some are more or less liable to shift. What stands fast does so, not because it is intrinsically obvious or convincing; it is rather held fast by what lies around it.

341. That is to say, the questions that we raise and our doubts depend on the fact that some propositions are exempt from doubt, are as it were like hinges on which those turn. (Wittgenstein 1969)

The "hinges" on which doubt about ordinary beliefs turn, such as whether it is a bird in the other room or not, are the *framework* propositions, the latter including such as empirically real objects can exist independent of their being perceived, and can be perceived by multiple perceivers, and so on. *Those* do not get doubted; they are not doubted because they are intrinsically obvious or convincing, or because one has satisfied himself or herself that they are true, but they are not doubted because they are part of the framework that underwrites the *possibility* of doubting – they form part of the inherited background in terms of which truth and falsity and certainty and doubt *can* be distinguished.

6.48   Reading Shepherd in light of Moore and Wittgenstein may allow us to work around concerns that her *arguments* in support of there being a *material* world, a world that exists independent of the mind, are circular. For, the belief in the existence of a material world, of a world that exists independent of the mind, is a "hinge," it is that in light of which doubt about other things is possible. It is one thing to doubt whether there is a bird in the other room, it is quite another thing to doubt whether there is a world, material or otherwise, that exists independently of one's experience. Where doubt is analogue to the swinging door, and certainty analogue to those hinges, if one wants the door to swing, the hinges have to stay put. That is, if one wishes to doubt, something must remain undoubted. Even if we endeavored to doubt the existence of an "external" world, which we might do when doing philosophy, the "hinges" are still there – for in doubting the existence of an "external" world, we are still certain about the fact that we are engaged in an act of doubting or in doing philosophy. To doubt that we are doubting would be conceptually impossible. It would be unintelligible. This is so because we would have lost the hinges, and the door could no longer swing. Doubting would have been rendered meaningless. The epistemic buck would stop there. This, it seems, is one charitable way of understanding Shepherd's view. And, it is fitting at the end of our study of the six principal philosophers that constitute the chapters in this book that we come full circle, for the point just made was where we began, with Descartes's first principle.

References

Atherton, Margaret. (1996) Lady Mary Shepherd's Case Against George Berkeley," *British Journal of the History of Philosophy*, 4(2), 347–366.

LoLordo, Antonia. (2019) Mary Shepherd on Causation, Induction, and Natural Kinds, *Philosophers' Imprint*, 19(52), 1–14.

Boyle, Deborah. (2022) Lady Mary Shepherd: A Snaphot, *The Philosophers' Magazine*. https://archive.philosophersmag.com/snapshot-lady-mary-shepherd/.

Boyle, Deborah. (2020) "Mary Shepherd on Mind, Soul, and Self," *Journal of the History of Philosophy*, 58(1), 93–112.

Moore, George Edward. (1939) Proof of an External World. https://rintintin.colorado.edu/~vancecd/phil201/Moore1.pdf.

Moore, George Edward. (1925) A Defence of Common Sense. http://www.sophia-project.org/uploads/1/3/9/5/13955288/moore_commonsense.pdf.

Wittgenstein, Ludwig. (1969) *On Certainty*, translated by G.E.M. Anscombe and G.H. von Wright, New York: Harper & Row, 1972. http://thatmarcusfamily.org/philosophy/Course_Websites/Readings/Wittgenstein%20On%20Certainty.pdf.

Readings

Primary Shepherd Readings

Shepherd, Mary. (1824) *An Essay Upon the Relation of Cause and Effect*. https://archive.org/details/essayuponrelatio00shepiala/page/n5/mode/2up?ref=ol&view=theater.

Shepherd, Mary. (1827) *Essays on the Perception of an External Universe*. https://babel.hathitrust.org/cgi/pt?id=loc.ark:/13960/t6vx1jj4m&view=1up&seq=9&skin=2021.

Secondary Reading

Bolton, Martha Brandt. (2017) Mary Shepherd, in *Stanford Encyclopedia of Philosophy (SEP)*. https://plato.stanford.edu/entries/mary-shepherd/.

EPILOGUE

It is never a bad idea to see the bigger picture when trying to make sense of a philosophical problem. The problem on which we have focused is The Problem of the External World. Seeing the bigger picture, not surprisingly, requires seeing the important role that Plato played in setting the scene, long before Descartes, Hobbes, Berkeley, Hume, Kant, and Shepherd were born. Let us take a quick look at one of Plato's discussions that will provide us with a tool with which we can compare and contrast the principal philosophers we studied in this book. So, let us turn to setting this up so that we can compare and contrast the views of Descartes, Hobbes, Berkeley, Hume, Kant, and Shepherd.

E.1 The Analogy of the Divided Line

At the close of Book VI of Plato's *Republic*, the main character, Socrates, tries his hand at laying out the underlying metaphysics that supports his account of how knowledge is possible. This account requires him to draw an important distinction between two "realms" of object: the realms of the *intelligibles* and the *sensibles*. They correspond to the two capacities we humans possess, namely, the *understanding* and *sensation*. Remember that the six principal philosophers studied in this book took this distinction seriously. Now, Plato's account employs an analogy: the analogy of a divided line. This analogy is importantly related to his more famous one, which is introduced at the opening of the very next book of the *Republic*, Book VII, which you probably know as *the allegory of the cave*. We do not need to see how the two are related to understand the analogy of the divided line, so we will forego any discussion of the allegory of the cave.

This Is Modern Philosophy: An Introduction, First Edition. Kurt Smith.
© 2023 John Wiley & Sons, Inc. Published 2023 by John Wiley & Sons, Inc.

Let us begin. Socrates instructs us to consider a line (*Republic*, 509d). Divide it into two unequal halves. It does not matter how long or short, just so that one half is longer than the other. Although there are a couple of ways of interpreting which half is supposed to represent which realm, for our discussion let the longer half represent the intelligible realm and the shorter represent the sensible realm. The line looks like this (Figure E.1):

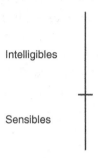

Intelligibles

Sensibles

Figure E.1 The divided line.

Let the greater length of the longer line segment assigned to the Intelligible realm represent Socrates's claim that objects in this realm are more real or more true than those inhabiting the sensible realm. Socrates will cast the "greater" relation in terms of ontological dependence: the objects that inhabit the intelligible realm are more real in the sense that the objects that inhabit the sensible realm depend for their being on the being of the objects in the intelligible realm. They do so in a way that the objects in the intelligible realm do not depend for their being on the being of the objects in the sensible realm. On the flipside, then, we take the shorter length of the line segment assigned to the sensible realm to represent Socrates's claim that the objects that inhabit the sensible realm are less real or less true than those that inhabit the intelligible realm.

Starting with the line segment assigned to representing the sensible realm, Socrates instructs us now to divide this segment in two, duplicating the exact ratio of long-to-short we introduced when dividing the original line. He assigns the shortest segment of the sensible line the role of representing what he refers to as "images." By this, he means to include things like reflections in mirrors. He in turn assigns the relatively longer segment the role of representing what he refers to as "originals," which are the things that the images are "of" (*Republic*, 509d–510a). So, thinking back to our earlier discussion of Socrates standing before the mirror, the shorter line segment represents items like the image on the mirror's surface, whereas the longer line segment represents items like Socrates. Socrates is the *original* of the image; he is what the image is "of." Just as with the relation between the intelligible and sensible realms, Socrates emphasizes ontological dependence between an image and its original: the image depends for its being (what it is an image of) on the being of an original in a way that the original does not depend for its being on the being of the image. So, the mirror image of Socrates depends for its being on the being of Socrates in a way that Socrates does not depend for his being on the being of the mirror image. There would be no mirror image of Socrates without Socrates, but Socrates could certainly exist (or be) without there being any mirror images of him. The line now looks like this (Figure E.2):

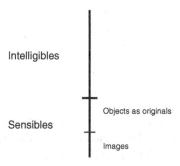

Figure E.2 Plato and Kant compared, continued.

Socrates next moves to laying out the Intelligible line segment. As with the Sensible line segment, we are instructed to divide it in two, in the very same ratio of long-to-short as before. Here is what that looks like (Figure E.3):

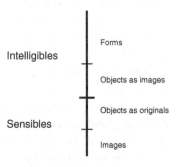

Figure E.3 Plato and Kant compared, continued.

To the shorter line segment, Socrates assigns it the role of representing the objects just considered in the category of *objects as originals*. But this time, he says, in their new category, that is, within the context of the intelligible realm, they are to be understood as *images*. So, Socrates or the Sun were considered in the sensible realm to be among the objects as originals, but now, considered in light of the intelligible realm, they are to be considered as images of something else. As you very likely know, if you have studied Plato, the something else here are the Forms. Socrates, for example, is an image of the Form of human being. Now, by image here, Plato took particulars like Socrates and the Sun to be instances of their respective Forms. The notion of image is only metaphorical. The thing to stress is the sense in which an image depends for its being what it is on the being of some original. So, Socrates depends for his being what he is on the being of the Form of human being, in a way that the Form does not depend for its being on Socrates.

It is important to see that the lengths of the line segment representing *objects as originals* and the line segment representing *objects as images* are the same. This is a trivial result of dividing the original line as instructed by Socrates. But the philosophical point of this is that they are the same length because they include (or represent) the very same objects. When considered in light of the sensible realm, the Sun is an original, something that can (and does) exist independently of the mind's subjective sensory images of it; whereas when considered in light of the intelligible realm, the Sun is an instance of some Form, the Sun depending for its being on this Form in a way that this Form does not depend for its being on the Sun. No Form, no Sun. But the Form remains whether or not there is the Sun; in the same way that the Sun is said to remain whether or not there are any subjective mental representations of it.

In light of our discussion of Kant, it should be pretty straightforward how his two distinctions align on Plato's divided line. Recall that Kant posits a distinction between *ideality* and *reality*. The first distinction is the empirical version: empirical ideality versus empirical reality. The second distinction is the transcendental version: transcendental ideality versus transcendently reality. The first distinction seems to align with Plato's Sensible realm, whereas the second seems to align with Plato's Intelligible realm. So (Figure E.4):

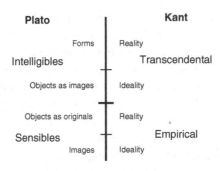

Figure E.4 Plato and Kant compared, continued.

Clearly, insofar as Kant says that "objects" in the category of transcendental reality are inconceivable, he would disagree with Plato's putting *the* objects of intelligibility, the Forms, in this category. It is perhaps odd to say that the Forms are inconceivable for Plato, but the claim here would be that one does not conceive the aspatial/atemporal Forms themselves, but instead conceives other things by way of the Forms. The Forms account for the very possibility of conceiving anything at all. According to Kant, the best that human beings can achieve, in terms of metaphysical *knowledge*, is to be found in the category of transcendental ideality. As we now know from our study, Kant says that such knowledge will be Synthetic *a priori*. What we learn is that the very intelligibility of the distinction drawn in the empirical distinction, between ideality and reality, is discovered *via* Kant's transcendental idealism, where the discovery is made by way of what Kant calls philosophical reflection, which is part of what he calls transcendental *philosophy*.

Given Descartes's Sixth Meditation proof for the existence of a material world that exists independently of his mind, Descartes would seem at the very least to be an empirical realist. That is, his view at the very least holds that we can know things about objects that exist independently of our minds – material objects such as the Sun. But he seems to hold something more, namely that our knowledge of the nature of body, of which the Sun is an instance, is made possible by way of reason. He made this claim as early as the Second Meditation. By the Sixth Meditation, he says that it is his innate idea of body that makes the nature of body (extension in length, breadth, and depth) intelligible. This could bump him up on the Divided Line, where he might be understood to hold some pre-Kantian version of transcendental idealism. Hard to say. Some might even be prepared to argue that the innate ideas serve along the lines of Plato's Forms, in which case some might hold that Descartes was what in Kant's terms would be a transcendental realist. If this was Descartes's view, Kant would surely disagree with Descartes (as he might disagree with Plato). Hobbes looks to be close to Descartes here, as a kind of empirical realist, even though he was a materialist and Descartes was a mind–body dualist. It should be noted that there are scholars who as a matter of fact think that Hobbes's introduction of the *phantasms* of space, time, body, and motion, which he took to account for the underlying conditions of the intelligibility of the material world, suggests that he may be closer to Kant than traditionally thought. And so, like Descartes, this sort of reading could bump Hobbes up on the Divided Line, making him a kind of proto-transcendental idealist. There is still much for scholars to do here to clear this up.

Kant and Shepherd would no doubt say that Berkeley was an empirical idealist, since Berkeley held that the only intelligible objects were the ideas of finite minds. Even so, as we noted earlier, it seems that with Berkeley's introduction of the Omni-perceiver, Berkeley could have accepted Kant's and Shepherd's accounts of the category of empirical reality – a world of objects that exist independently of any *finite* mind. So, perhaps there is an argument for supporting the claim that Berkeley was ultimately an empirical realist. Again, hard to say.

Hume looks to be an empirical idealist. However, Kant seems to have seen something in Hume's work that suggested otherwise. Remember it was Hume, Kant said, who had awaken him from his dogmatic slumber. But what exactly he saw is difficult to say. One possibility seems to be Hume's working out the underlying conditions of the intelligible orderly organization of perceptions – the three laws of the association of ideas. These laws themselves are not objects of perception, but even so, Hume argued, they emerge in the analysis as *necessary*, in that they are required in his accounting for the possibility of the highly ordered organization of our perceptions. In Kantian terms, the laws of the association of ideas run close to being part of a transcendental account of the possibility of experience.

We can also now better understand Kant's criticism of Descartes's and Berkeley's views. As we learned earlier, Kant says that if Descartes took himself to prove the existence of the "I" of experience, the perceiving subject, then he had *ipso facto* (by that very fact) proven the "object" of experience, the "not-I" that our ideas are "of," where the "I" and "not-I" form what we earlier called a concept-pair. What Descartes had failed to understand is that empirical ideality and empirical reality are concept-pairs, and cannot be understood in isolation of one another (in the same way that *up* can *down* cannot, or *inside* and *outside* cannot). And, as we also learned, Kant says that if Berkeley held that a world that existed independently of the subjective cognition of a finite mind was inconceivable, Berkeley had mistakenly paired empirical ideality (the subjective particulars of cognition) with transcendental reality (an inconceivable realm not subject to the conditions of space and time). The proper paired concept to empirical ideality, says Kant, is empirical reality (a realm subject to the conditions of space and time), not transcendental reality.

As Kant makes clear, the transcendental idealist can be a good empirical realist, that is, the transcendental idealist is able to accept a sense in which there exists a world that is "external to" the mind. This would be the *empirically real* world, the world that science in fact studies, the world whose inhabitants are objects such as Socrates, the Sun, apples, tables and chairs, and so on; the world that commonsense says exists. This was Kant's solution to the problem of the external world.

If Kant were to look at Shepherd's work (Kant had died long before she published her first book), he might classify her as an empirical realist, which would be consistent with how he would classify Descartes or Locke. Even so, Shepherd's examination of the underlying conditions of what counts as external and internal, and her account of cause and effect, look to flirt with what Kant referred to as transcendental idealism. This, arguably, might also be said of even someone like Hobbes, as noted earlier, who is traditionally taken to have been a materialist. For, his accounts of the *phantasms* of space, time, body, and motion, look to be spelling out the underlying conditions of the *intelligibility* of the distinction between the empirically ideal and empirically real. So, there is much scholarly work left to do!

Now, as we have seen, the six principal philosophers studied in this book attempted to address The Problem of the External World. Although Descartes, Hobbes, Berkeley, and Hume would appear to be at odds with one another, Kant, and maybe even Shepherd, showed us a sense in which the *rationalist* (Descartes) and *empiricists* (Hobbes and Berkeley), and even the *dualist* (Descartes) and *monists* (Hobbes and Berkeley), might find philosophical common ground.

INDEX